"Decentralization and democratization of our global platforms is a perennial battle worth fighting for. We lost much of that battle with the Web, but we have another chance with blockchain-based platforms. In this new book, Don Tapscott provides the vision and the leadership, and expert contributors provide realistic roadmaps on how to get there."

—Mary C. Lacity, PhD, Director of the Blockchain
Center of Excellence, University of Arkansas

"*Blockchain Revolution* was a trailblazer, introducing the key concepts and principles behind the technology. *Platform Revolution* is an amazing next chapter. It sets the scene for a paradigm shift in which blockchain serves as an open and neutral ledger for everything, enabling transparency, trust, and mass collaboration. Very good insights to position your enterprise for this next phase in the revolution."

—Ian I. Putter, Head, Distributed Ledger
Technology/Blockchain, Standard Bank Group

"Decentralized, immutable, trusted, efficient. Blockchain will transform how platforms operate today and will usher in a new era of value exchange. *Platform Revolution* cleverly explores how blockchain can deliver value and accelerate digital transformation across multiple industries."

—Debbie Gamble, Chief Officer, Innovation Labs and
New Ventures, Interac Corp.

"Secured, multi-cloud data networks open to all trusted participants are transforming how people work together in all industries. *Platform Revolution* eloquently explains the three pillar innovations—AI, blockchain, and the Internet of Things—that will be foundational to the next wave of innovation in the global economy. The game changers who have already embraced these emerging technologies have positioned themselves to thrive in this new era of radical transparency."

—Raj Rao, IBM General Manager, IBM Blockchain
Ecosystems and TradeLens

"A great map of the blockchain space and its quest to revolutionize the Internet, from currency to infrastructure to IoT. Bringing *trust* to the Web will unlock new superpowers we're only just beginning to explore."

—Molly Mackinlay, Project Lead, InterPlanetary File System

"Don Tapscott has brought together the finest minds in the industry on the convergence of blockchain, artificial intelligence, and the Internet of Things. With these innovations, we can build a future that benefits and empowers every single individual in the world, not just a select few. I highly recommend this book to anyone seeking to understand how technology and decentralization can help solve today's complex problems."

—Pradeep Goel, Chief Executive Officer, Solve.Care

"The future will be built on blockchain. Blockchain technologies can comprehensively revolutionize business processes, improve the quality of data, realize self-operation and self-management, offer greater cost efficiency, and provide security guarantees with its features such as enhanced security, immutability, and distributed ledgers."

—Adam Cai, *Chief Executive Officer, VirgoCX Inc.*

"Don Tapscott provides readers with a glimpse of the power of blockchain technologies in the global economy. *Platform Revolution* looks at blockchain's impact on the Internet of Things, artificial intelligence, and big data, and it underscores the importance of post-quantum cryptography. The future is clearly programmable, but we must be prepared."

—Sandeep Nailwal, *Co-founder and Chief Operating Officer, Polygon*

"Tapscott takes us on a journey to discover how blockchain already is changing, and will change in the future, the world as we know it forever."

—David Atkinson, *Commercial Director – Executive Team, Holochain*

PLATFORM
REVOLUTION

BLOCKCHAIN RESEARCH INSTITUTE
ENTERPRISE SERIES

C-Suite Revolution: How Blockchain Technology Is Changing
Enterprise Leadership
Edited with a foreword by Don Tapscott

Digital Asset Revolution: How Blockchain Is Decentralizing Finance
and the Management of Value
Edited with a foreword by Alex Tapscott

Financial Services Revolution: How Blockchain Is Transforming Money,
Markets, and Banking
Edited with a preface by Alex Tapscott

Platform Revolution: Blockchain Technology as the Operating System
of the Digital Age
Edited with a preface by Don Tapscott

Supply Chain Revolution: How Blockchain Technology Is Transforming
the Global Flow of Assets
Edited with a foreword by Don Tapscott

ALSO BY
DON TAPSCOTT

The Blockchain Revolution: How the Technology Behind Bitcoin Is Changing Money, Business, and the World, Penguin Portfolio, 2018
Co-author, Alex Tapscott

Blockchain Revolution for the Enterprise Specialization
INSEAD and Coursera, 2019
Co-instructor, Alex Tapscott

The Digital Economy: Rethinking Promise and Peril in the Age of Networked Intelligence, McGraw-Hill, Anniversary Edition, 2014

Macrowikinomics: Rebooting Business and the World,
Penguin Portfolio, 2010
Co-author, Anthony D. Williams

Grown Up Digital: How the Net Generation Is Changing Your World,
McGraw-Hill, 2008

Wikinomics: How Mass Collaboration Changes Everything,
Penguin Portfolio, 2006
Co-author, Anthony D. Williams

The Naked Corporation: How the Age of Transparency Will Revolutionize Business, Free Press, 2003
Co-author, David Ticoll

Digital Capital: Harnessing the Power of Business Webs,
Harvard Business Press, 2000
Co-authors, David Ticoll and Alex Lowy

Blueprint to the Digital Economy: Creating Wealth in the Era of E-Business, McGraw-Hill, 1999
Co-authors, David Ticoll and Alex Lowy

Growing Up Digital: The Rise of the Net Generation,
McGraw-Hill, 1999

The Digital Economy: Promise and Peril in the Age of Networked
Intelligence, McGraw-Hill, 1997

Who Knows: Safeguarding Your Privacy in a Networked World,
McGraw-Hill, 1997
Co-author, Ann Cavoukian

Paradigm Shift: The New Promise of Information Technology,
McGraw-Hill Companies, 1992
Co-author, Art Caston

Office Automation: A User-Driven Method, Springer, 1985

Planning for Integrated Office Systems: A Strategic Approach,
Carswell Legal, 1984
Co-authors, Del Henderson and Morley Greenberg

PLATFORM REVOLUTION

BLOCKCHAIN TECHNOLOGY
as the Operating System
of the Digital Age

Edited with a preface by

DON TAPSCOTT

Co-Founder and Executive Chairman, Blockchain Research Institute

BARLOW BOOKS
fine books for enterprising authors

111 Peter Street, Suite 503, Toronto, ON M5V 2H1 Canada

ISBN: 978-1-988025-73-5

Printed in Canada

1 3 5 7 9 10 8 6 4 2

Publisher: Sarah Scott/Barlow Books
Book producer: Tracy Bordian/At Large Editorial Services
Book design (cover and interior) and layout: Ruth Dwight

For more information, visit www.barlowbooks.com.

Barlow Book Publishing Inc.,
96 Elm Avenue, Toronto, ON
M4W 1P2 Canada

CONTENTS

LIST OF CONTRIBUTORS

Vlad Gheorghiu is CEO, president, and co-founder of softwareQ Inc. and a research associate at the Institute for Quantum Computing at the University of Waterloo.

Sergey Gorbunov is an assistant professor in the Cheriton School of Computer Science at the University of Waterloo. He works in cryptography and is building cryptographic primitives, protocols, and systems.

Dominique D. Guinard is co-founder and chief technology officer of EVRYTHNG, an IoT platform as a service managing billions of connected products from factory to consumer for big brands.

Christian Keil is chief of staff at Astranis Space Technologies Corporation, an enterprise focused on launching the next generation of smaller, lower-cost telecommunications satellites to bring the world online.

Alan Majer is founder and CEO of Good Robot and an active member of the local maker scene, frequenting spaces like InterAccess and HackLab.to.

David Mirynech is co-founder and chief executive officer of FanClub Sports Capital, a sports team investment platform that gives teams and minority limited partners access to liquidity.

Michele Mosca is CEO of evolutionQ Inc. and a founder and professor at the Institute for Quantum Computing at the University of Waterloo, where he is affiliated with the Department of Combinatorics and Optimization.

Bill Munson is director of research and policy analysis of Quantum-Safe Canada at the University of Waterloo, with a focus on cybersecurity. He is also a research associate at Institute for Quantum Computing.

Don Tapscott is chief executive officer of the Tapscott Group, executive chairman of the Blockchain Research Institute, and one of the world's leading authorities on the impact of technology on business and society.

Mark van Rijmenam is founder of Datafloq and Mavin. He holds a PhD in management from the University of Technology Sydney on how organizations should deal with big data, blockchain, and artificial intelligence.

Anjan Vinod is an investment analyst at ParaFi Capital, a former consultant at Blockchain at Berkeley, and a graduate of the Haas School of Business.

PREFACE

Something is rotten in the state of the Web—a view most vociferously articulated by none other than its creator Sir Tim Berners-Lee himself. The Web and its ideals of inclusion, free speech, and identity without boundaries—guided by "ethics, enlightened self-interest, and the commonweal"—have been undermined by powerful forces, commercial and governmental, threatening its existence.[1] Many of us spend most of our time on proprietary applications on a mobile device, bypassing the Web. Massive digital conglomerates are capturing our data and identities online, and the Web has become centralized and hierarchical.

Call it *digital feudalism*—we serfs create all the value, yet the big tech landowners let us keep only a cabbage or two. There are security breaches, fake news, trolling, and the end of net neutrality in the United States. Nefarious forces spread disinformation and influence the course of democratic elections. State censorship is on the rise, and Internet freedom is declining.[2] The Web is in deep trouble and, with it, the digital age.

For several years now, I've been studying how blockchain technology could support the Internet's founding ideals and restore the balance of power. Many of you have heard me talk about distributed ledger technologies as the leading edge of the second era of the Internet, one that could bring prosperity, autonomy, and self-actualization for all.

But the second era of the digital age hangs in the balance. We *must* address the problems of the first age—censorship, surveillance, the digital divide, fractured discourse, distrust in science and democratic institutions, cyberhacking and the quantum threat, etc.—all exacerbated by the pandemic, the global economic downturn, and the absence of the US government in facing the climate crisis. And we think we can and must tackle these problems systemically, through the technologies of the second age, all showcased in this book. We cannot let this global crisis go to waste.

There are different views on how to save the Web. Some propose government intervention, such as the European Union's General Data Protection Regulation (GDPR), to help users get access to their data and recover their privacy. Others propose technological solutions, such as Berners-Lee's Solid (short for *social linked data*). Solid is basically a set of standards and application programming interfaces (APIs) designed to "reshape the Web as we know it."[3] The goal of the Solid project is to enable users and organizations to separate their data from the apps that use them, so that people can look at the same data using different apps at the same time.

To explore this further, I decided to team up with our very capable researcher, Christian Keil, to write what has become Chapter 1 of this book. It frames the big issues, such as the lack of a data commons: the provenance of data is often unverifiable, the algorithms used are undisclosed, and institutional data are kept secret. To manage the scope of our research, we chose to focus on ensuring (1) open access, (2) fair participation, and (3) the recovery of our sovereignty as users. After conversations with numerous leading thinkers and practitioners, we concluded that, while other approaches have merit, blockchain could be the key to saving the Web as a virtual community, open to all on equal terms. For each issue, we describe how the world could look in the year 2040, if we apply blockchain to the Web today.

Chapter 2 looks at how blockchain will change the business of big data, fundamentally. Big data has become a new asset class, one that might trump all previous asset classes. Digital conglomerates such as Amazon, Facebook, and Google—all Internet start-ups at one time—have been stockpiling user data in their private silos rather than on the World Wide Web. Revelations of massive online surveillance and what I call commercial "data fracking" have driven people in established democracies to seek anonymity and encryption technologies such as those deployed in blockchain. With these tools, individuals can disguise their identities, mask their movement on the Web, and scramble their messages in transit and in storage so that only authorized persons may access them.

Those capabilities are essential in preserving both privacy and property rights to our own data, and blockchain technology enables us to collect, store, and manage it ourselves in a digital black box of sorts. We could establish the terms of usage and allow others to access it through *homomorphic encryption* and *secure multiparty computation*, meaning that we could share our data with Amazon, Facebook, or Google in exchange for a fee, and those parties could use it in computations without ever decrypting it or learning anything about us.[4] That's what MIT Enigma could empower us to do. "Enigma is a decentralized computation platform with guaranteed privacy" that enables "autonomous control of personal data."[5] That's exciting. It will turn this multibillion market upside down so that these revenues flow to the individual data creators. Serfs no more!

Changing the power dynamic will dramatically transform marketing, since every message will need to be compelling and useful enough to be accepted and viewed by its target audience. Ditto for recruiting new talent. Is this person accepting new clients or looking for new projects? If yes, then how much for a consultation? So blockchain will not only "disrupt the disrupters" but also radically change how all businesses operate. Business-to-business (B2B) data will be huge, too. Many large corporations have strong governance mechanisms for their hard assets. However, according to Dr. Elizabeth M. Pierce, a program chair for the International Conference on Information Quality hosted by MIT in 2015,

Information assets are often the worst governed, least understood, and most poorly utilized key asset in most firms because [information] is increasingly easy to collect and digitize, has increasing importance in products and services, is very difficult to price, has a decreasing half-life, has increasing security and privacy risk exposure, and is a significant expense in most enterprises.[6]

Dr. Pierce advocates for strong data governance—I couldn't agree more—which she defines as "specifying the decision rights and accountability framework to encourage desirable behaviors in the use of data." She makes an important distinction between data governance and data management: "Governance is about determining who inputs and makes the decisions and how. Management is the process of making and implementing the decisions."[7]

Dr. Mark van Rijmenam, our project leader, analyzed the parameters of data governance—sharing (or access), security, privacy, identity, and ownership—in practical terms for enterprise executives. We invited Mark to direct this research because he is among the top thinkers in this area. He has done an excellent job of underscoring blockchain's ability to support governance initiatives and rebuild the trust of consumers and collaborators.

In Chapter 3, my co-author Anjan Vinod and I examine the relationship between artificial intelligence (AI) and blockchain technologies. The use of AI is diffusing, making it one of the broadest technological revolutions ever. Consider what Google Nest and Amazon Robotics (formerly Kiva Systems) are doing in homes and warehouses. Blockchain technology has the unique ability to improve the reliability of AI training data and secure AI implementations through smart contracts and on-chain governance. We also explore the differences among centralized, decentralized, and distributed AI, the utility of autonomous agents, and scalability and governance challenges. I have since concluded that the convergence of these two inventions—AI and blockchain—with the Internet of Things will be foundational to the next wave of innovation in the global economy. We'll need all three to pull ourselves out of this recession.

Chapter 4 focuses on the Internet of Things (IoT), which will need a ledger of *every* thing and the ability to learn and adapt. It's where the rubber meets the road for blockchain. Beyond the purely digital applications of finance, communication, and intellectual property rights management lies the physical world where trillions of objects will be online—connected, communicating, and exchanging value without human intervention. Some will be collecting and transmitting data, others will be acting on these data and responding to changes, and still others will be selling their excess capacity for storage or processing in the open market. Some of the actions will be simple (e.g., shutting off a water valve when a sensor detects a leak in a pipe), whereas others will be more complex and might involve a smart contract.

Dr. Dominque Guinard is one of the world's top experts on IoT. He earned a PhD for his award-winning thesis on the Web of Things and followed that up with two excellent books on the topic. He is not just a scholar but a practitioner and co-founder of EVRYTHNG, which is collaborating with some of the world's most innovative companies to leverage connective devices. In this chapter, he provides context for the use of blockchain technology in IoT and describes how the space will unfold. Dom also does an excellent job of discussing the implementation challenges. Make no mistake about it: there will be IoT opportunities in nearly every industry. Those enterprise leaders who integrate their centralized IoT platforms with decentralized blockchain ecosystems will be better positioned to seize them.

Chapter 5 focuses on the challenges of an aging, overcrowded, and underfunded urban transportation infrastructure. Before the pandemic hit, local taxi and limousine commissions were battling Uber in many cities, and Uber drivers were pushing to be recognized as employees, not independent contractors.[8] City officials and public advocates were struggling to balance the consumer demand for affordable options with the need for public safety, qualified drivers, and city licensing revenues. The emergence of open and shared transportation platforms like the Eva urban mobility cooperative seemed promising, with apps developed and introduced by local entrepreneurs, community groups, municipal governments, and other stakeholders.[9]

Then came COVID-19. In 2020, Lyft lost $1.8 billion and Uber, $6.7 billion.[10] The Centers for Disease Control and Prevention (CDC) has set forth rigorous guidelines for what taxi, limo, and rideshare drivers for hire can do to protect themselves and their passengers and to minimize the spread of the virus.[11] Consider what we could do with the Internet of moving things. We could equip driverless electric vehicles with infrared digital non-contact thermometer guns that take passengers' temperatures before allowing them inside, and autonomous arms that mist, spray, or wipe down the interiors with sanitizers after each ride, depending on the infection rate in the zip code of every pickup.[12] Recharging stations might offer ultraviolet-C light treatments for hard, nonporous surfaces.[13] And a blockchain ledger would log every disinfecting transaction and share those data with prospective riders, giving the cleaner vehicles an advantage over less antiseptic rides.

Such platforms could adopt one or more business models: a *profit-making* model, supported by revenue earned on, say, a fleet of driverless vans; a *distributed co-op* among neighbors who invest in, say, ten vehicles reserved for members and shared via the ride app, rather like Eva; a *public service*, operating and maintaining express buses on high-demand routes or among a network of hospitals; or a *social enterprise* with a purpose, such as earning carbon credits, lowering carbon emissions, reducing traffic congestion, or replacing parking lots with playgrounds. These scenarios are increasingly feasible. Such apps will emerge in the next few years—likely in China, because it leads in autonomous vehicle testing, has established road safety laws that govern driverless vehicles nationwide, and is already using autonomous robots in disinfecting public spaces.[14] These apps will come to solve our transportation needs over the long term.

In this chapter, David Mirynech explores how blockchain technology will optimize the deployment of autonomous vehicles. As co-founder and chief executive officer of an innovative investment platform and the former director of research at Exponential Capital and Markets, David brings an investor's point of view to his analysis. He looks at the Mobile Open Blockchain Initiative, which involves 80 percent of global auto manufacturers and leading technology companies. He also looks at such implementation challenges as blockchain latency and scalability, communications network latency, and device security. Finally, he discusses data privacy and the management of personal information on immutable distributed ledgers as well as the legal liabilities and ethical considerations of autonomous vehicle ownership, usage, and the regulation of both.

Chapter 6 picks up on the autonomy-of-things theme and what we can achieve when these things and their owners collaborate on a massive scale. The sharing economy proved to be a promising early example of how a mass collaboration could manifest. The trouble was, the movement's leading stars such as Uber and Airbnb never represented true sharing. They are central authorities that control the ecosystem and collect rent for connecting borrowers and loaners or renters and owners.

In this chapter, author Alan Majer investigates how the start-up Slock.it is deploying blockchain technology to enable a true "universal sharing network." This network will enable people to rent their idle assets in a manner so non-intrusive and seamless that even microtransactions such as using someone's bicycle to ride to the store become viable transactions. This case study of Slock.it describes how the company's inspiration came from an attempted high-tech heist and outlines the conditions necessary for such a network to succeed. Alan's work is most prescient when he investigates technology at its cutting edge, especially when it incorporates robotics or the maker community. Alan is not only an accomplished researcher and writer but also a practitioner. His dual expertise readily benefits the readers of this chapter.

Chapter 7 covers a topic of utmost concern to every leader: the quantum threat to the cybersecurity of our global IT systems—and to everything we cover in this book. I first raised the issue in *Blockchain Revolution:* "Looming in the distance is quantum computing, the cryptographer's Y2K problem. It combines quantum mechanics and theoretical computation to solve problems—such as cryptographic algorithms—vastly faster than today's computers."[15] According to Steve Omohundro, an expert in artificial intelligence, "Quantum computers, in theory, can factor very large numbers very rapidly and efficiently, and most of the public key cryptography systems are based on tasks like that. And so, if they turn out to be real, then the whole cryptography infrastructure of the world is going to have to change dramatically."[16]

We have not yet reached "quantum supremacy," the point at which a quantum machine is able to perform a computational task beyond what any classical computer is capable of performing. But Google has contended that we could reach the commercialization milestone in the next year or two.[17]

The quantum race is on. According to the *Economist*, China is leading the pack in patent applications for quantum cryptography and quantum key distribution, and the United States is leading in quantum computing and quantum sensors.[18] Given that cryptography underpins blockchain technology and the very cybersecurity of our institutions and infrastructure, we believe this topic is too big to ignore. So we recruited four stars from the University of Waterloo—Vlad Gheorghiu, Sergey Gorbunov, Michele Mosca, and Bill Munson—and tapped their expertise in computer science, theoretical physics, cybersecurity policy, and two areas of mathematics: *optimization*, which works with the management problems of business and government, and *combinatorics*, which combines discrete structures in modeling the physical world. More companies are hiring this kind of talent.

In Chapter 7, they explain how quantum computing is a real threat to modern cryptography: there's a one-in-seven chance that a quantum computer will be commercially available by 2026. That's only five years away! By 2031, the odds become one in two. This chapter is a call to action. Some of the team's explanations are technically complicated, but we think it imprudent to oversimplify these issues: leaders need a level of detail for precision. Enterprise executives must understand their options for quantum-proofing existing blockchains and designing quantum-resistant blockchain networks. Their investors will expect it.

Chapter 8 underscores the need for governance of standards development at three levels: protocol, application, and ecosystem. Its author, Christian Keil, provides an in-depth and multi-faceted look at the different layers of the blockchain technology stack—from both logical and technical points of view. Combining economics and technology theory, he describes the importance of stakeholder involvement and the power of network effects.

Even within systems with charismatic leaders, agreeing on common standards is challenging. Implementing technological standards is even harder. The best way forward must accommodate a more distant future; yet, sometimes the immediate interests of a community trump the grand vision of the pioneers. Christian describes how to proceed amid uncertainty and depicts different versions of the technology stack. He identifies key obstacles that the community must overcome. He also tackles the problem holistically and correctly describes how semantic standardization will both require and lead to greater collaboration and even humility.

As I reflect on this platform revolution, I'm struck not only by the extent to which it changing how we live, but also by the speed with which the underlying technologies and applications are evolving. For example, our mobile devices have advanced well beyond phones, cameras, calculators, music, videos, games, and tracking chips. They now support AI, augmented reality, biometrics, digital wallets, and apps for managing our smart homes, our cars, our health, and a good many other assets.

Indeed, the convergence of these digital technologies—blockchain, artificial intelligence, and the Internet of Things, or what we're calling a *trivergence*—is driving the biggest ever transformation of assets from the physical to the digital. At the center of this transformation is data. We suggest a moratorium on new rules and regulations until there is a full consultation with stakeholders. The overall approach should be principles based rather than rules based.

One final note. We just celebrated International Women's Day 2021 at the Blockchain Research Institute, and so it is not lost on me that this book's contributors are all men. Through our network, we have sought and will continue to seek women in science, technology, engineering, and mathematics (STEM) to lead these types of projects in our research program. We welcome reader suggestions for achieving that goal. The lack of diversity, equal opportunity, and equal pay for women in STEM is part of the larger social, economic, and epidemiological challenges we face.[19] These all require acknowledgment, open discussion, the participation of multiple stakeholders, and a commitment to real transformation. All hands on deck. Let's not waste this global crisis but use it to change what needs to be changed in the world.

Don Tapscott
Co-Founder and Executive Chairman
Blockchain Research Institute

CHAPTER 1

SAVING THE WEB

How Blockchain Can Secure the Future of the Digital Age

Don Tapscott and Christian Keil

 ## SECURING THE WEB IN BRIEF

- With the rise of government censorship, gender inequality, and access gates, *open access* to the Web has been compromised. No longer can every individual connect to the Web without permission, limitation, or discrimination.

- Global megaplayers have formed walled gardens around their massive stores of data and, with the downfall of net neutrality regulation, may soon be able to pick winners and losers in the digital economy—putting *fair participation at risk.*

- Data troves have become the new oil, but large public and private actors have taken control of user identity, data, and the riches they both bestow. As a result, Web users are no longer *self-sovereign* participants; they are data serfs to digital landlords.

- Lack of access, systemic bias, and data feudalism are but three of the challenges facing Web users. To manage the scope of our research, we focus on these three. We propose leveraging blockchain technology to decentralize the Web again. This is what is truly "new" about the blockchain: never before have we had the ability to guarantee access to (and continuity of) data flows over the Web.

- Blockchain's elimination of rent-seeking intermediaries and enablement of new business models can promote fair participation. Users no longer have to trust legacy players, just that the blockchain code will run as guaranteed.

- Blockchain can drive adoption of public key cryptography and allow new means and methods for users' control of their own data and monetization. Together, these will revolutionize and restore Web users' self-sovereignty—what the Web was meant to achieve.

- There are several blockchain start-ups working on viable solutions to these problems. InterPlanetary File System is using blockchain-like architecture to develop a censorship-resistant alternative to HTTP. MetaX is building a community-curated list of the best advertising-supported websites. Companies like uPort, Civic, and Sovrin are working to provide individuals with authority and autonomy over their digital identity across applications.

INTRODUCTION

In its earliest days, the Internet was like a small town: everybody knew everybody else, and communal bonds were strong. The townspeople were almost exclusively academics, folks like Vinton Cerf (Stanford), Peter Kirstein (University College London), and Leonard Kleinrock (MIT), all of whom made decisions big and small that shaped the early Internet.[20] There were a few government cronies thrown into the mix—early Internet research was Pentagon-funded, after all—and some technologists like Ray Tomlinson (inventor of email) and Bob Metcalfe (Ethernet and his eponymous "Law"), but the small-town, close-knit feel was strong nonetheless.[21] In the words of Walter Isaacson, biographer of Steve Jobs:

> [A] notion of community ... was existent in the early days of the Internet with services like the WELL, started by Stewart Brand. When you logged on to the WELL, the first thing you saw was, "you own your own words." In another words, you had to take responsibility for what you said, even if you were using a pseudonym (which you knew could be traced to your true identity). The result was that a trusted community was formed there, and it had wonderful discussions.[22]

In the late 1970s, I worked at Bell Northern Research. I did controlled experiments on the use of "multi-function workstations" in office work. In my second week on the job, I attended a two-day seminar on *packet switching*—the term of art for what RAND researcher Paul Baran originally described as "hot-potato routing"—and something called ARPANET, short for the Advanced Research Projects Agency Network.[23] It was the first time I'd heard the phrase—my first exposure to the members of this small community.

Back then, we concluded that everyone would use a computer connected to a vast, open network of networks, and that this connectivity would change the nature of work and many other aspects of business and society. But the future took a while to unfold. In 1983, the ARPANET adopted transmission control protocol/Internet protocol (TCP/IP), a set of standards developed by Vint Cerf and Robert Kahn for determining how different networks would transmit data between them.[24] A year later, MIT's Jerry Saltzer, David Clark, and David Reed published their end-to-end argument, a precursor to net neutrality.[25]

Such a strong community was possible in the early days because of the Internet's size, surely, but also because of its homophily. The townspeople were all *like* each other. They shared similar aims, a similar passion for technology, and similar ideas about appropriate uses of the Internet. Together, this shared set of beliefs formed a social contract, albeit an implicit one, that governed the fledgling Internet and organized its early contributors.

Over time, the Internet grew and experienced the inevitable growing pains. For instance, as the Internet aggregated more and more networks, tracking hosts became infeasible, and so Paul Mockapetris came up with the domain name system (DNS).[26] But no scaling challenge was larger than that brought about by Tim Berners-Lee and his invention of the World Wide Web in 1990. Berners-Lee and his colleagues at CERN (Conseil Européen pour la Recherche Nucléaire) released the hypertext transfer protocol (HTTP), which standardized communication among servers and clients, thus creating the World Wide Web.[27]

The Web was a successor to the net: a series of technologies that built upon the foundation of the Internet and drastically expanded its potential impact. Web technology today is so omnipresent that it's hard to imagine the Internet without it—HTTP is found at the beginning of every Web address as "http://." The World Wide Web is, of course, "www," and the whole suite is accessed via a "browser."[28] Berners-Lee invented these standards and more. By so doing, he paved the way for the Internet and Web to alter the trajectory of modern life.

In 1994, with the launch of Marc Andreessen's commercial browser Netscape, millions and then billions of people began using the Internet for more than email.[29] Companies formed to build businesses atop this grand new global network. Shane Greenstein, professor at Harvard Business School and author of *How the Internet Became Commercial*, told us:

> In the development of the commercial Internet, the openness of the World Wide Web mattered quite a lot at a very specific moment in the mid-1990s. Up until that point, the Internet was just a big email system with the nerds figuring out how to send big files to do nerdy things like science. The principal designers didn't anticipate what nonacademic users would do.

> So, when diffusion began in commercial markets, they saw different uses and users, different distribution channels for news and content. There were thousands of experiments, and lots of them that nobody had foreseen. The fact that the Web was open enough and didn't limit use eventually allowed for unrestricted, unlimited experimentation.[30]

That era of experimentation on the Web brought the Internet to a new scale and imbued the platform with the potential to revolutionize the world's commercial, political, and social atmosphere.

The changes it experienced, however, were not only in degree but also in kind. In a very real way, the radical democratization of the Internet via the Web led to the downfall of its original social contract. The Web now is no small town; we're certainly not in Kansas anymore.

Today's Web is not academic, and not particularly decentralized. It is best understood as a series of walled gardens, each of which represents a self-governed, centralized, and usually commercial ecosystem. Together, these amount to a "counter web":

1. Access to the open Internet is at risk. Most Internet activity is not in the open commons at all but in corporate-controlled, proprietary apps running on proprietary hardware like smartphones. Such walled gardens include Facebook (WeChat, WhatsApp, Instagram), Google (YouTube), Alibaba, and more. Anti-democratic governments in many countries are censoring access to everything from critical information to search engines that might enable citizens to access unauthorized content. Consumers are using proxies and virtual private networks (VPNs) to get around those firewalls, but governments are stepping up their counteroffensive operations.

2. The Web isn't fair anymore. Massive social media companies seek to replace access to the open Web with their proprietary interfaces where they can collect data and monetize all access to content and communications. In developing countries, they will work to close the digital divide only if new users access the Web through their proprietary platforms. Some large telecommunications providers seek to replace the open and neutral Web with private highways where they can restrict access to content and charge consumers more for content consumption.

3. Finally, users have lost their sovereignty over the data that they generate through their online activity. Data, the new asset class of the digital age, are created by users but captured by large companies who use it to build vast fortunes. Citizens are denied the opportunity to derive wealth from or use their data to manage their lives, and their privacy has been undermined.

This is not the Web that Berners-Lee envisioned. "I'm still an optimist," he said in November 2017 when asked about the future of his invention. "But an optimist standing at the top of the hill with a nasty storm blowing in my face, hanging on to a fence. We [can't] take it for granted that the Web will lead us to wonderful things."[31]

In this chapter, we explore what the future may hold for the decentralized promise of the Web through the stories of three ideals: open access, fair participation, and self-sovereignty. The former two were more or less explicitly present in the Internet's original social contract; the latter only became necessary with the rise of the counter web. For each of these three ideals, we will discuss what they entail, how they came to be, and how the modern Web has fallen short of them.

We will also spend time in this chapter talking solutions. We are far from the first team to recognize the dire situation facing today's Web, and several actors have started working to improve the state of affairs:

1. Berners-Lee himself, along with the W3 Consortium, has made a proposal for a Solid protocol in which social data are decoupled from applications and controlled by users. The group has been working for several years and is beginning to show concrete results: a Node.js implementation and a basic data browser. It plans to release a software development kit in late 2018, and launched the Solid project.[32]

2. Governments are attempting to exert greater control over data privacy and information security, like with the European Union's GDPR. Simply, GDPR mandates certain data protection measures for companies that gather personally identifiable information about their customers, including mandatory disclosures (i.e., notifying users if sites are gathering cookies) and preserving the "right to be forgotten."[33]

3. Other entrepreneurs have proposed various data protection applications. We have seen approaches from peer-to-peer (P2P) networking to password/identity management to two-factor authentication proliferate over the last few years.[34]

These approaches, while well intentioned and promising, will not solve the root causes of today's problems without further partnership and innovation. We believe that a third evolution of the Internet is necessary: what started as the net and scaled as the Web will be secured by the chain. Or, less poetically, we believe that blockchain— the technological innovation behind a new era of open protocols and standards—can re-decentralize the Web and secure the ideals of open access, fair participation, and self-sovereignty for years to come.

THE FIRST IDEAL: OPEN ACCESS

Every individual should be able to connect to the Web without permission, limitation, or discrimination.

WHAT IS THE OPEN ACCESS IDEAL?

Open access was, to Berners-Lee, the primary reason that a "web" was needed. He saw a network to which only a select few could connect and developed decentralized protocols to radically democratize access to the Internet.

Open access, he argued, was as close to an inalienable right as exists in the modern, technological age, and any barrier to that right would act against the ethos of the Web. As he wrote in the original documentation for the Web, "The [World Wide Web] project is based on the philosophy that much academic information should be freely available to anyone. It aims to allow information sharing within internationally dispersed teams, and the dissemination of information by support groups."[35]

Professor Greenstein of HBS gave us context to the definition of "open":

There are two attributes that make a private firm or standard-making institution open: unlimited visibility into code, meaning clear definition or documentation of an API or clear visibility into the standard; and unrestricted use, meaning once the information is released, you can do whatever you want with it.

What you'll find is that few organizations will provide both attributes without qualification. There is an enormous number of variants and hybrids. Everyone claims to be open, but when you look carefully, that's very rare to see. There is this exception and that exception, and sometimes they are small, and sometimes they are large.[36]

In this context, we'll focus primarily on unrestricted use of the Web—but in so doing, we'll discuss the powerful corporate interests that lead to visibility restrictions as well.

HOW HAS THE WEB EXCLUDED POTENTIAL USERS?

As the Web matured, powerful actors—both private and public— began to use their considerable influence to limit access to the Internet. In practice, these limitations aren't (always) malicious, but can create significant challenges to openness when viewed in aggregate. As Greenstein continued:

> If every firm follows its own definition of open, and everyone incrementally does just a little variant that's convenient for them, and everyone forgets to post their documentation, and they all behave in a slightly different way, at some point we have lots of frictions in the system. The low-friction innovation economy we've grown to admire—the US testbed for innovative IT—becomes slowed down. That is why I worry so much about preserving the bright lines of openness. Without bright lines we may gradually slouch toward one hundred different frictions.[37]

Here, we will detail three such frictions: censorship, inequality, and access gates.

Censorship

It is no secret that access to the Internet is overtly prohibited in certain international jurisdictions. Canonical examples include North Korea with its *Kwangmyong*—a state-run intranet that offers curated websites and in-country email—and China, which earned the unenviable distinction of last place in a leading indicator of global Internet freedom, thanks to its "Great Firewall" that blocks Facebook, Wikipedia, Twitter, and YouTube.[38]

Importantly, however, Web censorship is also found in less extreme nation-states: more than two-thirds of the world's Web users are censored in some way by governmental actors, and more than one billion users around the world are using VPNs to bypass such government control.[39] Countries have restrictions that censor political content, pornography, hate speech, illegal downloads, particular sources of media, and more.

Globally, freedom on the Internet has declined for the eighth consecutive year. That's according to a new report issued by Freedom House, a human-rights nongovernmental organization (NGO) based in Washington, DC.[40]

Inequality

In certain nations, subsets of the population are limited in their ability to access the Internet. The Web Foundation's work on the "digital gender gap" is noteworthy and presents a striking conclusion: women are 50 percent less likely to be online than men.[41] The structural factors behind that gap are many but the end result is uniform: women are held back by their lack of Internet access. Michelle Bachelet, undersecretary general and executive director of UN Women and former president of Chile, wrote:

> There is much at stake, with much to lose, if women are left behind. Internet access enhances women's economic empowerment, political participation, and social inclusion through initiatives that support increased productivity and income generation, mobilization, and accountability, as well as improved livelihoods and expansion of services.[42]

Access gates

Free Basics is a program sponsored by Facebook that seeks to bring "Internet access and the benefits of connectivity to the portion of the world that doesn't have them."[43] To date, the program has brought more than 100 million people online for the first time, all by offering certain websites—like news, job postings, and, of course, Facebook—to users free of data charges.

The program may sound admirable, but to some it is an attack on open access. Ellery Biddle, advocacy director of activist group Global Voices, called the service *digital colonialism*. She said, "Facebook is not introducing people to open Internet where you can learn, create, and build things. It's building this little Web that turns the user into a mostly passive consumer of mostly western corporate content."[44]

CAN BLOCKCHAIN TECHNOLOGY IMPROVE ACCESS?

The emergence of immutable and censorship-resistant blockchain protocols may be a source of hope for those fighting for a truly open Web that can be accessed by all regardless of nation, politics, sex, or class.

Manipulation prevention

Blockchain ledgers are immutable; data that enters can never be edited or deleted. Ethereum founder Vitalik Buterin explained the importance of this feature:

> Blockchain solves the problem of manipulation. When I speak about it in the West, people say they trust Google, Facebook, or their banks. But the rest of the world doesn't trust organizations and corporations that much—I mean Africa, India, the Eastern Europe, or Russia. It's not about the places where people are really rich. Blockchain's opportunities are the highest in the countries that haven't reached that level yet. I think the technology, if we do it right, may go in history books.[45]

Trust is a useful tool for quantifying open access—for how can users know what they do not have sufficient access to see? (See Figure 1-1.) Users must trust those who claim that they are seeing the truth and the whole truth. Blockchain technology succeeds in this mission because its immutability offers citizens trust that their governments aren't restricting access to data on certain websites, altering headlines, or censoring certain types of news.

FIGURE 1-1

PENETRATION RATE OF INTERNET ACCESS

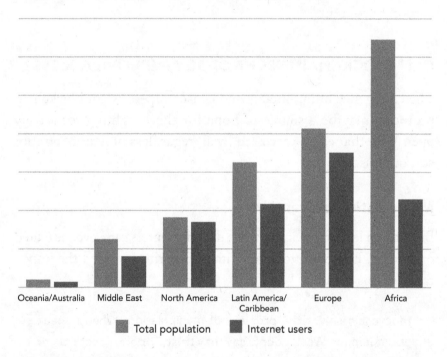

Source of data: "World Internet Usage and Population Statistics," Internet World Stats, Miniwatts Marketing Group, 30 June 2018. www.internetworldstats.com/stats.htm, accessed 16 Nov. 2018.

Censorship-resistance

On 29 April 2017, citizens of Turkey woke up without access to Wikipedia because their embattled, defensive government decided it was necessary to "protect" the public.[46] Luckily, decentralization trumps repression. Within the week, InterPlanetary File System (IPFS)—a company that uses a blockchain-like architecture to create a censorship-resistant alternative to Berners-Lee's HTTP—hosted live, uncensorable snapshots of Wikipedia in Turkish.[47] These immutable files now guarantee that Turkish President Erdoğan can never again censor Wikipedia.

This is perhaps the most compelling feature of blockchain technology ready for the big time today. Because entries in a blockchain can never be deleted, blockchains are better tools than databases for preventing censorship and ensuring open access to the world's information. Data published on a public blockchain can be viewed by anyone at any time, regardless of who they are—a powerful feature and compelling value proposition for those to whom open access to the Internet is less than guaranteed.

VIEWS OF ACCESS FROM THE DECENTRALIZED FUTURE

There are these two young fish swimming along, and they happen to meet an older fish swimming the other way, who nods at them and says, "Morning, boys, how's the water?" And the two young fish swim on for a bit, and then eventually one of them looks over at the other and goes, "What the hell is water?"[48]

The year is 2040. As David Foster Wallace's young fish knew nothing of water, so, too, do our youngsters know nothing of connectivity: it makes no sense for them to consider a world in which they—or anybody, or any device—isn't always freely, openly connected to the Web. Every person on the planet will have open access to the Web; connectivity is a right as fiercely protected as life and liberty.

"Connectivity" also holds a new connotation: it implies not only a point-connection to the current state of the Internet but also a clear view into the past. All Web pages are traceable back in time: consumers have perfect information on how headlines, prices, and corporate missions have changed. Accordingly, censorship is a political ill of an older age: the full history of the next-gen Web is instantly attainable, a reality no government nor corporation can sidestep.

Decentralized blockchain protocols have ensured access to all—without permission, limitation, or discrimination—and preserved one of the Web's original ideals.

THE SECOND IDEAL: FAIR PARTICIPATION

Once on the net, everything—all users, bits, and innovators—should be treated equally.

WHAT IS THE FAIR PARTICIPATION IDEAL?

In the earliest days of the Web, Berners-Lee made a deliberate decision *not* to monetize his world-changing innovation. At first glance, this might look like an inventor leaving the fortune of all fortunes on the table; but to Berners-Lee, the choice wasn't that simple. Trying to capture the value of his creation, he argued, could have destroyed it. He said, "Had the technology been proprietary, and in my total control, it would probably not have taken off. You can't propose that something be a universal space and at the same time keep control of it."[49]

Such counterfactuals are, of course, impossible to prove. Berners-Lee's decision to decline preferential treatment even for himself, however, is a powerful testament to the second ideal of the early Web: fair participation.

In its original form, the Internet was deliberately noncommercial. Per Kevin Kelly, founding executive director of *WIRED* magazine:

The fear of commercialization was strongest among hardcore programmers: the coders, Unix weenies, TCP/IP fans, and selfless volunteer IT folk who kept the ad hoc network running. The major administrators thought of their work as noble, a gift to humanity. They saw the Internet as an open commons, not to be undone by greed or commercialization. It's hard to believe now, but until 1991, commercial enterprise on the Internet was strictly prohibited. Even then, the rules favored public institutions and forbade "extensive use for private or personal business."[50]

The fair participation ideal can be understood as follows: don't extract value by offering preferential treatment for the rich; but if you must, stay away from core protocols.

HOW HAS THE WEB PERMITTED BIAS?

The Web has become an incredible, perhaps unprecedented commercial force. One of the most powerful companies in the world, Amazon, is a case in point: in 2017, Amazon's 300 million users spent $178 billion on goods from over one million small and medium-sized businesses, nearly every major corporation, and Amazon's own product lines, growing Amazon's market capitalization to north of $560 billion. (And as of this writing, it is nearly $300 billion greater than even that; its founder Jeff Bezos is now the richest man in the world.) The rise of e-commerce is not in direct conflict with the fair participation ideal, but does strongly imply that the original, research-oriented nature of the Web is long gone.

We would be wise, then, to ask what has replaced that ethos. We spoke with Tendermint CTO Ethan Buchman, who painted a compelling picture:

I like to tell the story in terms of the analogy to the evolution of human social organization. We went from villages and city states up into the era of large empires, or "somebody else's government." We eventually found that those empires weren't sufficiently responsive to capture the value of various communities, and adequately or accurately represent communities, and so we had this nation-state revolution. All of a sudden, there emerged democracies and independent but parallel rules of law that each particular country could take on, and call its own, and abide by.

We're starting to see the same thing happen in the digital networks realm, where we've gone into this world of digital network empires in the cloud, "somebody else's computer" instead of somebody else's government, and everyone offloads their sovereignty to Mark Zuckerberg or Jeff Bezos to make decisions on what they can do on the Internet.[51]

In this section, we discuss what trends commercialization—and the subsequent domination by a few large players whose business is entirely reliant on their ability to extract value from the richest players—have wrought on the Internet.

We identified two mega-trends that most threaten fair participation on the Internet: walled gardens and pay to play.

Walled gardens

Today, most Internet activity is not in the open Web, but within corporate-controlled, proprietary applications that retain complete control over the data generated within their walls.

Examples abound, but none is more top of mind than Cambridge Analytica's harvesting of Facebook user data and subsequent psychographic profiling for political ends. In the aftermath, reporters learned that Facebook was collecting data more holistically than many users expected, including its capture of detailed phone records like call lengths, phone numbers, dates, and times.[52] Of course, when Facebook reported the resulting impact to its user growth and revenue targets in July 2018, its stock lost nearly 20 percent of its value overnight.[53] That incredible response and backlash implies the question: should companies be able to use their positions as hubs of Web activity to harvest, own, and monetize the data that their users generate?

This is a complex question, but maintaining proprietary control over user data surely tilts the playing field—companies can build insurmountable moats in the form of calcified network effects that prevent even the most promising upstart social networks and search engines from meaningfully challenging the incumbents.

As a less polarizing example, consider the recent deal struck between Apple and Amazon, in which Apple products will be listed on Amazon for the first time by Apple itself. In the past, third-party resellers had filled the gap in the market. Now, with one flick of Jeff Bezos' pen, this deal dries up that well of revenue for the resellers by requiring them to apply for official authorization—such is the power of the ruler of a walled garden.

Pay-to-play models

In December 2017, the Federal Communications Commission voted to repeal net neutrality regulations and give more flexibility for the keepers of the Internet's pipes to productize and monetize their connectivity services. Those regulations had prevented pipe-holders from providing differential service for different types of content over the Internet; today, there is nothing preventing companies from charging users more to access YouTube or slowing down traffic to all Netflix competitors. Berners-Lee explained:

> Network neutrality is about the web being an open market, so anybody can participate, anybody can sell content, or anybody's blog will be accessible. Obviously, people like Netflix pay for

a massive amount of bandwidth because they've got a huge amount of downloads going from their place. They put a lot of money into the system. But if you've paid for bandwidth to allow me to view a video from your little movie site, then you should find it just as easy. There should be nothing impeding it, there should be no commercial or political bias in the delivery of the packets. That's what neutrality is about.[54]

Such preferential deals have yet to come to pass in the United States but have precedent in other nations like Mexico.[55] The impact of such higher rates for consumers would be significant—one study estimates that the average consumer would spend anywhere from $10 to $55 more for monthly broadband access in a non-neutral world.[56]

The debate around net neutrality has been discussed at such length elsewhere that we need not dive deep here to get across the main point: the net was first invented, in Berners-Lee's terms, as a "permissionless space for creativity, innovation, and free expression."[57] If net neutrality regulations are not re-introduced, powerful players can buy preferential treatment, which surely contradicts the ideal of fair participation.[58]

CAN BLOCKCHAIN TECHNOLOGY PROMOTE FAIRNESS?

Blockchain technology is the second coming of open standards development. In Buchman's words, blockchains are giving "new focal points for organizing around to actually deploy new generations of Internet infrastructure and services."[59] These services often disintermediate existing market leaders and offer new monetization pathways for Web companies. We'll cover these topics in general and explore how these principles play out in the case of content creation.

Eliminating rent-seeking intermediaries

Many corporations today build credibility as trusted third parties and convert that reputational capital into dollars on the open market. In the blockchain world, however, such third parties can be disintermediated by empowering network participants to create and capture value by themselves.

As a trivial example, Edgeless is a smart contract–powered casino with no house edge. This business model would be unthinkable in the analog world. But with the digital world's near-zero marginal cost and blockchain's disintermediation of escrow and money-holding, the impossible is now possible.[60] A more impactful example is what MetaX is building for the world of advertising: a "community-curated list" of the best ad-supported websites, in which sites must appease (i.e., not act maliciously toward) their users to stay on a whitelist.[61] Similarly, a number of teams (e.g., NYIAX and MAD Network) are hoping to create decentralized ad networks that can cut through the fat margins that Google and Facebook enjoy today—26 percent and 47 percent, respectively.[62]

Should these projects succeed, they will increase consumer surplus significantly by eliminating (or minimizing) the rent-seeking nature of market intermediaries. Blockchain entrepreneurs seem to have learned all too well from Amazon's Jeff Bezos when he said, "Your margin is my opportunity."[63]

Establishing a token economy

The core innovation behind many of the projects above—and far more as-yet undiscussed blockchain products—is the *token*, a digital asset designed to appreciate as the underlying network it supports creates ever-growing value for its participants. Olaf Carlson-Wee, founder and CEO of Polychain Capital, wrote:

These application-specific tokens, or app-tokens, are built on top of existing general-purpose blockchains like Bitcoin and Ethereum. For the first time, open-source project creators can directly monetize their open-source network. Historically, successful open-source projects like the torrent protocol or the Tor network were not directly monetized at the protocol level. Now, the founder of a decentralized file storage network can issue blockchain-based tokens that represent ownership in the network.[64]

There are questions about where tokens fit within the existing regulatory framework (e.g., as securities, commodities, or somewhere new), but some have created incredible wealth for their owners and sustained value for the users of their underlying products. This new business model gives teams the flexibility to integrate with existing lower-level innovations (e.g., open identity protocols) and level the walls around the gardens of old. In fact, it often makes economic sense for teams in the blockchain world to be as open as possible with their technology in hopes that future innovators will build on their infrastructure and appreciate the value of their existing, underlying tokens.

The best example of such a rising tide is the ERC-20 token (ERC for Ethereum request for comments). Rather than declare their own cryptocurrency—ether—the be-all-end-all, Ethereum developers designed an open standard for token interoperability, allowing *more* tokens to enter their ecosystem. Today, over 100,000 such tokens have been made. The top five ERC-20 tokens alone represent a collective market cap of $171 billion.[65] In the future, open networks may prove more fruitful than walled gardens.

Protecting property rights of content creators

To date, the Internet has been largely a publishing medium, as users communicate copies of content. This broke our property regimes for content ranging from articles to music.

For example, many thought the Internet might help democratize the music industry. Quite the opposite has occurred. "In the latter part of the twentieth century, if a song of mine sold a million copies, I would receive about $45,000 in mechanical royalties, and I was awarded a platinum record," said Eddie Schwartz, head of the Songwriters Association of Canada. "Today, a major music service pays me an average of $.000035 per stream, or about $35 for a million streams, thus reducing a reasonable middle class living to the value of a pizza."[66]

Big technology companies and streaming audio services have taken an additional piece of the pie, leaving artists with the crumbs—not to mention less control over their work and little knowledge of those who interact with it. The business has become so complex and powerful, so concentrated, that musicians like Taylor Swift and Jay-Z have taken themselves off the menu by launching their own companies. For most artists, that's not an option.

This could all change under blockchain-based platforms and clever pieces of code called smart contracts. The new technology runs on millions of devices, from desktops to smartphones, and is open to anyone. It's where information, money, and anything else of value can be transferred and stored securely and privately. Trust among participants is established not by powerful intermediaries like record labels, streaming services, or credit card companies, but by the collaboration of those whose devices are running the software.

Smart contracts essentially serve as templates for setting terms of service and usage for fans, distributors, sponsors, and licensees, and for directly and immediately distributing revenues to contributors, collaborators, and promoters of the work. Through smart contracts, artists would decide who could interact with their work, how, and how much each type of interaction would be worth.

Each of these parties could see all the transactions associated with the work on the blockchain and could track who was paying what amount for which right and who was receiving what proportion of revenues. There would be no opacity in accounting, no delay in payment, and no confusion over who owned or controlled which rights to the work.

Through a set of technical, ethical, and commercial standards, the ecosystem would enable an entirely new marketplace for music and services to thrive, eventually holding all music-related information ever recorded, all linked to a distributed blockchain network of personal computers. Those wanting to do business with the artists and musical works in the ecosystem would be able to do so without institutional friction—from sharing skill sets and finding collaborators to commissioning new works, booking shows, and hiring a tour manager or a local cellist.

VIEWS OF NEUTRALITY FROM THE DECENTRALIZED FUTURE

In 2040, strong net neutrality regulations passed by an international body have driven connectivity services toward full commoditization. The overwhelming momentum is toward disintermediation—networks, marketplaces, and other convening bodies feel increasingly insecure as larger and more significant businesses fall to open-source and crowd-governed protocols.

In the early days of the Web, applications enjoyed the fattest margins. In the early days of blockchain, those applications were replaced by, to use Joel Monegro's now famous term, "fat protocols." Today, the effort toward disintermediation drives platforms to allocate economic surplus to consumers, leading to the ultimate rise of the "fat consumers" (although this phrase has proliferated only in blockchain academia as it didn't *quite* catch on publicly).[67]

In 2040, all traffic is treated equally and third parties who extract rent are seen as prime targets for disruption, returning the Internet to its original ideal of fair participation.

THE THIRD IDEAL: SELF-SOVEREIGNTY

User data should be owned by users, not by governments, corporations, or nongovernmental organizations.

WHAT IS THE SELF-SOVEREIGNTY IDEAL?

As discussed throughout this piece, the creators of the Internet held a particular set of ideals. They wanted easier communication among researchers; they forbade commercial activity; they demanded open access and fair participation among all participants. Because of these desires, rules, and demands, a strong, if implicit, social contract was forged. With the mass democratization of connectivity that followed, however, Web access grew faster than the reach of that social contract—and quickly, it became apparent that the various actors connected to the Web did not share the same implicit ideals as those original researchers.

One such ideal lost in the scaling explosion was self-sovereignty, or the right of individual users to control their own identities. We use identity here as defined in *Blockchain Revolution*:

> We need to distinguish between identity, which is a social, cultural, and psychological construct, and identifiers in a namespace (a 128-bit IP address, a DD Form 214), needed both to participate in and to manage large centralized systems (Google email, Veterans Benefits Administration).[68]

A self-sovereign identity is one that is neither bestowed nor revocable by any central administrator and is enforceable in any context—analog or digital—anywhere in the world. It gives the power to the individual and by necessity removes centralized control by global conglomerates.

This means far more than just name and birthdate. Rouven Heck, project lead of the decentralized identity project uPort, told us that people still talk about identity in abstract terms:

> What's missing is that the game changer is verifiable data. The real game changing difference will be a signed piece of info about myself—like a university certificate, MIT confirms and signs the data, that I have an MBA. Since they're signed, the data can't be manipulated, and they're easily sharable. Once issued, the data are fully controlled by the user. The issuer is critical, but the user can use them in any way, without MIT's having to be asked. There's no trust issue between the user and the issuer anymore.[69]

That kind of sovereignty over one's identity—free, unrestricted use of what makes you "you" on- and offline—is what we propose the community ought to strive for in this new world.

HOW HAS THE WEB THREATENED SELF-SOVEREIGNTY?

At the outset, the creators of the Web made a design choice: delegate control of identity to the applications that run on top of it. While seemingly benign, this decision has since led to cataclysmic, if unintended, consequences. Irving Wladawsky-Berger, Blockchain Research Institute faculty member and former IBM Internet product lead, explained:

> To keep [the Web] as simple and flexible as possible, ... identity and security management became the responsibility of the applications ... [leading] to the explosive growth of Google, Facebook, Amazon, Alibaba, Tencent, Uber, Airbnb, and a few

other very large companies. The [application] layer has become highly centralized, dominated by a few huge companies whose primary objectives are financial in nature.[70]

Joseph Lubin, co-founder of Ethereum and CEO of ConsenSys, sees the problem similarly:

The technologists who built the Internet didn't have the tools to construct a well-architected, public key cryptography-based security infrastructure, and so security on the Internet has been built in layers over years, a patchwork of Band-Aids, effectively, and, maybe more importantly, was built without a native identity construct. So corporations have been able to create identity constructs that serve their business models, and it's evolved to the point where the technology that corporations can access is so strong that they can treat us as products and sell access to that identity construct.[71]

Blockchain Revolution spelled out the four pitfalls of this consolidation of power over identity:

One, they are system-centric, system-controlled, and vulnerable to cancellation, forgery, and theft. We're dependent on a system administrator who can freeze access, alter terms of access and usage, or delete our student IDs, healthcare insurance IDs, or land titles altogether.

Two, all the personal data we create and associate with each identifier (biometrics, college transcript, medical history) reside with and belong to the central system administrator, who may entrust it to untrustworthy vendors or sell some of it to unacceptable third parties without our knowledge. Such a system is opaque. If we want to switch colleges or countries, we bear the responsibility of porting our data from one system to the next—sometimes for a fee—and the rules for doing so are often complex and mercurial. Remember, we're going to be generating more of these data, not less.

Three, nothing about this identifier-centric system is user-friendly. Individuals—or, as noted, government or NGO representatives working on their behalf—have to repeat the registration process to obtain nearly every identifier, provide the same forms of über-identification, and maintain a portfolio of ID numbers, usernames, passwords, and the answers to personal questions. It is a system for the über-organized. It asks us whether we're robots and excludes robots from having their own identification—not good for all those robots that want to buy electricity.

Four, we bear most of the risk and responsibility for cleanup, should hackers break into these central systems and steal our identifiers and our data—but we enjoy none of the rewards of third-party data usage. Consider the legendary breach of Anthem, the largest US health insurer. It agreed "to settle litigation over hacking in 2015 that compromised about 79 million people's personal information for $115 million, which lawyers said would be the largest settlement ever for a data breach." Then it was breached again in October 2017 through one of its vendors, exposing the Medicare and health plan IDs of some 18,000 members. Fool me once.[72]

In the end, the necessity for an inalienable, self-sovereign identity is clear. That identity must not rely on traditional government- or corporate-controlled identifiers; it must be secure from misuse and loss by others, and it must be equally accessible by each individual. If not, we can expect little more than continued data breaches and government control for the foreseeable future.

Data breaches

Data recently surpassed oil to become the most valuable asset in the world, and your humble authors have spent enough time in Silicon Valley to know that the "data play" is the business model *du jour* as a result.[73] Modern enterprises have a voracious demand for data and, unless very deliberately and expertly protected, these vast, centralized data stores are landmines on a hair trigger. At a moment's notice, the private data of millions of users may be lost in one fell swoop (Table 1-1).[74] (A handy, if depressing, tool from the *New York Times* estimates that one of your humble authors has had his driver's license, home address, employment history, three credit cards, five phone numbers, eight passwords, and social security number exposed to hackers over the past few years.[75])

TABLE 1-1

LARGEST DATA BREACHES REPORTED IN 2018

COMPANY	PARENT	SECTOR	NUMBER OF ACCOUNTS	REPORTED PROBLEM
Aadhaar	Ministry of Electronics and Information Technology, India	Government	1,100,000,000	Poor security
British Airways		Transport	380,000	Hacked
Careem		App (transport)	14,000,000	Hacked
Facebook		Web (social)	2,200,000,000	Hacked
Firebase	Google	App	100,000,000	Poor security
Grindr		App (social)	3,000,000	Poor security

COMPANY	PARENT	SECTOR	NUMBER OF ACCOUNTS	REPORTED PROBLEM
LocalBlox		Web (storage)	48,000,000	Poor security
MyFitnessPal	Under Armour	App (fitness)	150,000,000	Hacked
Nametests	Social Sweethearts	App	120,000,000	Poor security
Newegg	Hangzhou New Century Information Technology	Retail	45,000,000	Hacked
Orbitz	Expedia Group	Web (travel)	880,000	Hacked
Panera Bread	JAB Holding Company	Retail (food)	37,000,000	Poor security
Saks Fifth Avenue, Lord & Taylor	Hudson's Bay Company	Retail	5,000,000	Hacked
TicketFly	Ticketmaster (Live Nation)	Web	27,000,000	Hacked
Ticketmaster	Live Nation	Web	40,000	Hacked
T-Mobile	Deutsche Telekom	Telecoms	2,000,000	Hacked
Twitter		App (social)	330,000,000	Poor security
View Fines	Total Client Services	Transport	934,000	Accidentally published

Source of data: David McCandless, "World's Biggest Data Breaches and Hacks," Information Is Beautiful, updated 15 Oct. 2018. www.informationisbeautiful.net/visualizations/worlds-biggest-data-breaches-hacks, accessed 16 Nov. 2018.

But regularity does not imply banality—these attacks are collectively and individually devastating, and if we can stop them, we must. Yuval Noah Harari, author of *Sapiens*, wrote in his next book, *21 Lessons for the 21st Century*:

More practically, and more immediately, if we want to prevent the concentration of all wealth and power in the hands of a small elite, we must regulate the ownership of data. In ancient times, land was the most important asset, so politics was a struggle to control land. In the modern era, machines and factories became more important than land, so political struggles focused on controlling these vital means of production. In the twenty-first century, data will eclipse both land and machinery as the most important asset, so politics will be a struggle to control data's flow ... . The most important contribution you can make is to find ways to prevent too much data from being concentrated in too few hands.[76]

Government control

Some governments today collect public data and refuse to release it, preventing the reinvention of government through open data initiatives that enable citizens and the private sector to self-organize to create collective value.

The upshot of the digital age is that data created by everyone have been captured by powerful institutions, and the largesse of the digital economy has been distributed asymmetrically. Wealth is growing, but prosperity is declining in most developed countries. Our economies are growing but the middle class is shrinking. Government corruption is rampant; the Turkish government, for example, "accidentally" forged a Google encryption certificate, which could have given the city government of Ankara the ability to perpetrate a "man in the middle" attack.[77] This is what fuels the anger, conflict, and populism that are turning countries inward and pitting people against themselves.

Such are the problems of centralized data control by state actors, and new, innovative solutions are necessary to avoid further large-scale social and political problems.

CAN BLOCKCHAIN TECHNOLOGY ENSURE SELF-SOVEREIGNTY?

While the perils of delegated identity control were not intended by the creators of the modern Web, we cannot say that nobody saw this coming—the "cypherpunks" surely did. This talented group of computer programmers and intellectuals met monthly in the early 1990s to discuss the intersection of cryptography ("cipher") and the Internet ("cyberpunk"). They were the kind of group to write a "manifesto," an excerpt of which reads:

> We cannot expect governments, corporations, or other large, faceless organizations to grant us privacy out of their beneficence. It is to their advantage to speak of us, and we should expect that they will speak. To try to prevent their speech is to fight against the realities of information. Information does not just want to be free, it longs to be free. ... We must defend our own privacy if we expect to have any.[78]

Prescient. The group included such members as Dr. Adam Back (Blockstream), Zooko Wilcox (Zcash), Bram Cohen (BitTorrent), and Julian Assange (WikiLeaks)—many of whom later made significant contributions to the rise of blockchain and decentralized technology. According to Samuel Falkon, editor of the *Social Club:*

> Cryptocurrencies are a dream for privacy and freedom lovers because they restore transacting power back to whom it belongs—individuals who have a right to control their own money. Cryptocurrency advocates understand the concerns of the original CypherPunks—privacy and freedom are inherent rights, not gifts to be bestowed by powerful ruling entities.[79]

We have identified three ways in which blockchain can help give control back to the users of the Web and live up to the cypherpunk dream: (1) mass adoption of public-key cryptography, (2) promotion of governmental transparency, and (3) assignment of ownership of and control over consumer data to the consumers themselves.

Mass adoption of public-key cryptography

The current security regime of the Web is, well, insecure. Normal password protection is limited: users reuse and rotate them, and nearly 2 percent of users use one of the same ten passwords (most popular: "123456," which matches 0.6 percent of all Internet accounts).[80] Similarly, secure sockets layer (SSL) certificates fall prey to all-too-human error, as the example of the Turkish government issuing a false Google certificate showed.

Luckily, the privacy and encryption standards built into most blockchain products are stronger than what exists elsewhere on the Web. It's safe to claim that very few average Web users used public-key cryptography before the rise of blockchain technologies like Bitcoin. But today, around 24 million people own private keys that can be used to access Bitcoin wallets.[81] Buchman put it well when he said:

> What's nice about the blockchain space is that even if it all fails, even if we never get cryptocurrency, at the very least, it will have increased the cryptographic competence of the professional class, because it's really, really stressing the importance and the significance and the power of some of these fundamental cryptographic primitives. And so, the more the Web is able natively to adopt basic cryptography, the more powerful it becomes, and the better able it is to secure the open access and the fair participation, both of which, to some extent, can actually depend on robust cryptography being used.[82]

Ancillary as it may be to blockchain's core value proposition, if blockchain drives the adoption of additional security standards for the average consumer—and increased academic, corporate, and governmental interest in cryptography—it will succeed in helping users take a more active role in securing their digital identities.

Promotion of governmental transparency

Government open data is used today to power our global positioning system, give weather updates, and issue product recalls; and research data generated by government entities is often released to the public.[83] Recent political developments in the United States have shown, however, how fragile such public data can be if government-controlled. Blockchain may offer a solution for politics-proofing open data initiatives.

Public blockchains are an incredibly useful tool for managing public data—they offer a verifiably permanent and tamper-proof record with which citizens can hold their governments accountable and secure the promises of public-maintained resources. That's why IBM is working on a suite of initiatives to promote "blockchain for government" with use cases as wide ranging as food safety and smart city development.[84] Nations like Austria and Estonia have also shown their interest in nationally sponsored blockchain open data initiatives, and we expect more nations to follow suit in the near future.[85]

Such efforts offer a new, but important, element to the concept of self-sovereignty—not only for data owned by single individuals but also for data owned by the collection of individuals known as "the public."

Restoration of consumer ownership and control of their data

Ultimately, these benefits all come back to self-sovereignty. Blockchain can give control back to the rightful owners of user data: the users themselves.

With blockchain, people can possess unique, immutable identities in a "digital black box." Such blockchain identity initiatives are underway from multiple sources. Companies like uPort, Civic, and Sovrin are working to provide individuals with authority and autonomy over their identity by creating horizontal solutions that work across applications—all possible because of the fundamental benefits of blockchain technology. Lubin explained:

> If properly constructed, blockchains are uncensorable and unrefutable. One can live in a totalitarian state and be comfortable that somewhere in the world, if they have access to this technology, that their identity and related data will persist. If one establishes that sort of data construction or centralized system, then one loses access to it, or the system goes away, then they're kind of out of luck. The ability to move across borders without possessions and still re-establish identity, either based on biometrics or some other kinds of information is also something that I believe would be better facilitated by global blockchain systems.
>
> Homomorphic data encryption technology will enable us to encrypt information such that the encrypted form will have the same shape, roughly, as the plain text form, and therefore enable computation to be run on the encrypted form and, if you have the right permissions, you'll be able to get answers about the encrypted information without the encrypted information ever being decrypted. So as the Cypherpunks wanted, cryptography may move us toward a world that's less exploitative of our data.[86]

Other solutions are taking a vertical approach. Take, for example, the much-hyped Brave Web browser. Made by Mozilla project co-founder and creator of JavaScript, Brendan Eich, the browser blocks ads natively, keeps all browsing data private to the user, and will ultimately allow individuals to support their favorite content creators through voluntary donation, not mandatory advertisement.[87] So far, consumers seem to love the prospects of additional security. Two million users now use Brave monthly, driving 12,000 publishers to register themselves to receive donations.[88]

Similarly, the blockchain-based social network AKASHA is giving users full control of their social data. Mihai Alisie, AKASHA founder and Ethereum co-founder, put it well:

> The toxic data that triggered [a] scandal [came] mainly from the second category because it includes very, very, very personal data about the users—starting from the number of seconds spent reading an article, to the clicks and pages visited after leaving Facebook. In comparison, AKASHA does not collect any kind of data to make ads better—since we have no ads or the desire to have them—and does not host the data that users share with each other since it is a decentralized network. Another very important distinction regards the user's identity: in the case of Facebook, the user has absolutely no control over "his" identity. In the case of AKASHA, the user has complete control over his identity.[89]

Of course, the unspoken conflict made clear from the above is that there are different approaches to this problem—some blockchain, some legacy Web. Consider Berners-Lee's Solid, an open-source Web-based protocol that re-architects how we store and share data and, as a consequence, how we develop apps.[90] Building on existing Web standards, Solid separates the apps from the data. Whichever app a user runs, it stores the data in the user's personal online data store—or "pod." Pods are like personal Web servers for a user's data.[91]

With Solid, a user can share anything with anyone, or no one, and each user has a choice of apps to use with the same data. Users are in control of their data and decide which entities and apps can access their data. Developers also benefit from being able to tap into a rich tapestry of data and can focus on the functionality of their app, without having to create a specific back-end for each app, since Solid provides a universal application programming interface. Inrupt was co-founded by Berners-Lee and his business partner John Bruce to fuel the uptake of Solid and provide a commercial force and additional accountability. Inrupt is currently working with Britain's National Health Service, NatWest Bank, and the government of Flanders, among others.[92]

Fast Company described Solid this way: "The app, using Solid's decentralized technology, allows Berners-Lee to access all his data seamlessly—his calendar, his music library, videos, chat, research. It's like a mash-up of Google Drive, Microsoft Outlook, Slack, Spotify, and WhatsApp. The difference here is that, on Solid, all the information is under his control."[93] We think that Solid certainly has potential, but that blockchain technology—with its security upgrade—has a better shot at securing self-sovereignty. Rouven Heck of uPort explained:

From what I know, Solid is based on traditional tech standards like DNS and HTTP. Relying on DNS doesn't give you actual control, since DNS names are rented from institutions and can be spoofed. Using a traditional server architecture with HTTP also doesn't provide much privacy, since the traffic between your service and applications will be fairly transparent, at least the metadata. Ultimately, with [self-sovereign identity], people will hold private keys, which allows more use control over their identity and encryption of data.

There are always trade-offs. We hope that every solution works, because different solutions have different use cases. We need to define protocols similar to SMTP [simple mail transfer protocol], which applications like uPort and others can adopt to be truly interoperable across various identity solutions.[94]

Heck hopes for collaboration and carving out areas in which multiple parties can play. Later in our conversation, he said that he doesn't expect there to be only one standard. That's why he compared uPort and other decentralized identity protocols to SMTP—supported and interoperable across other layered protocols like TCP/IP and user datagram protocol (UDP).

This is largely how Lubin sees the interaction of blockchain technology and legacy Web stack as well. He explained:

> Initially, it sits on Internet and Web technology and it consists of hundreds or thousands of decentralized protocols, over time. Some of them will be like Ethereum for trusted transactions, automated agreements, and smart software objects, others will sub-serve different needs, different utilizes, so decentralized storage, decentralized bandwidth, decentralized heavy-compute, proof of location, the identity construct, and many others.
>
> Many groups around the world are figuring out interoperability between all these different protocols and related systems, so it will be an inter-ledger world, and the protocols will be much less vulnerable because they'll be decentralized in nature. It may move. It may require less of the traditional stack, over time, and we can move virtual machines down closer toward bare metal.[95]

We think that type of hybrid approach would work well. In Chapter 8, "Standardized and Decentralized? Rethinking the Blockchain Technology Stack," we look at how blockchain technology itself decomposes nicely into a stacked architecture like that of the Internet today.[96] We need not have all layers fully operational to start seeing the impact of a self-sovereign Web; that is, we can gain incremental benefits from blockchain technology as a supplement, without wholly replacing HTTP and TCP/IP all at once.

For instance, uPort relies heavily on legacy Web infrastructure to offer a new, decentralized identity product. Very little of what they do actually occurs on a blockchain; but that small piece, having a distributed source of truth for key management and delegation, is incredibly important and gives uPort functionality that projects like Solid cannot have by their very nature. So, in the short term, we certainly think that blockchain products will play nicely with legacy Web products. (But, in the longer term, all bets are off. We'll see what happens with Filecoin, IPFS, and related projects, and write more on the long-term future of HTTP and related protocols.)

Promoting self-sovereignty through blockchain and other decentralized identity protocols will help us as a community to achieve three distinct and individually effective ends:

1. Consumers will be free to use their data to plan their lives. Without being locked into one particular platform that holds a monopoly over social data, for instance, consumers can plug their data into a series of platforms that allow them to learn what companies like Google and Facebook know today. Examples here span from judgments of personality and behavioral analysis to predictive analytics of everything from diabetes to pregnancy.[97] If users own their own data, they can use this information in unimagined ways.

2. Consumers will be able to monetize the data that they generate. The equation in this decentralized, self-sovereign world seems eminently fair: generate a valuable asset and benefit from its generation.

3. Consumer privacy will be protected. Blockchain technology can be a liberator of consumer data—pulling them out of centralized databases and giving them back to their rightful owners—preventing the magnitude of every data loss. Self-sovereign identity can also change the economics

for data frackers—conglomerates that mine cast pools of digital information and sell much of what they extract.

In short, we can remedy the problems of delegated identity by making a fundamental change—giving users direct ownership and control of their data and returning to the ideal of self-sovereignty.

VIEWS OF SOVEREIGNTY FROM THE DECENTRALIZED FUTURE

In 2040, I own my data. For all intents and purposes, the only data available to the public are those that I explicitly publish and authorize for use.

Data breaches are a thing of the past. Hospitals no longer worry about Health Insurance Portability and Accountability Act compliance because the data they "collect" is immediately transferred to the records that patients themselves own and control; similarly, alternate and fragmented social networks have popped up for extremely niche use cases—say, for one particular day at one particular club in Las Vegas—as each attendee owns their social graph and switching costs between platforms are effectively nil.

Now, all the data I generate is my property for safekeeping and monetization. Thanks to the advent of blockchain technology, the Web has finally and irrevocably guaranteed that users control their own self-sovereign digital identities.

 ## CONCLUSIONS AND RECOMMENDATIONS

Ultimately, we believe that blockchain can restore the decentralized Web and protect the ideals of open access, fair participation, and self-sovereignty. More importantly, we believe that it *will*.

This new era of open standards development has the potential to succeed even more than those of the past for two reasons: first, we have a historical example in that we know what the Web looks like today; and second, we know the downfalls of the last generation of protocol development. We know the importance of security and identity, we know the pernicious effects of profit-motivation, and we know that, left to their own devices, even open Web protocols can coalesce into walled gardens around mega-corporate data stores.

Similarly, we know that a collaborative approach is necessary in this new era of protocol development. Buchman told us that building with interoperability and future-proofing in mind was crucial to his technical approach in developing Tendermint and Cosmos:

> In a world of decentralization, no single developer team can figure out all the answers, so there's no way we could know the right solution for everyone. So, what we're trying to do is build technology that is as flexible as possible, that people can then take and adapt for their own needs. In the same way that HTTP is an incredibly general, flexible technology that people are adapting in a zillion ways the creators never even thought of, we're building the various pieces of Cosmos to be as flexible and adaptable as possible, so that people can use them in ways we haven't even thought of.[98]

We urge all business leaders and blockchain researchers to participate in this collaborative movement to re-decentralize the Web. "Blockchain has the potential of democratizing many aspects of the Internet we experience every day," said Yvon A. Audette, partner at KPMG. "Working through the enablement of this new paradigm will be critically important." It will not be easy. "Every user on the Internet would need some level of sophistication in managing his or her own personal information," he said.[99]

The companies and institutions that succeed in this new era will be those that are best able to collaborate with other actors in their ecosystems. As we have learned in the finance industry, the automotive industry, and many others, enterprise needs collaborative plays to generate value in this new era of open protocol development. Incentives matter. Howard Shrobe, the director of cybersecurity at MIT, wrote:

> We have demonstrated that it is possible to design a modern computer system that attackers can't break into and that can protect our information. The critical question today is not whether we can design safer computer systems, but really one of creating the right incentives for systems like these to become the new mainstream of computing.[100]

The trivergence of blockchain, AI, and IoT will take us to the next level, Web 3.0. It will be a ubiquitous Web where billions of people, trillions of devices, and countless decentralized autonomous organizations can transact, analyze huge sets of data, make increasingly better decisions, and take actions that sustain the planet—all in a secure, encrypted, and entity-to-entity manner.

We believe that the innate characteristics of blockchain technology—its immutability, censorship-resistance, new tokenized business models, elimination of rent-seeking intermediaries, strong cryptographic standards, transparency, and, most importantly, decentralization—will bring the Web back to its idealistic roots. We invite entrepreneurs, enterprise executives, and elected officials to join us in this important dialogue.

CHAPTER 2

THE CONVERGENCE OF BIG DATA AND BLOCKCHAIN

Disrupting the Business of Data Analytics

Mark van Rijmenam

 ## BIG DATA AND BLOCKCHAINS IN BRIEF

- Big data is eating the world. Slowly we begin to see the enormous implications of this mega trend. Big data offers organizations enormous possibilities to improve their products, services, and operations.

- Big data also results in enormous challenges for consumers, revolving around privacy, security, and ownership, as well as organizations, including changing data-governance practices and the sharing of data among industry players. Not meeting these challenges could undermine the competitiveness of every organization—or worse, directly undermine our democracy.

- Blockchain offers us a means of improving how organizations apply big data to preserve consumer rights to privacy and security. If designed and programmed carefully, smart contracts could help share data effortlessly and to the mutual benefit of the sharer and recipient.

- By using self-sovereign identities, consumers could recover and manage ownership of their personal data and the data they generate online. For consumers to assume better control of their data using blockchain, they will need to be educated on the use of public and private keys.

- We live in exponential times, and organizational leaders today should investigate how big data and blockchain will affect their business, if they want to be leading these organizations tomorrow.

INTRODUCTION

The phrase *big data* has been around since 2001.[101] Since then, the amount of data available has grown exponentially. Business Internet protocol traffic nearly tripled in 2017 compared to 2012 and will continue to grow at a compound annual growth rate (CAGR) of 21 percent to 2021, while global consumer Internet traffic is expected to grow at a CAGR of 24 percent for the next five years.[102] With the IoT, the world's total data volume will grow to 163 zettabytes per year by 2025, a tenfold increase compared to 2016.[103] By 2025, the average person will interact with a connected device nearly every 18 seconds, in effect digitally documenting every move, query, purchase, plan, and communication in such minute detail that, if this person cannot control access to his or her digital trail, privacy will have no meaning and security will remain uncertain.[104]

This increasing availability of data significantly changes organizations in terms of strategy, design, culture, and operations.[105] Already, for many businesses, the most likely path to creating competitive advantage is by subjecting big data to (advanced) analytics.[106] Today, big data has become a corporate standard, and data analytics is a prerequisite to remain competitive.[107] The impact of big data on an organization depends on the type of data collected (structured vs. unstructured) and the type of analytics applied.[108] There are several levels of practices, each increasing in complexity and the value they create: descriptive analytics, diagnostic analytics, predictive analytics, and prescriptive analytics.

Experts, consultants, and researchers have told organizations that the best approach to learning from big data was to centralize all available data, including customer, product, and operations data. Consequently, they have replaced large relational databases with data lakes running big data applications, creating a market worth well over $100 billion annually.[109]

However, the problems and challenges with big data are significant for both organizations and consumers, and we need to address them if we want to benefit from it in the future.[110]

FIGURE 2-1

ACHIEVING COMPETITIVE ADVANTAGE WITH CONVERGENCE OF BIG DATA AND BLOCKCHAIN

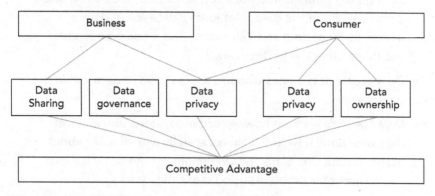

Created by Mark van Rijmenam, 2017, for use in this chapter.

CHALLENGES FOR ORGANIZATIONS

Large and multinational organizations span multiple jurisdictions and territories, where variables such as technologies, infrastructure, markets, customer demands, and consumer protection laws are different. Therefore, each business unit often develops its own data infrastructure solution, often with its own standards. Individual business units might operate their own data lakes, but have technical trouble pooling data across lakes. In addition, different departments often hold multiple copies of the same data source. How does an organization know which copy is the master copy, or the most up to date?

Sharing data across companies is even more challenging. Although companies such as DataStreamX and DataMarket facilitate the global exchange of information, sharing data with a competitor is usually tricky, even if it can bring substantial benefits.

Apart from sharing data within an organization or across industries, data governance remains an issue.

- *Data governance* refers to principles such as data quality, metadata, data access, and data life cycle.

- *Data principles* define how business users ought to manage and deal with available data.

- *Data quality* refers to the accuracy, timeliness, credibility, and completeness of the data. Metadata ("data about data") describes other data and helps us to find, understand, and use those other data effectively.[111]

- *Data access* determines who has access to what data within the organization.

- *Data life cycle* is about how we organize, store, and archive data over time. If we don't think carefully and critically about usage of data over time, then we might set our organizations up to encounter problems using these data later.

Departments, business units, and organizations might question the accuracy or ownership of the data when its provenance (its origin) is unclear or hackable.

Finally, security remains a big issue. Any organization can be hacked. The breach of Equifax, the consumer credit reporting agency, which exposed the personal data of some 143 million Americans in June and July 2017, is among the most recent and, some have argued, very preventable. Thus far, the Equifax breach has cost the company $4 billion.[112] The company's CEO resigned over the hack, as did its chief information officer and its chief security officer.[113] The Federal Trade Commission, the Consumer Financial Protection Bureau, the

Securities and Exchange Commission, a few state attorneys general, and other agencies in Britain and Canada have begun probes to determine whether the hack was indeed preventable, and whether several executives deliberately sold stocks before making their knowledge of the breach public.[114]

Equally troubling, in October 2016, hackers seized numerous unsecured IoT devices for a distributed denial of service (DDoS) attack, resulting in a widespread outage of websites. These connected devices could be hacked via their widely known default passwords.[115] Connected devices have a variety of vulnerabilities. Any smart device is a vulnerable device, according to Mikko Hyppönen, chief research officer at F-Secure, and Linus Nyman, assistant professor at the Hanken School of Economics in Helsinki, Finland.[116] Security issues include technical problems (outdated software, insecure data transmissions, etc.) and people problems (simple and default passwords, public Wi-Fi, etc.).[117] As more devices connect to the Internet and each other, without a security solution, the Internet of Things will become the Internet of Vulnerable Things.[118] How can an organization prevent the dissemination of valuable private data if its firewall is breached?

Big data sets enable organizations to improve operational efficiencies, but big data users must overcome significant challenges if they want to minimize risk. Consider Skullcandy, Caterpillar, and Avis Budget Group.

Skullcandy: Improving decision-making agility

The headphone manufacturer Skullcandy applies big data to communicate with its various teams.[119] Originally, Skullcandy used outdated business intelligence; employees who tracked performance metrics, such as forecasting and marketing data, kept getting varied results, despite using the same information. With data exceeding 100 million rows spread across multiple source locations, Skullcandy decided to implement a unified solution from Sisense: a central dashboard and reporting tool so that teams can assess their progress.

Considerations

- A centralized dashboard does not solve issues related to data quality and data provenance, nor does it verify that data can be trusted.
- Centralization of an extensive data source makes it vulnerable to security breaches and hackers.

Caterpillar: Using predictive analysis or maintenance

Caterpillar applies predictive maintenance analytics to reduce operational costs.[120] The company's marine division serves shipping vessel and tugboat fleet operators and uses analytics to discover ways to save fuel—an important driver for its customers' profits. The company used its intelligence platform, which integrates with the analytical platform and data integration of Pentaho, to discover a data correlation between refrigerated containers' energy consumption and fuel-meter readings, both of which are monitored by shipboard sensors.

Combining big data and predictive analytical maintenance helped validate this information and make better projections for the best operating range via changing generator power outputs. This tactic saved $30 per hour, which will have a big impact over time. For example, fleets with 50 ships that operate half the year (24 hours/day) would save more than $650,000 annually. Predictive maintenance analytics helps the company better serve its customers.

Considerations

- How trustworthy are data collected by these sensors?
- Can anyone edit this centralized database to show more favorable results?
- How secure are the sensor data if they are stored in a centralized database?
- How easy is it to share data with other companies?

Avis Budget Group: Using detailed customer profiles to improve marketing

Detailed, up-to-date, customer profile data are crucial to effective marketing campaigns. Car-rental company Avis Budget Group used big data analytics to accelerate its marketing activities. It garnered information from the 40 million customer records compiled from its reports, rental transaction system, and online transactions to produce one-year projections of customer rentals and profits on a continuous basis in comparison. It also infused data into the customer experience and focused on the customer lifetime value.[121] By using big data, the company was able to improve its operational efficiency and contact strategy.

Considerations

- Centralized customer data are highly sensitive to data breaches.
- Who has access to these sensitive customer data?
- How has it structured and stored data to generate reliable customer histories?
- Customers want to control access to their data and value their privacy.

CHALLENGES FOR CONSUMERS

The growing datafication of our society creates tension with consumers. Increasingly, consumers believe that privacy no longer exists. Organizations such as Google, Facebook, Microsoft, and Experian collect troves of data to offer personalized advertising, services, and products across the Web.[122] Not only do commercial organizations collect vast amounts of personal data but also governments aim to use big data to understand and control their citizens. The more data are linked together, shared, or sold to other companies, the more consumer privacy is violated.[123] Consequently, there is a trend toward restoring data ownership and control to consumers, which will require organizations to rethink their approach to big data.

For years, consumers have been handing over their data to companies that, in return, offer free services, such as email or social media. These companies use and abuse these data according to their take-it-or-leave-it terms of service. For example, Facebook allowed academic researchers to access its data without having secured users' informed consent.[124] Although consumers create the data, big corporations make billions of dollars off them. The centralized control of data ownership by large corporations is harmful for consumers and could even threaten democracy, as we have seen with Facebook's influence during the Brexit campaign and the 2016 US elections.[125] Consumers increasingly demand more control over their data, which could affect how organizations can collect, store, and apply customer data.

BLOCKCHAIN AND BIG DATA

Fortunately, the technology that solves the issues consumers have with today's big data practices will solve the organizational challenges companies face. Some have argued that blockchain would do for value what the Internet did for information: facilitate trustless P2P transactions without intermediaries.[126] Blockchain is a distributed ledger, and the data recorded on it are immutable, verifiable, and traceable.

These new characteristics of data will help organizations solve issues related to data sharing, data governance, data provenance, security, data ownership, and consumer or client privacy. As a result, the convergence of big data and blockchain will greatly affect how organizations should approach big data and how they can derive insights from it. This research explores these applications and looks at startups developing solutions to ensure data provenance, privacy, security, and data ownership.

HOW TELSTRA APPLIES BLOCKCHAIN TO SECURE SMART HOME SYSTEMS

The proliferation of IoT devices and its adoption by consumers have brought on security concerns, such as identifying the validity of a transaction and the identity of the person authorizing it.[127] Australian telecommunication company Telstra is tackling this issue for consumers. The company is experimenting with a combination of biometric security and blockchain technology for its IoT smart home product offerings. The company is using these technologies to enhance security across smart devices with the help of experiential tests using blockchains and leveraging the help of blockchain start-ups.

Telstra leverages blockchain to address technicalities

According to Katherine Robins, principal security expert at Telstra, Telstra intends to use blockchain to secure the IoT ecosystems of smart homes.[128] To do so, it works with numerous blockchain start-ups via its muru-D accelerator and Telstra Ventures, including Brontech, a start-up that aims to simplify the use of blockchain to help protect user identity.[129] The company tested its IoT smart home system on a variety of distributed ledgers, such as Ripple, Apache Hyperledger, and Ethereum, which resulted in exploring the viability of applying blockchain technology to IoT as a security enhancement solution for devices that were limited to storing small quantities of data.[130]

Initially, tests were exclusive to ADSL-T Gateway routers, but they were expanded to other home devices, including on-off switches and cameras.[131] However, as the number of IoT devices expands, so will the number of transactions, and keeping up with these transactions increases computational requirements, which can become a serious challenge.

Moreover, too much traffic can leave IoT devices vulnerable to other security issues, such as DDoS attacks. These attacks can bring down entire enterprise servers and halt the delivery of service to millions of customers, as we have seen in the 2016 Mirai DDoS attack that brought down much of the Internet. After the attack, more than 14,000 Internet domains (roughly 8 percent of Dyn's customers) dropped Dyn as their DNS service provider.[132] In addition, the time it takes to verify device firmware can cause difficulties, especially in settings where connections lack security or are inconsistent, such as rural areas or large farms.

Telstra, however, plans to mitigate these issues by incorporating blockchain technology to store device firmware's cryptographic hashes on private blockchains and reduce the time it takes to verify transactions.[133] This is possible thanks to Telstra's ability to detect tampering and receive data that is resistant to alteration in real time. Additionally, hashed user biometric data are integrated into the private blockchain to improve user identification and enhance verification.

Benefits of blockchain for Telstra

There are several benefits of using blockchain to secure smart home systems, including acceleration of resolution time, which can help companies identify users and verify transactions faster.[134] This becomes increasingly important as businesses create applications to enhance customer experiences with convenient access to their products and services, which is especially relevant for smart home systems.

Telstra extends the security provided by blockchain technology and combines it with biometric features, such as voice and facial recognition, which are stored encrypted on the blockchain, making it immutable, verifiable, and traceable.[135] The usage of blockchain makes IoT security significantly more efficient and cost-effective. In addition, the extra security can help reduce fraudulent transactions and mitigate unauthorized access of smart devices or networks.

As the IoT ecosystem increases, so will vulnerabilities and transactions. This makes it essential for heightened security measures to verify the validity of transactions and users at a faster pace. Telstra's use of blockchain technology will further improve security measures of smart devices within the home. This will enhance the customer experience by giving consumers peace of mind, knowing their information is safe and they have control over access to it.

DATA SHARING

For most organizations, the importance and advantages of data sharing are clear and have been clear for years.[136] Combining various internal and external data, so-called mixed data, offers organizations additional insights that can significantly benefit the organization.[137] Although sharing data across geographically dispersed business units can be challenging because of different standards or formats, sharing data with the competition is nearly impossible. After all, why would we share one of our organization's most valuable assets with our competitor, or with a broker such as Experian? Organizations therefore require an accurate, reliable, and data-preserving technology to facilitate such data sharing.

While existing companies such as DataStreamX or DataMarket offer novel solutions, none of them offer the benefits of sharing data that is trustable and private. Blockchain, however, enables organizations to keep control over their own data that they want to share or sell, since the data will remain within the organization. It enables organizations to segment data as they want, store each segment into a vault, and have full control over who has access to those vaults, governed by asymmetric cryptography and smart contracts. As a result, organizations "never make anything available that you can't, or that you don't want to," according to Marcien Jenckes, advertising president at Comcast Cable, which will be releasing a data sharing solution in 2018.[138]

Thanks to the usage of decentralized cryptography, the blockchain solution developed by Comcast is more secure than traditional solutions, which generally enable reverse-engineering the data to obtain any missing information. Comcast is collaborating with several organizations, including NBC Universal, Disney, Altice USA, Cox Communications, TF1 Group in France, Channel 4 in the United Kingdom, and Mediaset Italia, to figure out how the system should work.[139]

Another solution currently being developed for enterprise data sharing is the Fujitsu data exchange network, which allows organizations to share their data safely and quickly with their competitors without disclosing confidential information, and getting paid for every bit that is used by the third party.[140] It uses a Hyperledger-based framework that provides organizations full control over their distributed data; the objective is to promote interchanges of data collected by various organizations and companies. Every transaction will be recorded on the blockchain, making it immutable, verifiable, and traceable. This will help organizations understand who had access to what data when, how those data were used, and how much money the data generated. An added benefit of using a blockchain-based sharing platform is that organizations no longer have to hand over their data to companies such as Experian or Acxiom, since using distributed ledger technologies means these intermediaries are no longer necessary.

Data sharing will also be very useful for the IoT, where independent sensors can sell their data to the highest bidder (whether this is another sensor or an organization) using micro- or even nanotransactions. While microtransactions have never been possible due to the high transaction costs involved in traditional payments (or even nowadays in bitcoin), it is likely that future cryptocurrencies will enable sensors or organizations to pay for data by transferring thousandths or millionths of a cent. This capability will spur new business models for organizations that install sensors across the globe and sell the data collected by those sensors to interested actors.

The first platform to enable such data sharing is called Terbine, which has enabled a sensor data exchange for the IoT. While Terbine does not yet employ distributed ledger technology, it indexes all publicly available sensor data and grades the quality of those data, thereby creating a global frictionless IoT marketplace, according to David Knight, founder and CEO of Terbine.[141]

IOTA, on the other hand, has developed a revolutionary new blockchain technology that enables companies to share their data on an open marketplace in real time, without the need for fees. IOTA (Internet of Things asset) can settle transactions in real time among connected sensors through a blockless distributed ledger, called *tangle*, which is infinitely scalable. The tangle is built using a so-called DAG, or a *directed acyclic graph*, which is actually not a blockchain at all. IOTA has created a decentralized and self-regulating P2P network for the IoT that will enable anyone to share data among connected devices and sensors for free. With blockchain technology, or tangle in the case of IOTA, organizations can verify the integrity of and pay for the data shared across business units, organizations, and things. In 2017, IOTA launched a new data marketplace, data.iota.org, making it possible to securely store, sell, and access data streams, especially targeted at the Internet of Things domain.[142] A true paradigm shift for organizations, it enables including previously unthinkable data sources that will result in better products and services.

DATA GOVERNANCE

Organizations already consider data an asset and include it on their balance sheets. Secure data sharing enables organizations to monetize this asset.[143] As a result, organizations need a single version of the truth.[144] Therefore, how to govern the data is playing an increasingly critical role within organizations.[145] In fact, data governance has become such a necessity for organizations that they no longer can get away with expending minimal effort to that end.[146]

The importance of governance: Quality and compliance

Data governance is involved with creating guidelines and standards to achieve data quality management and ensuring compliance with the processes developed around data usage.[147] Master data management, an aspect of data governance, is growing in importance to ensure data quality, because decades of using and storing data in disparate stores and formats has resulted in many inconsistencies, making it difficult for companies to understand their data.[148] Improper master data management processes could result in a variety of problems that could harm the business, such as operational problems or incorrect customer data. As such, due to the increasing amount of data available, master data management is increasingly important to organizations.[149]

In theory, master data management will become more important since blockchain preserves data indefinitely. Resilience and irreversibility are two key attributes of blockchains; once transaction data are added and accepted by the nodes, they become immutable.[150] However, blockchain does not magically transform low-quality data into high-quality data in terms of consistency and correctness. Garbage in still means garbage out. If bad or low-quality data are presented in the right way, it will be appended to the blockchain. If a document contains false information but is presented in the right way, it will still end up on a blockchain.[151] Therefore organizations require a data governance framework that combines business and technical perspectives related to data quality to respond to strategic and operational challenges involved with data that is added to a blockchain.[152]

An industry perspective

Data governance is relevant for any industry, but the healthcare sector especially can benefit from blockchain-enabled data governance because of the sensitive data generated, stored, and shared. Already, several companies are investigating the potential of combining healthcare data with blockchain, including DeepMind, Google's health tech subsidiary driven by artificial intelligence. In March 2017, London's Royal Free Hospital and DeepMind announced plans to develop kidney monitoring software. The longer-term objective is to allow hospitals, the National Healthcare Service (NHS), and patients to track their health data and to share and combine data securely through distributed ledger technology.[153]

DeepMind co-founder Mustafa Suleyman and Ben Laurie, its head of security and transparency, called this a *verifiable data audit:* whenever an entity interacted with data, it added an entry to the ledger. The entry indicated which piece of data was used and why. For example, a doctor accessed a patient's blood test data to check it against the NHS national algorithm for acute kidney injury. Any access and changes made to the patient's data would be immediately visible. In other words, they are creating an auditing system for health data.[154] Ensuring that the data are accurate becomes all the more important when dealing with healthcare data to ensure patients' privacy and safety.

Healthcare is one area where data governance becomes increasingly important, but in fact, data governance should be a key consideration for any organization in any industry. Especially with the amount of data being created at increasing speeds, data governance becomes critical to ensure protection of the rights of consumers. Craig Mundie, senior adviser to the CEO of Microsoft and the company's former chief research and strategy officer, argued that the focus should shift from data collection and retention to how personal data are used. He suggested annotating datum at its point of origin and wrapping it with metadata that include how the data can be used by whom and under what circumstances.[155]

Alex "Sandy" Pentland, author of the book *Social Physics*, adds to this that consumers should have the right to full control over their data and that the protection of personal privacy ensures the future success of a society.[156] The approach of a "wrapper" with metadata and rules governing the use of personal data could definitely contribute to this protection—especially if that wrapper is recorded on a blockchain and governed by smart contracts to ensure that organizations cannot alter these rules without the consumer knowing. Implementing such governing rules would work similarly to the Fujitsu data exchange network, or the Blockchain Insights Platform developed by Comcast, albeit for consumers instead of enterprises.[157]

One approach to achieve this is using a keyless signature infrastructure (KSI) approach. This differs from a public key infrastructure (PKI) approach, which is the standard cryptographic toolshed for authentication of data using digital signature, as signatures can be reliably verified without assuming continued secrecy of the keys.[158] As Mike Gault, co-founder and CEO of Guardtime—a technology company with decades of experience defending networks from nation-state attacks—explained:

> Signatures generated by KSI can be used as a wrapper (or stored as additional metadata depending on the data model) for any size and type of data such that the signature is cryptographically linked to the underlying data. The cryptographic link allows assertions to be made at a later date regarding the time, integrity and provenance of the data.[159]

The result is a blockchain approach to include rules governing personal data that restores control to consumers over their own data—that is, bringing governance to the code. Smart contracts can then be used to change rules securely, depending on certain pre-set conditions. Therefore, with blockchain, data governance can become intrinsically linked to the data, preventing manipulation and protecting consumers and organizations.

DATA SECURITY

Blockchain not only improves data governance, it also positively affects data security. Despite the high market value, the Bitcoin blockchain has not yet been hacked, although it is likely that many hackers are trying, especially with a market capitalization of $675 billion, as of June 2021. Although a variety of cryptocurrency exchanges have been hacked, blockchain technology itself offers security on several fronts that is very useful for organizations dealing with big data. There are three main areas where blockchain can contribute in terms of data security: confidentiality, integrity, and availability.[160]

Data confidentiality

According to the National Institute of Standards and Technology (NIST), confidentiality refers to "preserving authorized restrictions on information access and disclosure, including means for protecting personal privacy and proprietary information."[161] Confidentiality is increasingly becoming important, especially in its ability to stop identity theft. Identity theft is especially known to harm consumers, although organizations can fall victim to commercial identity theft. This entails using fake identities to obtain information or to bill for services or products that have not been delivered. It happens to all types of organizations and as recently as April 2017, Facebook and Google disclosed being the victims of a $100-million commercial phishing scam.[162]

Although many organizations apply asymmetric cryptography or PKI to secure communication, PKI relies on a trusted central authority to issue the certificates (key pairs), an authority that can be compromised by hackers using, for example, a man-in-the-middle attack. Blockchain, however, can prevent such attacks by creating a public and audible PKI, thereby decentralizing the issuing of certificates. The KSI developed by Guardtime is one such decentralized approach; and in 2016, the company managed to secure all one million e-health records of Estonia.[163] Danube Tech is another tech firm that aims to develop a decentralized PKI and restore control of online identities to their rightful owners.[164] A third company is CertCoin, developed by MIT, which used a distributed ledger to remove the central authority for issuing certification.[165]

A common approach to identity theft is to obtain and exploit usernames or passwords of consumers illegally, sometimes by hacking centralized databases. Organizations are required to take the necessary security measures to prevent hackings. However, any security measure taken by organizations will be in vain if customers still use traditional usernames and passwords, such as *123456* or *password*. In such instances, a decentralized (certification) system can help. As Alex Momot, founder and CEO of Remme, stated, blockchain can move the responsibility of strong authentication from the user to the organization.[166]

The full encryption of blockchain ensures that data cannot be accessed by unauthorized parties while in transit through untrusted networks. In addition, inherent to blockchain is the immutability of data, preventing parties from illegally adjusting data for their own benefit. Therefore, for organizations to ensure confidentiality, blockchain has become key. Increasingly there are a variety of solutions, such as those offered by Guardtime, Danube Tech, and CertCoin.

Data integrity

The second contribution of blockchain in terms of data security is that it ensures integrity, which the NIST defines as "guarding against improper information modification or destruction, and includes ensuring information non-repudiation and authenticity."[167] The combination of hashing and cryptography as well as the decentralized nature of blockchain means that there is no central authority or actor that can adjust the data on the blockchain for its own benefit. Doing so would be known instantly to all other stakeholders with access to the blockchain, who would not verify such transactions.

With blockchain, any asset recorded on a blockchain can be retrieved or moved only with the corresponding cryptographic key. Therefore, the key becomes an asset that its owner can monetize, since it is backed by the underlying asset.[168] Protecting the private key is critical. Therefore, organizations should be aware of how to deal with the cryptographic keys and how to expect customers to deal with them. A lost private key can prevent data on a blockchain from being decrypted or, if it falls into the wrong hands, it can make the data public for those who have access to the private key. Therefore, to ensure integrity, organizations would need to educate consumers on how to deal with the private keys, since many consumers are not familiar with private and public keys and how they work.

As David Treat, managing director financial services and blockchain lead for Accenture said, "Leaving cryptographic keys in software sitting on a computer is the equivalent of leaving your house keys under the welcome mat."[169] So, although blockchain ensures integrity by making data immutable, there remains a responsibility for organizations and consumers.

Data availability

The third contribution of blockchain to data security is availability, which NIST defines as "ensuring timely and reliable access to and use of information."[170] Distributed ledger technology does not have a single point of failure, which would make a DDoS attack exponentially more difficult. After all, for a blockchain network to be brought down, all nodes within the network should be attacked. With some decentralized networks incorporating millions of computers, this becomes highly improbable to achieve. This is why a blockchain-based PKI is so valuable, since it does not have a single point of failure (the central authority that issues the certificates).

Despite blockchain's potential to improve data security, there must be a note of caution since the technology is still so new. In the (near) future, currently unknown security issues might appear that could have an impact on how the technology is used and applied. In addition, many start-ups are experimenting with various new blockchain technologies or cryptographic practices, which, if done incorrectly, could result in potential security breaches. Therefore, as with any digital technology, to protect consumers, customers, and employees, security should be a key component of any digital strategy.

DATA PRIVACY AND IDENTITY

Increasingly, big data is invading consumers' lives and affecting their privacy because the Web has become such a centralized platform.

Originally, the Web was designed to be decentralized so that everybody could participate by having his or her own domain and Web server.[171] Unfortunately, that did not work out, and as a result, there is a major problem with having centralized organizations collecting so much consumer data and using it to offer personalized advertising to their users.

As Jonathan Taplin discussed in his book *Move Fast and Break Things*, organizations that have access to so much data and use it to steer consumer behavior could directly undermine our democracy, as we have seen with how Facebook and Cambridge Analytics were able to influence both Brexit and the 2016 US presidential elections.[172] These centralized organizations do not forget or forgive. Since actions (i.e., data) speak louder than words, as long as consumers are not in control of their own data, it is possible that human beings are being defined by their data. This would be a serious threat to our humanity. An example of what such a world would look like can be seen in China.

Sesame Credit's impact on society and privacy

China is developing Sesame Credit, a social, transparent credit score for how obediently citizens follow the party line.[173] China's social credit scoring system applies innovative solutions that leverage the advantages of blockchain technology and big data.[174] Ant Financial, an Alibaba company, has been developing this social scoring system and it stands to impact society and invade the daily lives of Chinese citizens in a variety of ways.

Sesame Credit is a credit rating system that incorporates social scoring. It calculates credit scores based on online shopping habits.[175] Sesame Credit will impact society by ushering in the use of social trust as a part of credit scoring and reporting. The program helps China push the development of its social credit system on a national level. However, it comes with concerns regarding data privacy data and information transparency since, for example, many individuals were not aware that Sesame Credit rated them when the service initially began.[176] This is troubling, especially as the system is not 100 percent accurate.

Nevertheless, the Chinese government aims to fully implement these measures by 2020.[177] Sesame Credit uses big data insights to assign a social score based not only on a person's dealings with businesses but also on how he or she interacts socially online. This directly affects consumers by providing them with preferential treatment, such as skipping long lines at the hospital and access to loans. However, it could also affect consumers by way of penalties for breaking social trust, such as denial of consideration for public office or a loss of welfare and social security. The goal is to enhance market economy regulation and good behavior, such as buying diapers, and to penalize people and businesses for poor practices, such as selling toxic food or engaging in bribes.

Alibaba's Alipay brings social trust via Sesame Credit scoring system

Alibaba was one of the eight technology companies approved by China's central bank in 2014 to develop online and e-commerce rating systems based on social trust.[178] Alibaba's payment affiliate, Ant Financial, developed and integrated Sesame Credit into Alipay and assigns social credit scores to Alipay users who have agreed to use the credit-scoring service.[179] Sesame Credit can leverage Alibaba's robust database in conjunction with other factors, such as online transactional history, tax payment history, and traffic infraction history, to determine an individual's trustworthiness.[180]

For example, an individual who buys diapers might have higher scores than a person who spends money on entertainment, since the diaper transactions would be perceived as being more responsible. Alipay users with a Sesame Credit social credit score can access various perquisites depending on how high their scores are, such as expedited security checks at airports or deposit waivers for car rentals. Ant Financial is exploring incorporating blockchain technology to enhance the security of data and improve verification.[181] While the technology is still under development with Sesame Credit, Ant Financial plans to leverage it to make transactions cheaper and faster. It already has experience using it with its charitable donation site to track money.

Sesame Credit offers organizations several benefits, including rewarding better business decisions and penalizing poor decisions. As a result, organizations can verify the identities and trustworthiness not only of customers but also of suppliers and competitors. However, Sesame Credit might become a data-privacy nightmare for consumers.

Identity and black boxes

A solution to the privacy nightmare of Sesame Credit might be the incorporation of a *self-sovereign identity*, an identity that is owned and controlled by the person or the device itself. It is an identity that is portable, private, and protected. In other words, a self-sovereign identity is a paradigm shift from today's identity system, and it will drastically change how organizations are able to deal with customer data. To understand the importance of a self-sovereign identity, we need to understand what identity really is.

Identity consists of many different attributes, which are constantly changing and evolving in terms of priority and durability. Some attributes such as birthdates, place of birth, biological parents, and Social Security numbers will stay with a person for his or her entire life. Others, such as an employee number, student number, address, or telephone number could change periodically. Still other attributes could be very short-lived, such as a username on a forum or website. Each of these attributes has different, uniquely identifiable characteristics, and the combination of them constitutes a person's identity (although the person might perceive that differently).

The same goes for devices. As with people, machines have a variety of attributes that make up its identity. These include the type of device, its brand, color, characteristics, and capabilities. Although we have an identity infrastructure for people in place, at the moment we do not have an identity infrastructure in place for things. Despite that, we are rushing to connect devices to the Internet. This could pose significant future challenges, argues David Birch, an internationally recognized thought leader in digital identity and digital money. According to Birch, the only way to achieve this is using a decentralized solution, since a central database that stores everything about everything would be too dangerous.[182]

If an identity consists of ever-changing attributes, a self-sovereign identity restores control over who has access to those attributes to the consumer who owns that identity. So instead of social media companies or governments owning a person's identity attributes, the consumer is in full control and determines, for each interaction, who gets access to which data points. For example, when entering a bar, we could use a self-sovereign identity to prove that we are of drinking age rather than providing a driver's license, which discloses a variety of very personal details such as our name, date of birth, address, or license number, none of which the bar owner needs to know. Instead, we decide which information we want to release to which organization and when. As such, a self-sovereign identity offers many advantages to consumers. Building the infrastructure might be a challenge, however.

That is why David Birch believes that banks should be responsible for storing identity information, since they already have a secure infrastructure in place to deal with money. Birch argues that in the future, banks' function as stores of money might become outdated, which is why they should pursue guarding identity and reputation, albeit using a decentralized solution.[183] One organization that already enables financial institutions to ensure identity compliance, which could be a precursor for managed identities, is Cambridge Blockchain. Its product focuses on streamlining digital identity by offering users full control over their identities, while ensuring regulatory compliance for financial institutions. According to its website, "Cambridge Blockchain's distributed architecture resolves the competing challenges of transparency and privacy."[184]

However, Daniel Gasteiger, a member of the board of directors of the Global Blockchain Business Council, argues that we should be careful with adding attributes to a blockchain, since attributes change over time.[185] That is why a decentralized encryption method is required to provide individuals with full control over these changing attributes. As a result, consumers will become black boxes for organizations, and only the consumer will determine what kinds of data are shared with the organization. That will significantly change data ownership, how organizations can deal with customer data, and how they can derive insights from it. If Sesame Credit would incorporate such a decentralized infrastructure, it would offer Chinese citizens full control over who has access to their social credit score, while the government could guarantee that the scores are trustworthy, immutable, and verifiable at any moment.

Multiple organizations are working on developing solutions for self-sovereign identities. Each solution is slightly different from the other and has a different approach in terms security and encryption. These start-ups are focusing on digital identities related to passports; e-residency; online account logins; certificates of birth, marriage, and death; and so forth. Some of the pioneers in digital identity are as follows, in alphabetical order:

2WAY.IO (2way.io): a P2P reputation and identity platform that puts the user back in control. It offers services, which are blockchain agnostic, to organizations looking to implement an identity solution.

BanQu App (banquapp.com): a fintech company focusing on economic identities and extreme poverty. It offers a secure, portable digital identity that maintains transaction history through a proprietary blockchain-based platform for the poorest people.

Bitnation (bitnation.co): a platform company that offers the services traditional governments provide, but based on the blockchain. It calls itself the first decentralized borderless voluntary nation.

BlockAuth (blockauth.org): BlockAuth is developing a framework to verify user authenticity while also enabling an easy-to-integrate OpenID authentication system.

Brontech (bron.tech): a blockchain-based identity platform that aims to redefine the relationship between people, personal data, and money.

Cambridge Blockchain (cambridge-blockchain.com): a start-up that aims to put control of personal identity data back into the hands of the end user. The platform is focused on the financial industry and enables them to comply with know-your-customer regulations.

Civic (civic.com): an identity platform that uses identity verification and protection tools to provide businesses and individuals control over their identities.

Procivis (procivis.ch): a start-up that aims to develop and offer an "e-government as a service" solution, where digital identity empowers citizens and gives them control over their identity data.

ShoCard (shocard.com): an organization building a digital identity platform to protect consumer privacy and make it easy to use. It is built on a public blockchain data layer, and as such, it does not store any data or keys.

Sovrin (sovrin.org): a self-sovereign identity blockchain developed initially by Evernym, which has since open-sourced the platform. It aims to build the missing layer for secure identity on the Internet.

uPort (uport.me): a start-up that aims to develop an open source, self-sovereign, blockchain-based identity system on Ethereum; it partnered with Microsoft and it is developed by ConsenSys.

These start-ups, and many more, aim to develop solutions around identity for all industries. Any industry can benefit from digital identities that are verified using the blockchain. However, three early adopters are most advanced in their development of applications for digital identity: the financial services industry, healthcare, and government.

DATA OWNERSHIP

Many people have handed over personal data or agreed to be monitored in return for free services. However, increasingly, consumers are concerned about who has access to their data: a 2016 Pew Research survey showed that 74 percent of consumers said it was "very important" to have control over who could get information about them.[186] In addition, consumers might not realize that they have given their consent because the terms and conditions of usage or service are long and complicated and take time to read and understand; or they have a sense of resignation about corporate surveillance.[187] Such centralized control of data ownership by large corporations is harmful for consumers as it gives centralized organizations enormous power and puts consumers in a vulnerable position. Consumers can see only their own transactions and interactions, not how third-party vendors or applications are using their data.

However, with blockchain technology, we can solve this situation by giving consumers full control over their data, enabling consumers to decide which organizations can use their data, how, and when. Since data on a blockchain are immutable, verifiable, and traceable, it enables data provenance. Data provenance shows how ownership and permissions have changed over time, as well as how the data were created and used, and who is in control of those data. As such, it speeds up the process of verifying an identity of third parties and offers consumers a choice to select, for each piece of data that they create, whether or not they want to allow third parties to have their information, and to verify that these third parties are authentic.

In addition, consumers can get paid for it. When consumers have full control over their data, organizations will have to find new ways to get consumer consent to analyze those data. Consent moves away from a simple "I accept terms and conditions" to technologically implementing solutions that not only obtain real-time consent from users but also reward consumers for usage of their data. This shift will become a significant but not impossible technical and cultural challenge for organizations to meet: the first solutions similar to the Fujitsu data exchange network are already in development. They work as if every bit of data had its own vault, including smart contracts linked to it, which regulates who has access to the data, for how long, and for what price. Every transaction can be traced, and the data owner can benefit in real time.

Of course, what we can develop for enterprises can be developed for consumers. For example, the start-up Blockstack is working on a new Internet using decentralized applications where users own their data. With Blockstack, users obtain digital keys that enable them to control their data. They use these keys to sign into the applications locally, and they own any data they generate while doing things on the Internet. It combines a decentralized domain name server system with blockchain technology to deliver these capabilities. If it succeeds, Blockstack will significantly change the game for organizations. Given the technical and cultural challenges of such a solution, organizations should begin preparing for this future.

SHIFTING ATTITUDES AND POLICIES

The convergence of big data and blockchain will require new solutions and approaches from organizations, regulators, and individuals to ensure that, in the end, everyone can benefit from this convergence. It is a paradigm shift when, suddenly, the creator of the data is in full control, rather than the organization collecting the data. Here are five ways the convergence of big data and blockchain will directly affect individuals, organizations, governments, and policymakers.

First, organizations need to ensure data privacy and security, especially when related to individuals and things, and if they want to share data across organizations. Distributed ledger technology is key for organizations if they wish to achieve this. Data sharing requires standards to ensure that organizations and consumers can easily share their data across borders and organizations, while remaining in control, keeping data private, and being able to monetize it.

Second, regulators and governments need to ensure that consumers remain in full control of their own data, taking it away from organizations, and to ensure that organizations take data security seriously. A self-sovereign identity will become the new normal, for individuals as well as things. Governments and policy advisers, therefore, need to understand what a self-sovereign identity entails and need to draft legislation to force organizations to move to self-sovereign identity systems and restoring control to the individual.

Third, individuals need to become aware of the opportunities and responsibilities that come with being in control of their data, such as keeping a private key truly private. Therefore, it is vital to build awareness of what the convergence of big data and blockchain means for consumers. This requires, most likely, long-term education of consumers on how to deal with private keys.

Fourth, control of data will move to the individual, organization, or device responsible for creating it. Data vaults will become the new normal, governed by smart contracts that execute automatically once certain pre-set conditions have been met. Watchdogs should ensure that these smart contracts are ethical and treat each customer fairly and equally in similar situations.

Fifth, we will see organizations bringing governance to the data and the code by applying smart contracts and cryptography to ensure trust in a trustless society. Governance within organizations will shift from boardrooms to developers, who will be responsible for incorporating governance within the code.

The convergence of big data and blockchain will not slow down in the coming years. On the contrary, we live in a time of exponential progress, and the coming years will see the development of a plethora of new solutions developed with the customer in mind, offering data ownership, privacy, and security while enabling individuals, organizations, and things to share and monetize their data. It is a paradigm shift that requires actions for all stakeholders involved, including governments, policymakers, and regulators, to ensure that moving to this new paradigm is done in accordance with the law and protects consumers.

CONCLUSIONS AND RECOMMENDATIONS

With the amount of data created increasing exponentially over the years and the rapid improvement of distributed ledger technologies, the convergence of big data and blockchain offers many opportunities for organizations and societies to develop products and services that are more secure, fair, and private for consumers.

WHAT EXECUTIVES SHOULD KEEP IN MIND

Data ownership will take on a new meaning. Data sharing will become possible as data provenance opens up new revenue streams for organizations, while data governance will be improved significantly. As a result, the convergence of big data and blockchain offers four key takeaways:

- Blockchain will protect consumers' privacy and ownership and offer consumers full control over their data, but will also require education regarding the opportunities and responsibilities that come with this new paradigm.

- Data security will become increasingly important as the number of connected devices increases, and blockchain can ensure trust among connected devices.

- Data sharing will enable organizations to gain better insights, while ensuring data privacy across departments and organizations. In addition, consumers will be able to monetize their data if they have full control over it.

- Blockchain will revolutionize data governance by bringing governance to the code, whereby smart contracts add a metalayer to every bit of data, determining the conditions related to those data.

WHAT ORGANIZATIONS CAN DO TODAY

Take action today if you want your organization to benefit from the convergence of big data and blockchain. Regulators will soon awaken and impose rules and regulations that offer more control to consumers over their data. That will significantly change the playing field for organizations. Consumer data will become a black box that will require technical consent to access and a monetary reward to use.

Investigate how you might better monetize your existing data. Could such solutions as the Fujitsu data exchange network enable you to share data securely and privately with other organizations? Could you incorporate external data into your own insights? These efforts will result in improved products and services for both consumers and organizations and an improved bottom line.

Explore mutually beneficial partnerships with competitors or other industry players. Would sharing data help you to improve your products and services? Organizations can test this process with an internal data-sharing project across geographically dispersed business units to understand what it means before sharing data with external organizations.

Consider which of your processes could benefit from smart contracts that govern data and automate decisions.

Especially when working with connected devices, smart contracts can automate transactions and offer a new data source that can lead to new insights. In addition, they can ensure data integrity, which could result in more secure applications.

Imagine not having automatic access to customer data. How would lack of access affect your operations? What if access required more than a written consent and complicated terms and conditions? How would it change your processes? What new solutions would you need to implement? Would you need to create them yourself or could you leverage existing solutions?

Understand the impact of self-sovereign identities on your business. Such IDs for individuals and their devices might still be far away, but consumers will demand increased privacy and more control over their data. Find out how they can help your organization become an early adopter of self-sovereign identities, similar to what Telstra is doing.

Investigate how blockchain can make your own connected devices more secure. For many organizations working with IoT, which is almost every business today, security is not a priority and could leave the network vulnerable to massive DDoS attacks such as the one in October 2016. Blockchain solutions such as the IOTA tangle—which offers infinite scalability and free microtransactions—could prevent such attacks, and so leaders would be wise to consider them and create a more secure organization.

We live in a time of exponential progress, and accelerated change is the only constant, especially for those using big data and exploring blockchain technology, two mega trends that are fundamentally transforming how we work and live. Therefore, organizational leaders should start discussing the impact of these trends on their organizations and preparing for a connected world where data are more secure, private, and owned by consumers.

CHAPTER 3

DISTRIBUTED ARTIFICIAL INTELLIGENCE

Blockchain as an Operating Platform for AI

Don Tapscott and *Anjan Vinod*

 DISTRIBUTED AI IN BRIEF

- Although heavily used as a buzzword, AI is emerging as one of the biggest technological revolutions ever. The ability for computing systems to absorb and interpret large data sets in a meaningful way evolved in the twentieth century and has advanced rapidly for about the last 10 years. The biggest disruptions are yet to come.

- With a market size projected to reach $70 billion by 2020, the opportunity to discern actionable insights from data using AI will transform a variety of industries from transportation to healthcare, finance, manufacturing, retail, and so many more.[188]

- As adept as the human mind is at finding opportunities, systems now have the ability to pore through thousands of times more data in a way that ultimately will augment our decision-making skills. Seventy-two percent of business leaders see AI as being fundamental for the future.[189]

- As powerful as AI is becoming, blockchain technology has the unique ability to push the AI revolution forward through a decentralized, trustless set of features. In this chapter, we look at what AI is exactly, and what are some of its most powerful aspects.

- We look at centralized AI solutions, the solutions blockchain technology could provide, and the issues posed by these emerging fields. We then analyze what the power of decentralized AI could unveil.

- Blockchain has the potential to be the operating platform for AI, whether for existing centralized entities or for emerging uses of decentralized AI.

WHAT IS ARTIFICIAL INTELLIGENCE?

At an extremely high level, artificial intelligence is the design of intelligent systems capable of learning and simulating human cognition. The field of AI encompasses a variety of techniques such as natural language processing, neural nets, and deep learning.

We can divide AI into two classes: the first is symbolic AI, and the second is machine learning (ML), also known as *connectionism*. The former uses mathematical logic to formalize the complex tasks that artificial intelligence machines will perform. For tasks too difficult to formalize, such as pattern recognition—say, a set of rules to distinguish a picture of a cat from that of a dog—machine learning is particularly powerful. It is a set of techniques that model cognitive processes directly from experiences. Given a large set of examples, machine learning algorithms can perform complex tasks (e.g., market predictions) by identifying patterns in the data set.

We are surrounded by tangible AI applications daily. In fact, 77 percent of consumers use an AI-powered service or device.[190] AI-based enterprise applications are projected to grow from $1.6 billion in annual revenue to $31.2 billion by 2025. This estimated 52 percent compounded annual growth rate is fueled by such applications as image recognition, recruitment, data analytics, and cybersecurity. With investment in AI start-ups increasing sixfold since 2000, the amount of attention, money, and development in the space is unprecedented.[191] Enterprise adoption of AI is growing rapidly as well, with a reported 61 percent of businesses implementing AI in 2018.[192]

Recommendations on Netflix and targeted ads on Facebook are both supported by AI-powered systems in some manner. IBM has deployed Watson, its AI platform and *Jeopardy!* game show champion, for a variety of companies.[193] Korean Air leveraged Watson to analyze years' worth of maintenance records for its fleet, cutting down the maintenance analysis time by 90 percent.[194] Amazon leverages machine learning to optimize the thousands of robots it uses for fulfillment and to map voice commands to real-time execution in Alexa.[195]

There are various AI-powered applications in the market today. How does AI actually work? How are computers becoming "intelligent"?

TRAINING DATA

The answer lies in the computing systems' ability to interpret and extract meaning from large data sets. These data sets, sometimes called *training data*, serve as an input into a system. The system interprets the data thoroughly, ideally to provide a decision or outcome that achieves some goal. The power lies in ML, a subset of AI, which trains a system to *learn* from its experiences. Programming a computer to complete a task step by step has become impossible for complex tasks such as image recognition or market predictions. However, ML pushes the boundary by ultimately allowing a system to identify its mistake and retry one of many actions to achieve its goal. The system notes the mistake and can reference past errors in future decision-making processes.

This incredible technology has resulted in Terminatoresque theories of the future, even while technology giants are investing billions in research to drive AI development. Google's acquisition of Nest for

$3.2 billion brought a powerful suite of ML and products driven by IoT to the Google portfolio.[196] Amazon's $775-million purchase of Kiva Systems integrated a suite of robust robots into the company's core warehouse operations.[197]

Many of our most ambitious societal objectives—from self-driving cars to cures for diseases to space exploration—rely and will continue to rely on the progress of machine learning. AI is here to stay, and while the revolution is just beginning, blockchain technology may help accelerate its growth.

AI AND CENTRALIZATION

"Data is the new oil" is a common expression that reveals the value of data.[198] However, we need our AI algorithms to be processing data—extracting, refining, distributing, and monetizing it—in ways that respect human rights and create more opportunities for people, not just for corporations.[199] ML requires a massive amount of data for these training models to accurately develop and learn over time. Developers feed these data sets into systems to interpret and adjust their decision-making skills.

One key issue arises: how can we trust the data fed into these models? How can we better understand how a particular system or algorithm is actually making its decision? For example, if an automotive manufacturer discovers a major fault in a testing simulation in its self-driving program, the company needs to turn to an auditable, trustless source of the data used for the simulation. This provides an intuitive way to verify the data used.

Additionally, a handful of large technology companies control the vast majority of data used for AI development. Google and Facebook collect gigabytes' worth of data per user, millions of data points that include every message exchanged through Messenger, location history, music preferences, and so many more.[200]

Acquiring these data is impossible for smaller companies, allowing a few large players to serve as gatekeepers to AI development. Public data sets, for the most part, are very limited and may have covenants for commercial use. There are multiple public data sets available (Table 3-1), but these data can be unstructured and not as insightful as the more proprietary data sets.

TABLE 3-1
PUBLIC DATA SETS

SOURCE OF DATA	TYPE OF DATA
CERN Open Data Portal	Particle physics experiments
eBay Market Data Insights	Online sales and auctions
US Federal Bureau of Investigation	Uniform crime reporting at national, state, and county levels
Financial Times	Global market data including stock price indexes, commodities, and foreign exchange
FiveThirtyEight	Polling on public opinion of politics and sports
Glassdoor	Job openings, salaries, company reviews
Google Trends	International Internet search activity and trending news stories
International Monetary Fund	International finances, debt rates, foreign exchange reserves, commodity prices, and investments
Microsoft Machine Reading Comprehension (MARCO)	Reading comprehension and question answering
United Nations Comtrade	International trade
US Bureau of Justice	Adults on state and federal probation and parole, jail inmate populations, jail capacity, arrest-related deaths, capital punishment
World Bank	Population demographics and economic and development indicators

Source of data: Bernard Marr, "Big Data and AI: 30 Amazing (and Free) Public Data Sources for 2018," Forbes.com, Forbes Media LLC, 26 Feb. 2018. www.forbes.com/sites/bernardmarr/2018/02/26/big-data-and-ai-30-amazing-and-free-public-data-sources-for-2018/#6e0d8b7e5f8a, accessed 6 March 2019.

Some start-ups, including Spil.ly, needed hundreds of thousands of images for their image recognition development. Unable to pay for the input data required, Spil.ly was forced to create synthetic data from computer-generated graphics to feed its AI models.[201]

How can we democratize these data so that developers all around the world can easily gain access and use it to build AI data sets? Could a decentralized marketplace help democratize the data required for AI training in a trustless manner?

BLOCKCHAINS AND ARTIFICIAL INTELLIGENCE

Blockchain, at its core, is a distributed database stored by parties in a decentralized network. Over the past two years, we have seen an explosion in attention and resources in the blockchain space with hundreds of billions' worth of cryptocurrency purchased and traded. We saw an initial coin offering (ICO) boom in 2017 in which ICOs raised over $4 billion, promising disruptive changes in practically every single existing industry.[202]

Bancor, a network for token exchange, raised $153 million in three hours, even though it had no significant consumer adoption or use. There has been little connection between the prices of tokens as digital assets associated with different blockchains and the real value of the underlying technology as a decentralized structure for storing data. The space is evolving from low-throughput decentralized systems to industrial-strength high-velocity differentiators.

There has been no better time than now to begin understanding the powerful abilities of the blockchain. Satoshi Nakamoto's Bitcoin white paper emphasizes the importance of placing value in "cryptographic proof instead of trust."[203] This seemingly simple idea unveiled a completely new realm of interactions. Rather than placing our trust in individuals and enterprises prone to human error, let us trust the objectivity of cryptography and mathematics. The Bitcoin white paper introduced a new way of thinking that AI may serve to benefit from one day.

Two of blockchain's most powerful characteristics are its immutability and decentralization. Both of these present opportunities to improve AI's centralized state.

IMMUTABILITY

Not only do AI training models require vast amounts of data but also the data used needs to have a clear audit trail to ensure quality. Blockchains can store data in an immutable manner, to avoid any deletion or alteration.

For example, on the Bitcoin platform, a valid transaction is broadcast and confirmed by a set of "miners" that know neither the other miners nor the sender. Once a transaction is confirmed and added to the ledger, it cannot be altered or reversed without an immense amount of money and computing power. This helps provide a level of confidence in the transaction and, looking higher level, can translate into secure data points available for analysis.

KenSci, a prediction platform powered by artificial intelligence and machine learning, is focused on healthcare data analytics. Leveraging large sets of medical records and training sets, the company relies on the accuracy of the data input into the models, because patients' lives are on the line. As co-founder Ankur Teredesai underscored, "We're talking about real patients, real lives" when running these AI models to provide healthcare recommendations to doctors and insurance companies.[204]

However, AI has the potential to reinforce existing cultural and social biases embedded in the data sets that it relies on. For example, Google faced backlash for offensive tags related to image recognition in its photo app, and so did Microsoft when its Twitter chatbot used unverified and inappropriate input data to determine responses.

As companies undertake tests on a particular system, they will be able to point to a specific data point found at a particular time stamp on the blockchain. For example, a multinational clothing retailer may want to understand how its products are selling across various channels such as brick-and-mortar and e-commerce. It could input point-of-sale data from each channel into an inventory-management training model that could automatically adjust forecasting and inventory based on consumer trends. Over time, this model could help predict shifts in consumer tastes.

Retailers such as Walmart and Nike have been investing in the data analysis tools required for increased sales and customer engagement. Companies are looking at customer sentiment and inquiries on Twitter during and after their shopping experience.[205]

The data from these various channels must be as accurate as possible. Multiple parties and companies are selling the retailer's products; the data are not stored in one place. With a shared blockchain, data from each channel could be hashed and uploaded to a blockchain so that the retailer could be confident that the data used in its model had not been altered. All parties to transactions would need to reach consensus on any changes to the data, and so no single player could rig the data in its favor. Requiring consensus would serve as a governance tool: it would not be completely decentralized yet would prevent a single entity from having control over sensitive data.

Current solutions involve external parties aggregating and selling data to interested companies; however, these data cannot truly be audited for accuracy, and the aggregators bear none of the risk associated with its use. So there is moral risk in this market. Companies relying on this information to make key decisions do so at their own risk.

Blockchain technology may help provide a high-quality, ever-growing stream of transparent data to which AI models could refer regularly over time. Once hashed, the data would be available in a secure manner, only to parties involved. There would be no central entity or aggregator of the retail data. Bob Tapscott, blockchain and AI author and strategy consultant, explained how computers' ability to forget nothing is incredibly important for AI:

> Deep learning loves data. The larger and more credible the data set, the more intelligent AI's interpretation and predictions based on that data will be. With AI, 20 years of actual data and the subsequent human decision-making can be reviewed, learned, refined, and critiqued overnight.[206]

For example, given a large enough data set of magnetic resonance imaging data and the actual patient outcomes, an AI routine was able to detect colorectal cancer with 86 percent accuracy; and AI routines have the potential to predict precancers earlier than human beings can.[207] Where there are massive amounts of data, AI routines can readily see subtle correlations in millions of images that we cannot.

It is all about the data. If we run a remote text-based diagnostic shop (be it for sick people or broken machines) and have the text for 100,000 queries, responses, and subsequent satisfaction scores, with current AI technology, we can train a computer to perform those tasks to get consistently higher satisfaction scores than human beings. Then the computer can simultaneously translate the results into 20 different languages, depending on customer preferences. Of course, processing natural language can still be quite challenging, depending on the complexities of the written requests.

Note that these models are improved with the accuracy of data. With vacuum-cleaner repair, the right answers and the most pleasing answers are likely the same thing. With medical patients, these answers may not be the same. The more data we use to train a model, the more accurate the model will be.

"Based on 100,000 previous observations, when something goes wrong the computer can filter out anomalies to the data," Tapscott said.[208] In other words, the computer could learn from mistakes and apply its learning to future decision making. Tapscott touched not only on the importance of having data but also on the ability to *verify* the data inputted.

When data are put on a blockchain, we can identify the exact point of entry or faulty input and then correct it, for a decision at hand and for future decisions. The decision-making process improves through each iteration. AI, supplemented by blockchain, will allow us to understand a problem or pattern as no human could.[209]

BLOCKCHAIN AND DEMOCRATIZATION

Our identities are increasingly becoming linked to data that may not be accurate or kept securely (Table 3-2). With current centralized data-capturing systems such as Amazon, Facebook, and YouTube, we have less and less control over our data. As a result, our digital identities have too often been mismanaged and compromised, sometimes without our knowledge. Corporations should not be able to sell our data without providing us with some financial incentive.

TABLE 3-2

LARGEST DATA BREACHES REPORTED IN 2018

COMPANY	PARENT	SECTOR	NUMBER OF ACCOUNTS	REPORTED PROBLEM
Facebook		Web (social)	2,200,000,000	Hacked
Aadhaar	Ministry of Electronics and Information Technology, India	Government	1,100,000,000	Poor security
Twitter		App (social)	330,000,000	Poor security
MyFitnessPal	Under Armour	App (fitness)	150,000,000	Hacked
Nametests	Social Sweethearts	App	120,000,000	Poor security
Firebase	Google	App	100,000,000	Poor security

Source of data: David McCandless, "World's Biggest Data Breaches and Hacks," Information Is Beautiful, updated 15 Oct. 2018. www.informationisbeautiful.net/visualizations/worlds-biggest-data-breaches-hacks, accessed 16 Nov. 2018.

A key advantage of blockchain technologies is their potential for ownership of personal data, ensuring increased privacy and security. Blockchain also has the potential to democratize the availability of data. A handful of corporations control the vast amount of data that AI models require. The real insight lies in data such as customer buying patterns or app usage, yet only a few corporations can leverage this information. Imagine if a variety of firms and developers of all sizes could gain permission to access large sets of data to push innovation forward.

Blockchain can facilitate this democratization of data, ultimately producing a new type of data marketplace. Networks of companies could purchase data directly from users, with the data available on the blockchain. The availability of data peer to peer would allow users—including companies traditionally excluded from the data ecosystem—to garner completely new insights. Here's how it would work:

1. A buyer creates a smart contract containing a data set and commissioning an AI/ML model that must meet certain criteria. For example, an online retailer could write a contract that would release a data set of 20,000 orders and request an AI model that could identify fraudulent orders with greater than 90 percent accuracy, in exchange for some amount of ether.

2. The buyer publishes the smart contract to the Ethereum blockchain for anyone to access.

3. Machine learning engineers access the contract and download the data set. The race is on!

4. Each engineer uses the data to train an AI/ML model.

5. When an engineer has trained a model sufficiently, the engineer runs this model on the Ethereum blockchain.

6. If the model indeed meets contract requirements—that is, it identifies fake orders with greater than 90 percent accuracy—then the smart contract sends the model to the buyer and issues payment to the engineer.[210]

Buyers who offer money in exchange for training an AI model open up the possibility for AI to reach the hands of all types of developers and companies looking to gain insights from their existing data sets.

What if we could share the data among participants with a governance protocol in place? For example, what if automotive manufacturers sold autonomous testing data to one another, or gave data sets away in exchange for the insights derived from them? Enabling this kind of sharing could help accelerate the development of new vehicles.

Autonomous vehicles are generating terabytes of data, with one car capable of producing hundreds of terabytes' worth of radar, lidar, and camera data for analysis (Table 3-3). Rather than settling for current data silos, we could attempt to create a data marketplace for automotive manufacturers.

TABLE 3-3

DATA GENERATED BY CAR AUTOMATION SENSORS

SENSOR TYPE	QUANTITY	DATA GENERATED PER SENSOR
Radar	4–6	0.1–15 Mbit/s
Lidar	1–5	20–100 Mbit/s
Camera	6–12	500–3500 Mbit/s
Ultrasonic	8–16	<0.01 Mbit/s
Vehicle Motion, GNSS, IMU		<0.1 Mbit/s

Source of data: Stephan Heinrich, "Flash Memory in the Emerging Age of Autonomy," Flash Memory Summit, 7 Aug. 2017. www.flashmemorysummit.com/English/Collaterals/Proceedings/2017/20170808_FT12_Heinrich.pdf, accessed 6 March 2019.

The data would be on the blockchain, so that all players would have an understanding of data sources and time stamps. There would be no central party controlling, aggregating, or removing the data, decreasing the chances of manipulation. Participants uploading suboptimal data could be voted out of the blockchain by other participants.

SMART CONTRACTS

One of the biggest issues behind using data for AI is the privacy and sensitivity of the content. Smart contracts have the potential to help govern the actual use of these data in an AI environment. The ability for a smart contract to face "computational scrutiny" without relying on a third party could result in new governance platforms.[211]

Dr. Henry Kim, associate professor and co-director of blockchain.lab at York University, explained that we "may be able to use a governance smart contract." While the data are in use, entities must still "observe privacy" and confirm that they have access to the right data. Dr. Kim touched on the importance of a smart contract in dictating the governance policies of the data. The smart contract itself could contain the set of rules for using those data and rewarding the corresponding party for providing those data. The question comes down to whether we may use that person's or party's data in exchange for payment?[212]

BLOCKCHAIN GOVERNANCE

For example, if a company chooses to use a particular data set, the governance details behind that data set could be stored on-chain for all interested parties to verify. This is incredibly important as data privacy laws come under even more scrutiny. The Ponemon Institute found that 71 percent of companies would face global detriment to their businesses for failure to comply with EU GDPR.[213]

Rather than having a grand mesh of data aggregated centrally by a single party, a company could extract the data sets relevant to its needs, verify the data, and then use the sets according to governance rules in the smart contract. An on-chain smart contract would be available for all participants to verify, compared to a simple two-way contract. Network participants could be voted out for malicious behavior.

In addition, AI has the potential to analyze smart contracts for errors. As millions of smart contracts are developed, engineers could input the contracts themselves into a training model to determine where errors might lie and whether they could construct a more efficient contract.

DECENTRALIZED ARTIFICIAL INTELLIGENCE

Now that we have discussed the applications of blockchain in existing centralized solutions, we can begin looking at the functional potential of blockchain in a decentralized AI system. Decentralized artificial intelligence (DAI) is a subfield of artificial intelligence that analyzes the interaction and activity of autonomous agents. DAI attempts to understand how agents distribute themselves, interact with one another, and adjust to changes in their environment, without the oversight of a central body.[214] An entirely new and autonomous data ecosystem could emerge.

DISTRIBUTED AI VERSUS DECENTRALIZED AI

Distributed artificial intelligence establishes a different setup from a completely decentralized entity. In a distributed AI system, a central system still manages the overall setup and has greater permissions over activities such as data aggregation. For example, imagine a system that tracks the number of photos taken by a group of smartphones in each period.

A central entity oversees distributed artificial intelligence, which depends on the entity to use and process the data carefully. However, what if agents—sensors embedded in cars or factory equipment, or distributed throughout corporations—could begin learning and transacting with one another? That is where the combination of AI and blockchain gets really exciting.

DAI AND BLOCKCHAIN'S ROLE

In DAI, a multiagent system could one day emerge. For example, in the future, an autonomous vehicle may be able to pick up riders, earn fares, and pay for insurance, maintenance, and gas all without human intervention. The car could then begin to participate in the sharing economy by offering rides to passengers. Through an AI model, and millions of rides later, the car could learn various trends that a human driver would never consider. The ability for one car to teach another car where kids tend to play on the street, for example—to transfer what it has learned about a neighborhood to a car that has never traveled in that neighborhood—has the potential to improve safety dramatically for all. The veteran car could even sell its learnings to the new car on the block.

The car may begin positioning itself in areas with high densities of passengers. It may understand when it needs a maintenance check and could scan local mechanics for the best pricing. The vehicle may understand how to receive the most affordable insurance policy by adjusting its driving habits or "negotiating" with autonomous agents at other entities such as insurance companies and vehicle manufacturers.

DAI will need an operating platform to run on. Were this platform run by a centralized authority, the agent itself could be compromised through a technical back door, which allowed the centralized entity to take over. Blockchains are run not by some central organization but by the nodes themselves. These nodes decide how to govern the future of the network. As stakeholders, they must first approve any protocol upgrades or developments prior to implementation.

Autonomous agents need a platform on which they can vote and help direct the future of the protocol itself. Blockchains would not care nor discriminate whether a node were a human or an autonomous agent, but they could assign more weight to the votes of nodes that have learned more.[215]

George Polzer, director of education at Blockchain 48 and task force chair of the Enterprise Ethereum Alliance, sees blockchain "as an enabler ... to gather data from multiple nodes" helping to achieve "collective intelligence."[216] In a more decentralized world, autonomous agents need not rely on a handful of data sources but could move from one data source to another, leaving an auditable trail for the data used. Imagine a massive number of nodes pooling their data, contributing to a data commons of sorts, rather than dealing with the very siloed and centralized pools of data that exist now.

In addition, blockchains would allow autonomous agents to interact without having to trust each other. Because data is immutable on the blockchain, agents can quickly verify that an agent is not falsifying its data for its own interest. The trust lies not in the agent itself but rather the cryptographically secure data produced by the agent's actions.

Reviewing our autonomous vehicle example, we can see that a multiagent system needs to achieve consensus or agreement on terms. For example, how could the insurance company know that the vehicle had not altered its data before requesting a new policy?

Autonomous vehicles could leverage a blockchain by continuously uploading their data, through hashes, for other agents at other entities—insurance companies, vehicle manufacturers—to verify. This verification would provide an important level of trust and assurance that the data had not been tampered with for the agent's benefit.

Also, blockchains introduce an incentive layer on top of DAI. Governance protocols could require agents to stake or set aside their tokens in reserve while they interact with other agents. If a particular agent decided to act maliciously, other agents could vote to remove that agent from participating in the ecosystem and retain some portion of that agent's staked tokens as a penalty. The governance protocols could reward honest nodes for performing well (e.g., picking up passengers on time, driving safely) and could penalize malicious nodes (e.g., temporary denial of access, higher transaction fee, more tokens required in reserve).

AUTONOMOUS AGENTS AS AI REPRESENTATIVES?

One possible economic structure could be the use of delegated proof of stake (DPoS). DPoS is a consensus mechanism used by other blockchain projects such as EOS and VeChain. Similar to the workings of the US legislative system, each token holder in these blockchains can vote on a representative to validate transactions on its behalf. A group of nodes, between 10 and 100, are the sole individuals who can validate transactions in the network.

Autonomous agents could begin representing other autonomous agents as delegates. As delegates, these agents would have to "stake" or put away some token in reserve, which would be slashed if the agent acted maliciously.

Imagine a system where one autonomous vehicle is elected to represent other autonomous vehicles for better bargaining power over insurance policies. Because each transaction would occur on the blockchain, other agents could verify that the delegate is performing in the interest of the network.

Toufi Saliba, CEO of Toda.Network and chair of the Association for Computing Machinery, described how we might see an environment where "machines can ensure each other's governance accordingly; the machines, they can compete between each other."[217] Saliba pointed to programs that follow a set of protocol rules and exchange information, yet still act individually. Each program plays a role in challenging malicious actors and removing them from a shared protocol. If a miner is malicious on the Bitcoin network, then it will be punished financially, as it is forced to spend vast amounts of money to achieve a 51 percent attack. In an autonomous world, autonomous miners can begin to punish malicious miners automatically, voting them off the network.

The crux to this governance is that no central authority would dictate which agents could join, leave, or take a percentage of the agents' earnings. A group of autonomous agents would run the system:

each would provide its resources for the greater good while still receiving rewards for its individual efforts.

Saliba reminded us that people do not "want to acknowledge that there's fear of attack from within."[218] Central authorities control the keys to vast amounts of permissioned information and data. This centralization puts these data at greater risk of hacking than data distributed across a cryptographically secure network, as we have seen happen at dozens of corporations (Table 3-2). Institutions that many people "trust today," Saliba said, may be the same institutions that individuals "don't know if they can trust tomorrow." The simple yet groundbreaking topic of trust brings us to a new concept of organization and autonomous agents.

LOOKING TO THE FUTURE: DAO

Autonomous agents can make their own decisions and learn over time through trial and error without human intervention or risk of human error. But can we create something more complex than an autonomous vehicle?

Looking at the distributed economic entities visual (Figure 3-1), we can gain an understanding of where autonomous agents fit within the ecosystem. An autonomous vehicle or a vending machine that can understand customer demand and inventory management falls under relatively high automation and low complexity.

We can automate a few tasks such as replacing products in a vending machine or paying for insurance over time. However, what happens when we venture toward a complex corporation run on the blockchain? That is where the idea of a decentralized autonomous organization (DAO) comes into play. A DAO is an entity run entirely by its stakeholders rather than an executive team. Because of its decentralized nature, any stakeholder can propose a change to the organization's actions or structure with other stakeholders voting.

FIGURE 3-1

DISTRIBUTED ECONOMIC ENTITIES

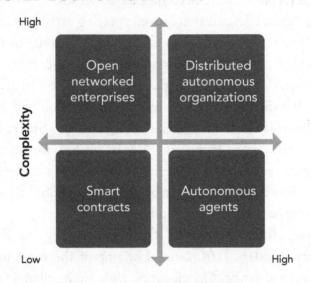

Source of concept: Don Tapscott and Alex Tapscott, Blockchain Revolution: How the Technology Behind Bitcoin and Other Cryptocurrencies Is Changing the World (New York: Portfolio Penguin, 2018): 120.

Over time, a DAO can begin to learn who its competitors are, what proposals stakeholders are supporting, and what market trends to follow. An ambitious future would have organizations running entirely on their own, making business decisions, hiring employees, and responding to market changes.

Imagine a US toy factory that knew exactly when to order raw materials, based on plastic production in China. The factory would use Web scrapers to analyze toy searches and trends from millions of websites and videos to know which colors, styles, quantities, and trends to produce. The factory would then begin production, optimizing each piece of equipment for constructing a particular part of a toy. During production, the factory would contact the largest buyers in Europe, South America, and Asia and would negotiate with external agents to achieve the target profit margin. It would then ship the toys and receive payment without any human intervention. The factory would keep track of its earnings and analyze its competitors' earnings in its objective to become a market leader.

George Polzer argued that "anyone playing an intermediary role [such as] financial institutions or credit bureaus" would be disrupted by DAOs along with "any industry that is not currently transparent in transactions." These intermediaries could be governed by smart contracts that dictate the movement of information and value that these intermediaries have traditionally controlled. Smart contracts could "provide an independent, decentralized inner economy." The governance of DAOs is a critical topic that is currently being researched; however, "governance by a council [DPoS] … [is] a novel idea worth experimenting and building."[219]

Although the DAO model faced scrutiny by the Ethereum community in 2016, DAOs could be one of the most important advancements of artificial intelligence, with unprecedented use cases.

CHALLENGES WITH BLOCKCHAIN NETWORKS

Blockchains provide a variety of use cases for AI development, but there are challenges with using a decentralized system. For example, one of the most pressing issues with a blockchain is the issue of scaling.

SCALABILITY

As people and things generate more data, storing those data in a decentralized manner can be challenging. Public blockchains are very expensive for storing vast amounts of data; and beyond the cost, quickly retrieving those data can be computationally intensive. Computing systems will need to retrieve, analyze, and compute algorithms in a very short period.

Not only will data need to be collected and distributed to all relevant stakeholders but also that same data will need to be structured and trained within a short period of time. Current blockchain solutions do not offer the scalability required for such types of aggregation and computation (Figure 3-2). With terabytes of data passing between products and companies, existing solutions will not suffice.

Fortunately, innovators are developing solutions for scaling. One is the IPFS. Its users download the IPFS protocols for storing and indexing files on their own and each other's devices, in a distributed network rather than on a central set of servers. Its storage capacity grows with the number of users and the available space on their collective machines. Users can host data and create a hash of the data set, so that others can locate and access the nearest copy of it, if not the original host's copy.

For example, when an application needs to reference a large data set on a blockchain, it could refer to just the hash of the data rather than the whole data set. The hash should always match the data set, unless the set has been altered.

FIGURE 3-2

COMPARISON OF TRANSACTIONS PER SECOND

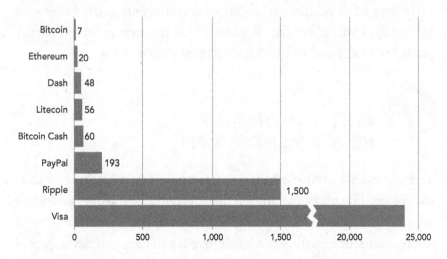

Source of data: Raul, "Transactions Speeds: How Do Cryptocurrencies Stack Up to Visa or PayPal?" howmuch.net, 10 Jan. 2018. howmuch.net/articles/crypto-transaction-speeds-compared, accessed 6 March 2019.

GOVERNANCE

Establishing the governance of these blockchains and the data they hold is incredibly important. AI will require myriad data from various sources, but data owners will want to keep those data private and secure on the blockchain, so that only permissioned parties have some level of access. We could see some integration of homomorphic encryption, which allows engineers to use data sets for training without compromising the confidentiality of those data.

Amid AI model development, user data stored on an immutable ledger may also become problematic. What if we wanted to transform and map the data from one raw format into another format so that we could work more easily with the data set downstream, say, for business analytics? Or what if governments placed limitations on the types of individual or household data that organizations may collect and use for commercial purposes?

How will we remove data sets that are supposed to be immutable and safe from deletion? Or is it a matter of changing the smart contracts governing access and usage of such data? Moreover, in these early days of development, as autonomous agents learn to interact, blockchains will likely face latency issues; the rate at which participants broadcast and validate transactions may be slow.

CONCLUSION AND RECOMMENDATIONS

The trivergence of blockchain and AI with IoT is an exciting frontier to explore. The idea of an immutable, decentralized ledger providing an auditable data source for hungry AI models could vastly improve if not revolutionize existing models. There is still plenty of development work, testing, and redevelopment to be done before this enterprise capability is ready for mass deployment. However, the future could not look more exciting.

AI is becoming more prevalent on the enterprise side. In numerous industries, this technology has shown immense utility, and its growth will continue with enterprise adoption. However, AI is extremely centralized in our current infrastructure. The question for enterprise leaders is, "Do we want to entrust autonomous agents to a handful of corporations, or do we want to advocate for a more decentralized architecture and open governance?"

Blockchain can provide a decentralized infrastructure for the AI ecosystem. Currently, AI data sources and development are very centralized, preventing smaller players from working on novel AI solutions. A decentralized blockchain-based solution may allow a more democratized yet secure means of transmitting and using the data required for AI training models.

Blockchain adds an *incentive layer* on top of an Internet-based sharing economy. Such an infrastructure could open completely new channels for companies to share data sources and tap new resources and provide some incentive for doing so. Organizations could develop reputations for the quality and utility of the data they share.

Imagine the impact of millions of AI agents running on a few centralized servers. While the focus today may be on centralized AI, *decentralized* AI will lead to cars, machines, and even companies that are more autonomous. Pure autonomous systems will need decentralized platforms to run on. Blockchain may provide better insights over centralized, and possibly biased, data sets.

Current blockchain solutions are not ready for wide-scale deployment. Work is underway on scaling solutions ranging from layer-one improvements to layer-two scaling solutions such as the Lightning Network. Each solution comes with trade-offs in throughput as well as governance, and so no player dominates. As scaling solutions mature, enterprise leaders should discuss where blockchain fits in the AI stack of their enterprise.

Consider hybrid models of decentralized and centralized infrastructure. Which data sets could have greater value in such a hybrid model? If those data sets were ready, we could begin exploring blockchain platforms and determining which worked best. Private blockchain initiatives such as R3 and public blockchains such as Ethereum are competing for enterprise adoption. While private blockchains are often not as decentralized as public ones, initial tests on permissioned networks could inform more decentralized solutions down the road.

Distributed ledger technology cannot solve all AI's problems. Blockchain may help address some, but not all, of the issues that AI developers face. For example, to learn and develop over time, these models need access to high-quality streams of data. The vetting of these data is crucial. While blockchain helps to track provenance, it does not yet verify accuracy or quality of inputs.

The great creation of value is yet to come. Remember, with the Internet, we did not immediately understand the potential for such use cases as e-commerce, social media, and cloud computing. These took years to reach mass adoption. Yet, as the infrastructure matured, start-ups and enterprise innovators alike created tremendous value by developing and running applications on top of the Internet. Distributed applications programmed to run on top of blockchains may generate as much or more value over time.

CHAPTER 4

THE LEDGER OF EVERY THING

What Blockchain Technology Can (and Cannot) Do for the IoT

Dominique D. Guinard

 ## BLOCKCHAIN AND IoT IN BRIEF

- The IoT revolution is changing how we live at home, how we interact with our cities, and how we handle consumable goods. New use cases are demonstrating the complexity of managing our data privacy, security, and scalability—the same complexity that blockchains are designed to handle as a backbone for IoT solutions.

- The combination of two overhyped concepts—blockchains and IoT—risks applying complex solutions to simple problems. In this chapter, we first look at a spectrum of IoT use cases. So grounded, we then analyze which parts of the IoT could benefit from blockchain and under which circumstances. We then examine the unique challenges introduced by blockchains, and we created a framework for weighing risks and benefits. Finally, we develop a way to achieve the best of both worlds: integration patterns for combining IoT platforms with blockchain technologies.

- Blockchains have taken the world by storm. Never before have we seen such a fast pace of development and adoption. As a consequence, six months after our original research for this chapter, quite a few things have changed.

- First, several blockchains such as Bitcoin and Ethereum have faced the ransom of premature success, and scaling problems have become increasingly more concerning, leading to big bottlenecks, delays, and higher transaction fees.

- Second, the energy consumption of most blockchains has continued to creep up, despite the lack of scale. This escalation cannot go on. It has led to a large number of initiatives in the blockchain community, both on technical and market-fit levels.

- A wind of realism has hit the space: no, the blockchain is not the universal solution to all IoT problems. It is a powerful but immature technology that we must use very wisely or risk making our solutions impossible to scale, incredibly power-hungry, and very expensive—all of which are linked.

- Hybrid models such as the one presented at the end of this chapter have become the real-world norm: do as much as you can off-chain! For instance, store your data in traditional systems, aggregate all your transactions, and anchor only what you absolutely need on-chain. More generally, we now refer to these techniques as "Layer 2," because they perform numerous operations off-chain.

- This pragmatic use of blockchains does help, but our efforts should not stop there. The vibrant and relentless community has been very active in proposing technical solutions to the scalability challenges. New proofing algorithms have appeared to propose alternatives to the very power-hungry and slow (by design) proof-of-work consensus mechanism. As an example, proof of stake (PoS) and proof of authority (PoA) have been tested on several public test networks (e.g., Ethereum) and adopted by new blockchains.

- Concerns remain around these weaker consensus and proofing algorithms. Most attempts to relax rules have led to large and healthy debates. Ultimately, these alternatives run the risk of weakening what distributed ledger technologies have to offer: trust in decentralized protocols, not in a central authority.

- All in all, the blockchain space for IoT has moved past its peak of inflated expectations and is now proceeding more carefully, focusing on those challenges we really need to solve for future-proofing the technology and understanding where the technology can truly help and where it cannot. In other words, the world has learned to become more critical and is now slowly looking at use cases beyond the hype. We are entering the phase of real-world testing, preparing for the long road to the plateau of productivity.

INTRODUCTION

This revolution isn't without its own set of issues; it forces us to start thinking about new ways of dealing with unprecedented challenges. First, the sheer size of the network requires us to design increasingly more distributed and decentralized systems, both in terms of connecting things and processing their data. Then, as the IoT matures, it will gather increasingly more useful but also intrusive datasets that will make for the best possible, personalized applications but also threaten our privacy. Establishing a network worthy of trust will be instrumental to ensuring that the technology gives consumers the right ratio of cost to benefit.

Blockchains and, more generally, distributed ledger technologies (DLTs) were proposed as revolutionary architectures that could resolve a number of these problems, such as decentralizing computing tasks, but also remove the need for pre-established trust. However, combining IoT with DLT is about as high on the hype curve as we can go. Hence, we need to think beyond the hype, analyze the broad use cases of IoT, and draft a systematic approach to determining where blockchains can help us and where they can't. In particular, this research focuses on the readiness of blockchains and DLTs for IoT use cases. It also proposes a hybrid integration architecture that could enable us to use blockchains today and limit the risks inherent in a relatively immature set of technologies.

WHAT IS THE INTERNET OF THINGS?

There are hundreds of definitions of the Internet of Things in circulation. Let's use the one we proposed:

> The Internet of Things is a system of physical objects that can be discovered, monitored, controlled, or interacted with by electronic devices that communicate over various networking interfaces and eventually can be connected to the wider Internet.[220]

With this in mind, we need to clarify the term *things*. Things on the Internet are not just smart light bulbs or connected plugs. Things can be whole environments such as smart homes, smart buildings, or smart cities, or they can be objects with a radio frequency identification (RFID) tag or a quick response (QR) code. They can be devices or machines like an iBeacon with Bluetooth low energy, an Arduino board, or a Raspberry Pi. They can range from the simple to the complex, from low to high computational power.

From the concept of tagged objects—which originated in Auto-ID Labs, an international cluster of research laboratories founded at MIT—came the larger concept of the Internet of Things! In 1999,

Auto-ID Labs focused on automatically identifying goods using RFID tags to create a global network of electronically tagged products, ultimately to optimize logistics and supply chains. Lab members came up with the "Internet of Things" to describe this global network.[221]

In more technical terms, the IoT is about giving real-world things a combination of four properties: connectivity, identity, sensing, and actuation. Connectivity is the first and most relevant aspect: an application that does not involve connecting real-world objects to the Internet should not be called IoT!

Identity is also an important property of IoT. Without a unique identity for things, many use cases are simply not possible: how would we know where a product comes from if we have no way of uniquely identifying it? We need to address and identify things in the IoT uniquely and securely just as computers on the Internet require a unique IP address.

Once they are connected and have an identity, things in the IoT can offer sensing and/or actuation services. *Sensing* is the thing's ability to report about the real world. Sensors can, for example, monitor freezer temperatures, pollution levels in a particular street, or the foot traffic in a retail store. With sensing, communications travel from the thing to the Internet and into the cloud. *Actuation* is the thing's ability to receive and act on communication from the Internet. Think about command and control, turning lights on or off, shutting off water valves, or reselling energy on the grid.

We now recognize that IoT is an umbrella term for many domains and use cases (Figure 4-1). Some of these domains differ so much from one another that we must look closely at each domain before concluding that blockchain can help IoT. In broad terms, we can think of the following domains of application:[222]

- Smart homes (aka home automation)
- Wearables (aka the quantified self)
- Smart cities, grids, and buildings

- Smart manufacturing (aka industrial IoT and Industry 4.0)
- Smart logistics (aka connected supply chain)
- Connected marketing (aka direct to consumer)

These categories are sometimes further clustered into three broad domains:[223]

- *Consumer IoT*, including smart homes, wearables, consumer marketing, and the product provenance side of smart logistics
- *Commercial IoT*, including smart logistics, smart buildings, and connected medical devices
- *Industrial IoT*, covering smart cities, smart grids, and smart manufacturing

In this chapter, we mainly cover the impact of blockchain for the consumer and commercial IoT, but most of the challenges and solutions we discuss also apply to the industrial IoT.

TYPICAL ARCHITECTURE OF AN IoT DEPLOYMENT

We now have a common understanding of the IoT domain but there remains one more step to be able to understand what opportunities blockchains could bring to the table: we need to understand the typical architecture of an IoT deployment. While generalizing such a big domain is challenging, there is a fair amount of common patterns used in IoT deployments.

A typical IoT deployment consists of these six building blocks:

- *Things*: the things themselves, which range from smart appliances to tagged items in the smart supply chain
- *IoT networking protocols*: the low-level protocols that things use to become part of a network
- *Gateways and edge computers*: machines slightly more powerful than the things themselves (the typical routers, set-top-boxes, or voice assistants responsible for translating lower-level protocols into Internet and Web protocols)

- *Internet*: the backbone of the IoT, composed of several protocols such as IP, TCP, and UDP (things that do not connect to the Internet either directly or via gateways are not considered part of the IoT)
- *IoT and Web of Things platforms*: the platforms, typically centralized, that communicate with and manage things
- *Applications and systems*: the users of things in the IoT (apps typically interact with the IoT via platforms, as the apps themselves are not usually on the same network as the things themselves)

Let's look at the role of these building blocks when it comes to the four properties of IoT use cases: connectivity, identity, sensing, and actuation.

Connectivity: Cost, power, and context

Connectivity is about linking things to the Internet. Ideally, we would have a connectivity network covering all possible use cases, but the world of IoT connectivity is a wild one wherein thousands of standards compete with one another: NFC, Zigbee, Bluetooth, Zwave, EnOcean, Thread, low-power wireless fidelity (Wi-Fi), LoRa, NB-IoT, SigFox to name a few!

While some of these protocols result from big alliances in a rush to grab IoT land by re-inventing the wheel (e.g., Zigbee vs. Zwave vs. Thread vs. Bluetooth or LoRa vs. SigFox), we have several good reasons for different protocols to connect things to the Internet. Our experience is that we can distill these reasons into three factors.

- Cost influences the choice of connectivity. For instance, a device that leverages existing Wi-Fi infrastructure will likely cost less than one that requires a SIM card or access to a low power wide area network (LPWAN) such as SigFox, NB-IoT, or LoRa. Similarly, the chosen type of connectivity affects the bill of materials, as costs vary among connectivity chipsets. Traditionally, those that spin out of large alliances with relatively open specifications (e.g., Wi-Fi, Bluetooth) tend to be the cheapest, though that distinction erodes as the technology advances.

- Energy is another factor, since some protocols are more power hungry than others. For example, LPWAN-powered devices can run on battery for several years whereas a Wi-Fi device cannot. Power consumption is an important aspect to consider when comparing blockchain solutions, which tend to be quite power hungry—especially when requiring a proof of work (PoW).

- Context will influence the choice of the protocol. For instance, a remote outdoor environment is unlikely to be able to leverage Wi-Fi and would benefit from a long-range solution such as LoRa or a mesh-network such as Zigbee, wherein each device itself becomes a network relay. On the other hand, a smart home solution would work well on Wi-Fi as most homes have Wi-Fi connectivity.

These differences make clear that we will not live to see a unique IoT network. While consolidations will happen (e.g., we see Zigbee and Thread getting closer and closer to each other), IoT networks will remain fragmented. A direct consequence is that some block-chain solutions, for instance, those looking at securing things, will have to deal with this heterogeneity.

Identity: Addressability and authentication

Identity is key for most IoT use cases. It encompasses two broad concepts: addressability and authentication: How do we address a thing and how do we ensure the thing is who it presents itself to be? In the Web of Things, we handle addressability by giving each thing a unique IP address or even unique URL (uniform resource locator).[224]

The Web can help the IoT with authentication as well and several IoT solutions now use Web security in the form SSL/TLS certificates and public key infrastructures. Blockchains could help improve how we identify things by proposing more flexible and scalable identification systems based on widespread cryptography and, in particular, hashes.

Sensing: Reporting on the real world

Once a thing is on the Internet and boasts an identity, it usually starts sensing its environment (e.g., a door sensor detecting intruders, a temperature sensor on a container) and sending these data to services in the cloud.

The services are quite often referred to as *IoT platforms* (Figure 4-1). The primary role of an IoT platform is usually to manage connectivity and store the data sent by the things. However, IoT platforms usually offer numerous other services, such as analytics engines and dashboards, rules engines, machine learning, device monitoring, security management, and so forth. There are several IoT platforms: from those created by software giants such as Amazon, IBM, or Microsoft to those pioneered by start-ups, such as Xively, ThingSpeak, ThingWorx, or EVRYTHNG.

These platforms are usually high-availability and scalable systems. However, they are owned by a single commercial entity that controls the platform. Manufacturers of things do own some proprietary platforms (e.g., Nest, SmartThings) while others are independent and serve several manufacturers (e.g., EVRYTHNG, Xively). Other players include device manufacturers and service providers (e.g., Google, Amazon). Blockchains have the potential to decentralize platform control.

Actuation: Receiving and acting on communication

We can manage actuation by controlling the thing directly using Web protocols (e.g., HTTPS) or proprietary application protocols (e.g., Zigbee). On top of local control, we can implement control via the Internet for remote control of things explicitly or through a rule or a machine-learning algorithm. In this area, most current blockchain solutions have significant limitations because of the time it takes to reach consensus or because of the relatively slow speed of execution of transactions on the current blockchains.

FIGURE 4-1

IoT PLATFORMS

Some of the features IoT platforms typically offer range from managing device connectivity and storing very large data sets to integrating with other services and enterprise systems and providing analytics and machine learning.

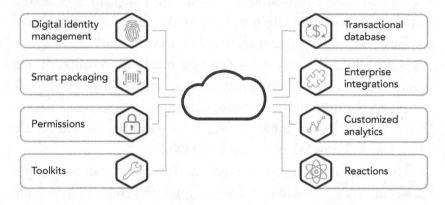

BLOCKCHAINS AND IoT

In its July 2017 report, Gartner placed blockchain in the peak of inflated expectations of its hype curve with about five to 10 years for it to reach the plateau of productivity. Hence, when we have a blockchain hammer, everything today looks like a nail. The IoT is no exception, and blockchain solutions offering to solve IoT problems have mushroomed. In such an overhyped climate, we must carefully study the challenges of the IoT to understand if blockchains and DLTs offer true solutions to these problems.

CHALLENGES OF CENTRALIZED IoT AND WHAT BLOCKCHAINS CAN DO

Let's look at the unique properties of blockchains and decentralized architectures that have the most potential to help the IoT. First, blockchains are usually *distributed* and *decentralized*. Recognizing the differences among centralized, decentralized, and distributed architectures is essential in evaluating the benefits of blockchains (Figure 4-2). The key point is that no single player can control a decentralized or distributed system and so it is more resilient and difficult to terminate.[225]

FIGURE 4-2

CENTRALIZED, DECENTRALIZED, AND DISTRIBUTED SYSTEMS

In the context of computation, a truly decentralized system is much more resilient and cannot be easily shut down or controlled by a single entity.

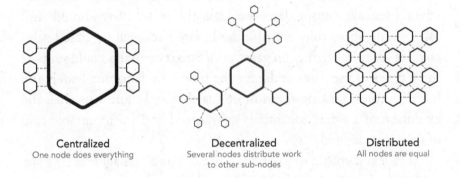

| Centralized | Decentralized | Distributed |
| One node does everything | Several nodes distribute work to other sub-nodes | All nodes are equal |

For example, the Ethereum platform allows users to build applications (called Dapps) that run on various decentralized nodes on the network. Moreover, there is no central Ethereum server but rather a distributed network of nodes with equal privileges. This distributed network is a fundamental difference from traditional centralized IoT platform architecture. Decentralization means not only that control is distributed but also that things can communicate autonomously with one another. All these aspects are important for the future of IoT, especially when we consider scale and durability.

Another important property of blockchains for IoT is their *immutability*: transactions in a blockchain are recorded forever and, once executed, cannot be tampered with or deleted. This property is a fundamental difference from centralized IoT platforms, which are controlled by the manufacturers of things, manufacturers with power over what gets recorded and whether it gets modified. Closely linked to this immutability is the widespread use of hashes as identifiers in blockchains. *Hashes* are one-way functions that serve as a fingerprint of data; and this ability to provide secure identities for things is vital to all IoT use cases. Hashes, combined with other properties of blockchains, could form the basis of efficient identity solutions for the IoT.

Finally, *smart contracts* are a powerful concept for IoT use cases. An important feature of IoT platforms is the ability to run real-time business rules as a response to sensing or actuation events. For instance, when a leakage sensor detects a leak, the water valve should shut off. Usually, these rules are running in large-scale cloud-based rules engines (or rules engines on gateways). Smart contracts could support these types of use cases and have the power to distribute widely the business rules, making them more scalable and more trustable: the execution of a smart contract is guaranteed and an immutable trail of data is generated.

If blockchain is a toddler, then the IoT is a teenager: as its hype curve continues, several significant challenges have emerged for consumer IoT. In our view, here are the most important.[226]

Interoperability: A Web—not an Intranet—of Things

The IoT is very fragmented when it comes to protocols. While many dream of a single IoT protocol to rule them all, several networking protocols exist with good reason (e.g., cost, power, and deployment environment) and because of powerful and highly political alliances in—or battles over, as between giants Apple and Google—the IoT space.[227]

This is a big paradox for the IoT, which should be synonymous with *convergence* and *interoperability*. Consider smart homes. With protocols such as X10 appearing as early as 1975, smart homes are not new, yet have developed little to no interoperability. Instead, the field has suffered from extreme fragmentation, where smart home protocols are unable to communicate with other devices from other vendors using different, sometimes proprietary protocols. The IoT largely continues to exacerbate this trend by creating Intranets of Things in homes rather than an Internet of Homes.

As IoT researchers and practitioners, we felt this heterogeneity failed the IoT's mission to bring about the interoperability of things. We searched for an abstraction layer wherein different protocols could converge—from which the concept of the Web of Things emerged circa 2007.[228] The core idea of the Web of Things is that, no matter what the underlying networking protocol might be, things should speak Web protocols (e.g., HTTP, Websocket) to allow interoperability at the application layer. In the last 10 years, a large number of companies has adopted this path of converging IoT protocols, and additional Web standards for IoT are in development.[229] Yet, the interoperability battle for the IoT is far from over.

Blockchains and DLTs are likewise typically active at the application layer, creating new protocols on top of Internet Protocols (IP, TCP, UDP, etc.). Because these protocols are distributed and understood by a wide range of players, they have potential to help provide IoT interoperability. Interesting alternatives to traditional Web protocols such as IPFS are emerging and could provide interesting new aspects for IoT devices, particularly in terms of decentralization and P2P communication.[230] However, in their current state of frenetic development, blockchains bring much fragmentation and suffer from a lack of interoperability.

Trust: Decentralized, tamper-proof, and compliance-ready

Perhaps the biggest potential contribution of blockchain to the IoT could be the resolution of the trust issue. As noted, most IoT solutions are built around a centralized platform. The level of user trust in these platforms must be high because they gather data from and about users. Consumers need to trust that the IoT platforms will manage their data securely and not abuse or modify the data. What if our health insurance, which was connected and running on top of an IoT health platform, was modifying the data of our health-tracking device in order to deny one of our claims? What if a major coffee brand was modifying provenance data so that it could label itself "fair trade coffee"? What if the company behind our IoT door lock went out of business—would we be able to enter our home?

Recent events lead consumers to be increasingly dubious. For example, when a consumer gave the Garadget Internet-connected garage-door opener a bad review, Garadget's creator denied server connection to the consumer's unit (ID 2f0036), thus eroding consumer trust in the brand.[231] Such loss of trust affects not only the smart device market but also the food and apparel industries: organic or fair-trade labels—and, more generally, product provenance—no longer hold much consumer trust.[232]

This is where blockchains have the most potential to help. First, blockchains support distributed and decentralized platforms—with no central authority—in contrast to the centralized structure of IoT platforms. An IoT product on a distributed network and decentralized platform depends on no single entity to operate as expected. In fact, the most serious IoT platforms on the market are built as high availability systems that are well distributed. However, they are owned by a single commercial entity that controls the platform and the things connected to it. Hence, control is centralized.

Second, blockchains are trustworthy. This is particularly true for public blockchains but no less for consortium-based blockchains with a sufficient number of players. Since blockchain transactions cannot be tampered with, we can trust that the data sensed by IoT devices are the data the network will record. Blockchain has the potential to repair the public's distrust in product provenance, a positive for the commercial IoT and smart logistics.[233] Numerous blockchain players (such as the aptly named Provenance) have understood this potential and are building blockchain-based trust systems for consumer goods.[234]

Finally, blockchains—particularly, smart contracts—hold unprecedented potential for regulatory compliance. Regulations can be programmed as smart contracts with fully auditable and completely automated enforcement. This capability is useful in numerous IoT domains, especially the commercial IoT. The start-up Modum, for example, built its use case around a new regulation that forces partners of the pharmaceutical supply chain to track the temperature of medicinal products.[235] By combining smart IoT sensors with low-power communication technologies and smart contracts on the Ethereum blockchain, Modum makes possible the assurance of auditable and tamper-proof regulatory compliance.

Privacy: Data cryptographically secure and not centrally owned

There is consensus that privacy on the Internet is dead, its demise long predicted.[236] The IoT exacerbates the situation by gathering an unprecedented amount of personal data. This is an important paradox: many benefits of IoT are possible only because of the personal data gathered. Nest thermostats learn our habits at home and automatically set the right temperature at the right moment.

Regulators have started to tackle such privacy issues by creating new laws that affect the digital world and the IoT. For example, the European GDPR is enforcing a set of strict guidelines on the rights of citizens regarding their digital profile.[237]

A blockchain solution would not necessarily change the nature of the data collected. However, decentralization would mean that the data would not belong to a single, all-mighty entity. Rather, data could be audited and leveraged by several players. This solution could also help consumers to regain control of their personal data and offer better ways to monetize those data. While centralized IoT platforms enclose much consumer data, we must acknowledge that they also protect those data from unwanted public access, whereas public blockchains, by definition, make those data available to everyone. Hence, putting the right cryptographic and obfuscation mechanisms in place is important for preserving privacy in blockchains.[238]

We should not underestimate the implementation challenges. Several studies have shown that even properly anonymized data can be used to identify individuals with very good accuracy.[239]

Scalability: Beyond autonomous devices and processing at the edge

Scalability is a serious concern in the Internet of Things. To understand the scale we are talking about, let's consider Twitter, a social network used worldwide. As of March 2021, about 800 million tweets reach the Twitter servers every day.[240] To handle this volume while maintaining a decent latency, Twitter has developed quite an impressive infrastructure. Now, consider a fleet of 100,000 IoT devices sending an update every second to an IoT platform—that's about 86 billion transactions per day—about 132 times the number of tweets a day, and still a tiny fraction of the 50 billion devices expected to be on the Internet by 2020.[241]

The IoT represents an unprecedented challenge both in terms of network and data scalability. The success of IoT products puts ever more pressure on their respective platforms and can lead to service outages that impact the physical world. As the IoT infiltrates every aspect of our daily lives, the volume of data generated will put ever-increasing pressure on the Internet infrastructure and on central-ized IoT platforms.

Massively distributed systems are usually a sensible way of dealing with such issues. Making devices more autonomous and processing an increasing amount of data on the edge (e.g., gateways) are two parts of the solution. By definition, blockchains are massively distrib-uted and, hence, have a potential to help with decentralization and the autonomy of things. However, the community still has work to do for blockchains to scale.

Durability: Upkeep distributed across the network

Finally, durability is an important issue for current IoT products. The question is not only "Will this IoT product last for 10 years?" but also "Will the IoT platform that it's connected to still be around in five years?" This isn't science fiction: numerous IoT products have been discontinued and numerous IoT platforms have gone bankrupt, leaving consumers with bricks instead of smart devices. Think of the smart home start-up Revolv hub, which Nest shut down after acquir-ing it, rendering the devices connected to it unusable. Or how about the Eyefi card that connected cameras to the Internet: it became obso-lete through a firmware update.[242] The increase of such problems led the director of the US Federal Trade Commission (FTC) to send an open letter to the makers of IoT devices.[243]

Decentralization means distribution of control. Public block-chains are not controlled by a single entity but by all (or some, depending on the implementation) participants in the network. The powerful effect of this distribution is that it is quite difficult to shut down a blockchain, even if some of its main participants stopped using it. Blockchains can exist for as long as a few people decide that running a few nodes is worth the cost (e.g., energy). Imagine, for instance, that Revolv hub had been based on DLT: device owners could have taken over and continued operating the system. Moreover, we could use smart contracts to implement the rules engines of IoT platforms. Smart contracts are a real plus for durability because they put intelligence in the network and can drive use cases in a totally decentralized manner.

The benefits of decentralization apply not only when considering the cloud part of IoT devices but also when considering the longevity of the devices themselves. Blockchains could, for instance, ensure firmware updates are made available to devices far beyond what is commercially sensible to commit to for device manufacturers: as long as one device in the network has the latest firmware, all devices could benefit. IPFS is tackling this issue by implementing an alternative to HTTP. Using DLT, IPFS is distributing files across the network, making it resilient, should a server disappear.[244]

LIMITATIONS OF BLOCKCHAINS FOR THE IoT

To recap, blockchains hold the promise to help the IoT overcome such challenges as resilience, durability, scalability, trust, privacy, and interoperability. Now let's consider the challenges that blockchains can't yet solve, the new challenges that they bring, and the remaining challenges of distributed ledger technologies deployed in the IoT (Figure 4-3).

Scalability, latency, and transaction costs

Scalability is one of the most complex and controversial challenges that the best-known blockchains implementations have yet to resolve and, in some cases, even exacerbate. In particular, such public blockchains as Bitcoin and Ethereum in their current state are known to process a relatively low number of transactions per second: about seven for Bitcoin and 25 for Ethereum at the time of this writing.[245] This latency results from different factors, some of them artificial, linked to the PoW and distributed consensus requirements of these public blockchains, which make them slow and limited in concurrency by design.

FIGURE 4-3

CHALLENGES OF BLOCKCHAIN-BASED INTERNET OF THINGS

Blockchains and distributed ledger technologies have the potential to tackle several challenges for the IoT—but also to introduce new challenges.

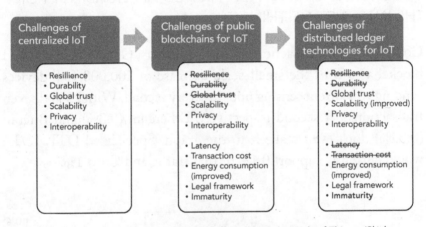

Source: Dominique D. Guinard and Vlad M. Trifa, Building the Web of Things (Shelter Island, NY: Manning Publications Co., 2016). webofthings.org/book. Used under CC BY 4.0 license.

Consequently, microtransactions in public blockchains are stamped with a very high level of fees. At the time of this writing, the median fee for a one-to two-dollar transaction was 34 percent for Bitcoin and eight percent for Ethereum.[246] This makes frequent microtransactions with little value (such as uploading the new temperature value of a sensor) totally unrealistic. Add the processing power and time required to perform encryption and confirm transactions, plus the increasing storage needed to record the ledger, and we have systems with very limited IoT applicability, particularly ill-suited for very large-scale sensing with frequent sampling.[247]

Figure 4-4 compares the transaction volume of a small-scale Internet of Things (100,000 devices connected to an Internet-based platform) with the volume of Twitter posts, Google searches, and transactions on blockchain. The latency to confirm transactions—in the order of minutes—renders most current blockchains unusable for actuation in industrial or consumer environments. Imagine having to wait a minute for a light to turn on or a garage door to open!

FIGURE 4-4

BLOCKCHAINS HAVE VERY LIMITED APPLICABILITY FOR THE INTERNET OF THINGS

Comparing the transaction volumes of tweets, Google searches, and blockchains with the small-scale use case of 100,000 IoT devices sending concurrent sensing updates every second. With 25 and seven transactions per second respectively, Ethereum (0.3%) and Bitcoin (0.09%) don't even make it to the graph. Specialized DTL IOTA would currently support 0.1% of that traffic and Coco 1%.

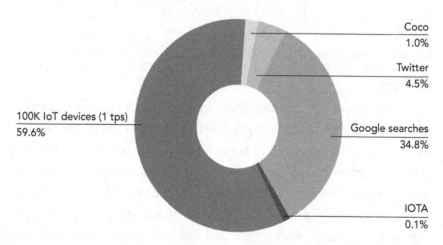

Source of data: Dominique Guinard, 2017.

Scalability and the latency that comes with the lack of it are major concerns for the future of these blockchains, and major efforts are underway to address these issues. Since public blockchains such as Ethereum and Bitcoin will not help out of the box with IoT scalability challenges, the community is thinking about higher-level protocols.

For example, the Ambrosus project is looking into instrumenting and sensing the food chain using Ethereum.[248] However, instead of naively pushing microtransactions (e.g., the temperature readings of a pallet of strawberries) to the Ethereum blockchain, Ambrosus is looking to massively aggregate these events prior to synchronizing with the blockchain and to store only references to events, thus pushing the actual events to a decentralized database. This method makes the system more viable for sensing IoT use cases but would not resolve use cases requiring high frequency updates or the latency issues that actuation use cases would face. This is why Ambrosus is focusing mainly on instrumenting the supply chain with IoT, a sensing-centric use case.

The idea of aggregating transactions is very sound, and several other initiatives are looking at such a pattern. For example, batching transactions is one of the reasons the Coco Framework currently reaches about 1600 transactions per second on top of the Ethereum network.[249]

Others have been thinking about radically new protocols inspired by blockchains but with fundamentally different implementations. Consider IOTA, a blockchain without the blocks and the chain, meaning that it isn't really a blockchain—it's distributed ledger technology. In essence, IOTA is based on the idea of the *tangle*, the core principles of which are similar to those of blockchains: the tangle is a distributed ledger based on a P2P network.[250] However, how its participants achieve consensus is fundamentally different from well-known blockchains such as Ethereum or Bitcoin: every transaction on a tangle has to attest that two previous transactions are valid. This method effectively creates a directed acyclic graph (DAG) and leads also to indirectly attesting that a subsection of the graph (the tangle) is respecting the protocol's rules.[251]

This small difference has two very important consequences: first, it means that the *entire* network—rather than a smaller group of miners—is involved in the approval of transactions, and so there are no transaction fees in IOTA. This design resolves the issue of the prohibitive fees for the microtransactions required by IoT sensing and actuating use cases.

Second, the tangle protocol enables parallelized consensus, making for a shorter confirmation time and leading to more transactions processed per second. As a reference point, 250 IOTA nodes can manage about 100 transactions per second with confirmation times of 10 seconds or less.[252] While this rate is still far from the performance of centralized IoT platforms, it is encouraging, and the IOTA team is confident that the number of supported transactions will increase significantly.

While blockchains and DLTs might not be able to help the IoT with scalability today, they could help in the long term by fostering P2P communication among things—a significant paradigm shift from how things operate today. Rather than relying on full connectivity to a centralized platform, things could initiate communication in smaller and more local networks. Add the idea of value exchange in the form of tokens at the core of several blockchains, and we could have a self-organizing network in which things could execute and get "paid" for operations without intermediaries. This use case is precisely the kind that blockchains such as IOTA are exploring by allowing the execution of feeless microtransactions on the network. For example, the Brooklyn Microgrid project is applying these principles in its energy grid in which citizens can automatically monetize and exchange the energy produced by solar panels and other renewable sources of energy.[253]

The IOTA tangle, Ambrosus, and Coco are not the only frameworks and protocols attempting to resolve the scalability issues of current DLTs and blockchains. New protocols and solutions appear daily and push the art of the possible one step at a time.[254] Benchmarks and systematic scalability testing of these new solutions will be instrumental to foster realistic adoption.

Legal aspects: Regulation lags behind innovation

As with every fast-moving technology, blockchains are a step ahead of regulators, resulting in multiple legal gray areas. This has been especially well documented when it comes to financial market regulations. For the IoT, blockchains raise several unanswered legal questions. For example, Article 17 of GDPR stipulates the "right to be forgotten," meaning that an individual can demand that a data controller erase any or all data that the controller holds about that individual.

This stipulation is clearly problematic with a blockchain where, by design, transactions cannot be deleted. This is perhaps the most striking but not the only example of how regulations are not ready for decentralization and blockchains.

Interoperability: Decentralize and standardize

Blockchains have the potential of creating an IoT where things talk to one another autonomously rather than through large centralized platforms. However, for this communication to work at IoT scale, we need interoperability: things must speak a common set of protocols to enable autonomous, decentralized interactions—clearly far from a given in the blockchain ecosystem. Indeed, new blockchains or DLTs appear daily, creating more incompatibilities.

This is not dissimilar to how the IoT itself evolved. At first, networked embedded systems were speaking largely incompatible and proprietary protocols, creating many intranets of things, which is still largely the case. However, all these protocols have started to converge to Internet protocols such as IP and TCP/UDP and interoperability is happening through Web protocols at the application layer. In many cases, blockchain solutions are building competing application protocols on top of the Internet, adding another layer of incompatibilities.

For example, the Bitcoin protocol is not compatible with Ethereum's. These two protocols form separate massively decentralized networks. Communication across the two requires translations layers. While translation is viable for large systems, embedded systems in the IoT are unlikely to be able to support many decentralized protocols in order to communicate with one another. We need convergence if we want worldwide P2P and autonomous communication to flourish for the IoT.

Numerous initiatives are looking at cross-blockchain and DLT standardization within standards bodies such as the International Telecommunication Union or World Wide Web Consortium.[255] Other initiatives design new distributed protocols to enable interoperability, for instance, Polkadot multichain technology or the Icon Hyperconnect system.[256]

However, convergence and true interoperability will take time. It took years for embedded systems to converge toward Internet and Web technologies in the IoT and that journey is ongoing. The road to standardization of DLT for the IoT is long but it is an important series of steps to materialize the decentralization potential of DLT for IoT.

Energy consumption: Too high for resource-constrained devices

The power consumption of blockchains is an easily overlooked challenge. In 2014, a study established that the power consumed by the Bitcoin blockchain was comparable to Ireland's electricity consumption.[257] More recent results demonstrate the power consumption of Bitcoin compared to other countries (Figure 4-5).[258]

Not all blockchains are equal when it comes to energy consumption. The most power-hungry ones rely on PoW. For example, to validate transactions, bitcoin miners have to find value, that satisfies a particular equation involving the SHA-256 cryptographic hash function. This is a very computationally expensive operation—comparable to a lottery where we can pick our own number—and it requires a significant amount of energy. The requirement for such an expensive operation is important in protecting the blockchain against attackers: it makes attacks financially and computationally difficult. Beyond PoW, decentralization and redundancy generally consume power. This is a challenge because it makes blockchain solutions not very sustainable and also significantly more expensive than centralized solutions. Creating optimized hardware and using new consensus algorithms could resolve or mitigate these challenges. For example, PoS does not require power-hungry machines to produce as many hashes per second as possible.

FIGURE 4-5

ENERGY CONSUMPTION BY COUNTRY

If the Bitcoin blockchain were a country, it would rank 38th in terms of terawatt hours of energy consumption per year, higher than Austria, Bangladesh, and Chile.

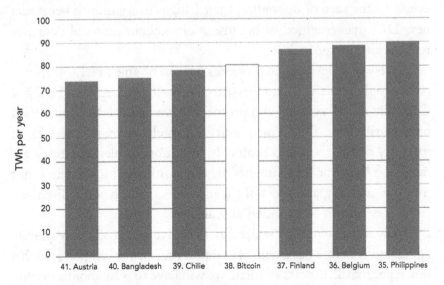

Source of data: "Bitcoin Energy Consumption," Digiconomist.net, as of 9 March 2021. digiconomist.net/bitcoin-energy-consumption.

The high-power demand of blockchains is also an issue for the things in the IoT. Numerous IoT use cases run low-power devices because they need to run on batteries for a long time or because low-power hardware is cheaper. This means that numerous blockchain and DLT protocols are not well suited for resource-constrained devices: they can work on the gateways but not on some of the more constrained nodes of the IoT.

Aside from scalability, resolving the power-consumption problem of blockchain technology is an important challenge with a high priority to ensure the sustainability and future-proofness of solutions in development.

Immaturity: Not production ready

Finally, perhaps the most important challenge introduced by DLT for IoT is the immaturity of the current solutions. The biggest difference between IoT and pure Web applications is the fact that IoT deployments have an impact in the physical world where the rules of engagement are fundamentally different. People are likely to be averse to the idea of upgrading their fridges every month because a new DLT has emerged or because a blockchain protocol does not really scale as expected.

Real-world devices and processes need to be able to rely on proven technologies that will last for years without fundamental changes. Centralized IoT systems and protocols have just reached some level of maturity. The DLT community is largely aware of the lack of maturity of the tools and protocols, and most implementations are tagged as "beta" or "experiments" by their authors: "blockchain is not production ready, and most of the use cases that are being discussed right now cannot be executed at scale."[259]

However, the pace at which DLTs evolve is actually very encouraging: rarely before has a field of computer science developed at such a quick pace. Still, experts estimate we will have to wait about a decade before DLTs reach maturity and mass adoption.[260]

IMPLEMENTING BLOCKCHAINS FOR IoT

The particular blend of advantages and challenges that DLTs and blockchains bring to the table does not necessarily make the design choice very straightforward. As we have seen, a few criteria such as potentially better scalability have yet to be proven. Therefore, we should focus instead on the unique features of blockchain relevant to our IoT use case. We consider three questions in particular:

1. Do we need to fix distrust?

2. Do we need to conduct multiparty transactions?

3. Do we need to decentralize and distribute computation?

If we answer yes to all three questions, then blockchain might be a viable solution.

PRESENT AND FUTURE-PROOF INTEGRATION ARCHITECTURE

If blockchain makes sense for our use case, then the next question is, "How do we architect an integration?" We could rebuild the features of IoT platforms on top of blockchain or DLT ecosystems, but we propose an approach that minimizes risk by leveraging existing IoT platforms while creating a bridge to DLT innovation.

The core of the idea is to continue connecting things to the IoT via centralized platforms but to start propagating some of the data to blockchains or DLTs. Figure 4-6 illustrates the Web Thing model.[261] A thing connected using this model has a Web identity in the form of a URL. We use a blockchain hash corresponding to the identity of the device (e.g., using a blockchain identity service) to extend the thing identity, thereby leveraging the security and trust of identities on the blockchain while preserving addressability on the Web.

FIGURE 4-6

EXTENDING THE WEB THING MODEL

Here is how we have extended the Web Thing model in the EVRYTHNG platform to synchronize important events in blockchains.

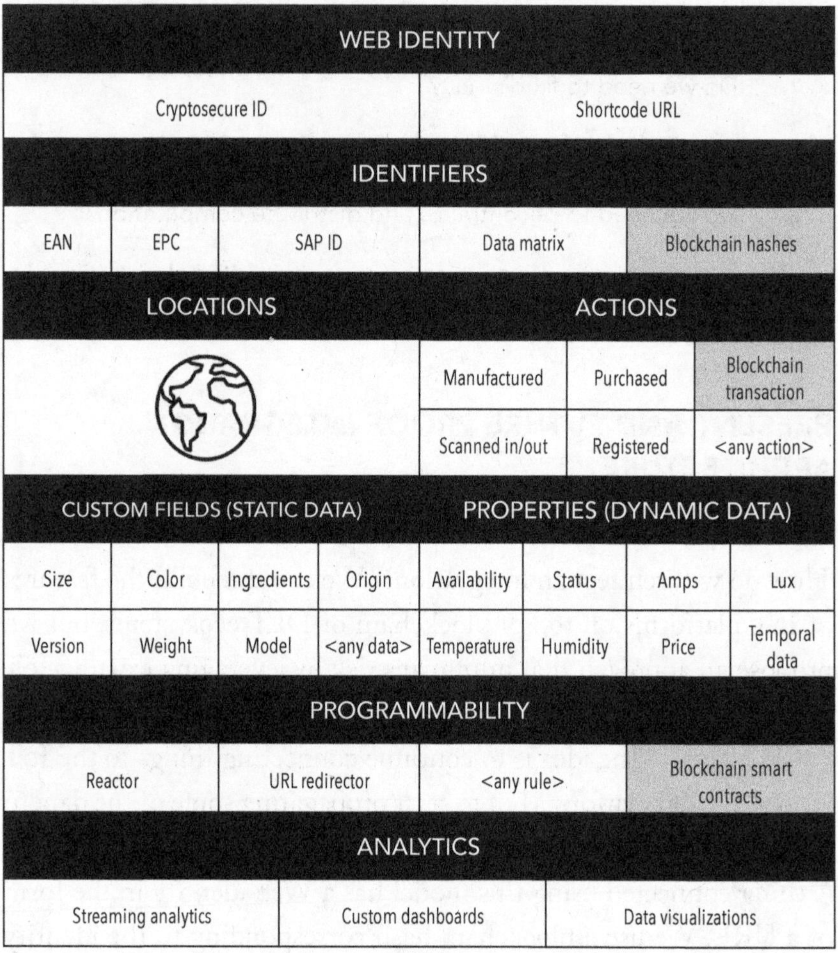

WEB IDENTITY							
Cryptosecure ID				Shortcode URL			
IDENTIFIERS							
EAN	EPC	SAP ID		Data matrix		Blockchain hashes	
LOCATIONS				**ACTIONS**			
				Manufactured	Purchased	Blockchain transaction	
				Scanned in/out	Registered	<any action>	
CUSTOM FIELDS (STATIC DATA)				**PROPERTIES (DYNAMIC DATA)**			
Size	Color	Ingredients	Origin	Availability	Status	Amps	Lux
Version	Weight	Model	<any data>	Temperature	Humidity	Price	Temporal data
PROGRAMMABILITY							
Reactor		URL redirector		<any rule>		Blockchain smart contracts	
ANALYTICS							
Streaming analytics		Custom dashboards		Data visualizations			

Similarly, with this model, a thing receives a number of actions representing the actuation commands it receives from the IoT platform. We could hash and store these actions in a blockchain as transactions (e.g., Ethereum transactions) or as batches of transactions, which would provide a trustable and immutable trace of the actuation.

Properties represent the data sensed by a thing. Storing these data at scale in a public blockchain might be problematic because of transaction fees and scalability, but we could aggregate and synchronize them to the blockchain on a regular basis or send them to a decentralized database.[262]

Finally, IoT platforms offer a rules engine for running the business logic and rules. These form contracts between the devices and the platform. In the centralized platform, we could keep real-time rules triggered when sensing or actuation data reaches the platform (e.g., temperature threshold, preventive maintenance of an appliance). We could transform specific rules requiring strong auditability or multiparty agreements into smart contracts on a blockchain such as Ethereum.

This architecture presents the advantage of keeping the core operation of the thing in a proven centralized IoT platform while preparing to leverage the future benefits of blockchains for a number of data points, operations, and rules.

PRIVATE BLOCKCHAINS

In answer to some of these challenges, alternative models have appeared: from public blockchains, some developers moved into the concepts of "private blockchains" or the hybrid "consortium-based blockchains" (aka federated blockchains) or DLTs. For example, the Hyperledger blockchain stack or the Corda DLT projects support numerous researchers or businesses as private or consortium-based blockchains.[263] These projects are not publicly accessible distributed systems; they are closed systems accessible to a limited number of partners. They are to blockchains what intranets are to the Internet.

While we see little value in private blockchains, there are two advantages in taking a consortium-based approach. First, it can be run as a controlled experiment, thereby alleviating the immaturity issues. Second, it can hide scalability issues by limiting and controlling the throughput of applications. Nevertheless, nonpublic blockchains or DLTs lose several advantages of their very proposition: though based on decentralized technologies, they are put in place by a small set of actors who control the destiny of the system.

GUIDELINES FOR DURABLE IoT SYSTEMS

Since things are still communicating with a centralized platform acting as a proxy to blockchains, this hybrid architecture is not fully decentralized and, hence, does not guarantee resilience and durability. Here are four guidelines for ensuring that things connecting to the IoT today will be able to transition to different decentralized systems tomorrow. The guidelines are simple:

Use open protocols. Things should connect to the Internet using open protocols, rather than proprietary ones. Whenever possible, choose Internet protocols such as IP and TCP/UDP (either directly or via local gateways) for network connectivity and open application protocols (e.g., HTTP, Websocket, MQTT, CoAP, etc.) with wide community support for application connectivity. This ensures that switching from one IoT platform to another is possible without the need to rethink completely the protocol a device uses.

Expose open APIs in the cloud. IoT platforms should expose open APIs using well-supported Web protocols such as HTTP and Websocket to ensure that consumers could retrieve the data and configuration, should they want to transition from one platform to another.

Rely on local operation—no cloud dependency. The core functionality of things in the IoT should work even if a cloud provider disappeared. Furthermore, platforms should offer local APIs (e.g., a local HTTP or CoAP API) or at least a local interface that allows switching to a different cloud provider or uploading a different firmware locally.

The combination of these three guidelines ensures that consumers will be able to switch their devices to other providers should their IoT provider disappear. Easy switching ensures a certain durability of IoT devices; devices will be able to evolve into more decentralized systems in the future.

Put the right legal framework in place. Regulators should implement rules that protect consumers and ensure that IoT is sustainable over time. To ensure compliance, we could implement these regulations using blockchains.

 ## CONCLUSIONS AND RECOMMENDATIONS

Very few technologies have developed so rapidly and have had the impact of blockchains and DLTs. The interest around these new systems clearly shows that they will revolutionize numerous markets, including IoT.

DLT could solve some of the problems the IoT faces. In particular, it could help to overcome the important scalability challenges the IoT will face over the next decade. Indeed, by proposing autonomous and contract-based communication between things, DLT could help to achieve the decentralization of things in the IoT and make them rely on resilient global networks instead of a handful of centralized platforms.

The future of the IoT will most likely lean toward the all-digital. Billions of networked devices will have to be able to work autonomously and dynamically adapt to fast-changing rules. This hyperscale IoT will be sustainable only with decentralization and autonomy. This is where blockchain and more generally DLT have the potential to help: they will certainly be at the root of massively distributed and decentralized networks of the future.

DLTs are still in their infancy, not production ready. Their current evolution is an unprecedented real-world research project, where studies are trials that have a direct impact on the world outside research (e.g., the world of finance). Consequently, the domain will likely evolve much faster than what we are accustomed to in the traditional world of research. Nevertheless, the makers of this new technology are no fools and realize that they are not engaged in production ready at scale.[264] Before deployments at scale, there are several big challenges to address, most important scalability and energy consumption.

The IoT is here and now—in all markets! The IoT market revolves around connectivity, identification, sensing, remote monitoring, and actuation. Companies are busy deploying connected things in all sectors, touching all markets. Corporations that are not embracing digitization are already facing the risk of obsolescence.

Decentralization can wait; digitalization of the physical world cannot. Choose an IoT strategy very wisely. Experts estimate that up to 90 percent of blockchain-based pilots will fail over the next two years.[265] While we can hide the immaturity of a technology in layers of abstraction in the digital world, we cannot ignore update cycles, physical constraints, and safety regulations in the real world, and those make it very hard to base things in the IoT on emerging technologies.

Many IoT use cases work without a blockchain or DLT. Scrutinize the capabilities—trust, multiparty transactions, and decentralized and distributed computation—before onboarding a full blockchain implementation. Beware of alternative implementations of blockchains such as private blockchains, which tend to expose companies to all immaturity challenges without the benefits of public blockchains. Remember what CompuServe was to the Web and how it disappeared.

The potential of DLT for the IoT is undeniable. Start with hybrid architectures, where data from centralized systems can be shared on blockchains and leveraged. Experiment with decentralization and global trust. Start thinking about which subparts of centralized solutions these new distributed ledger technologies could replace. Finally, build the IoT of today with mechanisms that prevent lock-in to proprietary, centralized platforms so that things will be ready to adapt to distributed ledger technologies.

EDITOR'S NOTE

Now that we've covered big data, AI, and IoT in terms of block-chain technologies, let's pause for a review. The World Wide Web was a read-only platform (Web 1.0) for publishing information, searching by syntax, and consuming content. It was a distributed network stewarded by passionate technologists. The social web we use today is a read-write platform (Web 2.0) not only for inter-acting with content and its creators but also for collaborating with people on a global scale. While the underlying technology still has its Web 1.0 stewards in terms of standards, the network has been co-opted by state interests in authoritarian regimes and commer-cial interests in democratic ones. Control over access, privacy, and free speech is far more centralized.

The trivergence of IoT, blockchain, and AI ushers in the seman-tic web (Web 3.0), a decentralized network where trillions of devices on the IoT generate sensor-direct data, a distributed ledger records and secures those data, and AI analyzes the data, communicates with the things, alerts their owners, and continuously adjusts and improves the efficiency of the ecosystem and the sustainability of its effects on the environment (Figure 4-7).

FIGURE 4-7

THE TRIVERGENCE OF BLOCKCHAIN, AI, AND IoT AROUND DATA

Web 3.0 will run in distributed clouds, not on enterprise computing platforms.

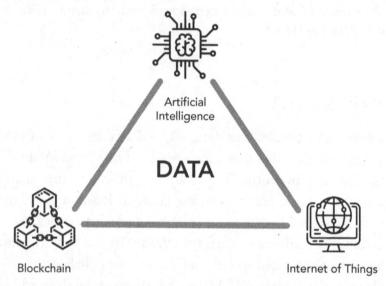

Artificial
Intelligence

DATA

Blockchain   Internet of Things

"Blockchain," "Chip," and "World Grid" by Freepik, used under Flaticon June 2019 license.

The days of enterprise computing are coming to an end: Web 3.0 will run in a distributed cloud, some combination of public and private servers dispersed geographically and with edge computing capabilities. These will be important for securing public resources such as transportation networks with autonomous vehicles and charging stations, the topics of Chapters 5 and 6.

We must ensure that the governance or stewardship of this network remains distributed and is quantum proof, where citizens, advocacy groups, entrepreneurs, developing economies, and small to medium-sized businesses have as much say in the network's governance, operations, and standardization as large corporations, nongovernmental organizations, and global powers. Those are the topics of Chapters 7 and 8. Read on!

CHAPTER 5

AUTONOMOUS VEHICLES AND BLOCKCHAIN

How a Distributed Ledger System Could Fund the
Next Generation of Transportation Infrastructure

David Mirynech

 ## NETWORKED AUTONOMOUS VEHICLES IN BRIEF

- From the pages of science fiction to a pavement near you, autonomous vehicles are beginning to navigate our roads and highways. Intense competition among firms has attracted capital, prominent stakeholders, and other resources to fuel the technical development of this industry.

- Yet, a world of ubiquitous driverless vehicles comes with challenges, such as how to fund road construction and maintenance; how to secure devices on the Internet of mobile things; how to preserve the privacy and safety of owners, users, and their data; and whom to hold responsible for accidents when vehicles malfunction.

- Blockchain technologies are proving effective not only in lowering the costs of IT infrastructure associated with identity and credit card systems but also in increasing the profit functions of vehicles. To finance state and federal roadway networks, governments could capture these revenues through instantaneous remittances.

- Blockchain could also reduce information asymmetries in used car markets, improve accuracy and verifiability of insurance claims, automate claims processing, and support trusted P2P autonomous vehicle leasing systems. The need for safety and accountability is pushing sensor technology and machine learning to new heights.

- An important consortium is the Mobility Open Blockchain Initiative (MOBI). It is replacing siloed and secretive research and development (R&D) with collaboration among technology developers, automotive manufacturers, transportation authorities, and other stakeholders to provide a road map for overcoming barriers to adoption.

- Telecommunications is critical. The need for high-frequency data input is spurring the build-out of fifth generation (5G) national networks. Demand for blockchains that can support high user volumes is prompting advances in scalability solutions such as state channels, side channels, sharding, and interoperable chains.

- Vehicle owners or operators may one day receive compensation for sharing other basic resources, such as renewable energy and Internet connectivity. This blockchain-based sharing economy could extend to electric vertical takeoff and landing (eVTOL) vehicles and personal aircraft that facilitate air transportation.

STATE OF OUR INTERNATIONAL HIGHWAY NETWORK

In the last 100 years, automobiles have become the dominant mode of transportation in North America.[266] To accommodate personal transit, an international network of highways has expanded across most continents. These highway systems serve as economic pipelines for people and products to move efficiently across borders. Because of these networks' ability to stimulate economic movement and remove the friction in transportation, demand for new roads, particularly in developed and large metropolitan areas, has grown enormously. The result has been increased traffic and roadway congestion, continual road maintenance and repair, and a greater desire for new serviceable roads and highways.

To keep up, governments have had to determine how to pay for the next batch of roadway maintenance and construction. Over the last 50 years, municipal, state, and federal bodies have done so through such payments as tolls, petrol taxes, parking fees, vehicle registration fees, traffic fines, and other charges for motor vehicle infractions.

While automobile innovation has accelerated at a rapid pace in recent times, two emerging technologies in the automotive industry are reducing governmental ability to modernize these networks. The first is the electric car, an environmental breakthrough that has lessened our reliance on fossil fuels but not necessarily the government's dependence on taxes collected from fuel sales. The second is the autonomous vehicle, which is fundamentally changing our culture of driving and our need for personal ownership of cars.[267] As a result, important revenues from traffic tickets, vehicle registration, driver licensing, and parking are at risk.

Governments must be creative in finding new pools of public money to pay for the upkeep and development of our roadways. In 2017, a group of economists from Jacobs Engineering Group and Volterra Partners jointly submitted a proposal for funding better, safer, more reliable roads in a way that was fair to road users, good for the economy, and beneficial to the environment.[268] These economists proposed a mobility-based, pay-per-use system that combined blockchain technology with on-demand ride-sharing services like Uber and Lyft as well as connected and autonomous vehicles (CAVs), and their solution was named a finalist for the esteemed Wolfson Economics Prize.[269] While they identified the broad properties of DLT that could aid in their solution, they didn't discuss many of the specifications and challenges inherent in such an implementation of blockchain. Nevertheless, their research is quite interesting.

In this chapter, we investigate the feasibility and merits of a blockchain-based system for collecting funds through tolling systems and mileage-based user fees. In particular, we examine several use cases and analyze the technical properties of such a system, the limitations of blockchain and obstacles to adoption at scale, and the stakeholders most affected by the transition.

AN INDUSTRY-WIDE PIVOT

For many optimists, the transition to an electric and autonomous age of vehicles seems all but a given, in light of the powerful interests who have put significant resources behind this paradigm shift. In 2009, the digital behemoth Google began developing a secret driverless vehicle project that became known as Waymo.[270] In 2013, traditional industry players like Bayerische Motoren Werke (BMW), Mercedes-Benz, Ford Motor Company, and General Motors (GM) all launched their own self-driving car initiatives. In 2014, brands such as Tesla, Uber, and Apple followed.[271] By mid-2018, Google announced that its autonomous cars had driven over eight million miles.[272]

For traditional auto manufacturers, the emphasis on autonomous vehicles is a stunning transition in vision and strategy. For years, the classic car dealership model has focused on driving sales ahead of the release of next year's models. Yet, manufacturers must shift from a business model focused predominantly on selling units to one with multiple revenue sources.

For example, today's cars sit parked almost 95 percent of the time.[273] As assets, self-driving cars can work constantly, delivering value to owners around the clock with fees based on such factors as time, distance, and weight or value of cargo. Once in circulation, autonomous vehicles become shared resources for rental, use, and insurance on demand. That challenges the very concept of vehicle ownership. If we can simply hail a vehicle from our phone rather than pay the high costs associated with a lease or sale, parking, maintenance, mandatory insurance, and vehicle inspections, then our need to own a car falls. This shift directly affects the number of vehicles on the road, the volume of vehicles sold, the manufacturers' bottom line, and the government's fees collected. Therefore, an industry outsider might wonder why these corporations are investing in R&D to disrupt themselves.

To their credit, manufacturers are looking to capitalize on a new business model known as mobility-as-a-service (MaaS). MaaS represents a new user-focused mobility paradigm.[274] Chris Ballinger, the CEO of MOBI, said that this future has arrived because of two distinct occurrences: "Vehicles are now connected, and they are getting smarter. Those two things allow vehicles to participate in the service economy in ways they never could before."[275]

Ballinger elaborated: "Twenty years ago the automaker's value chain ended with the sale of the car and a listing price stickered to the windshield. The extraction of rent and value came from financial services such as leasing and from vehicle maintenance. Now this extraction is poised to happen well into the life of the car."[276]

According to Deloitte, consumers favorably view new mobility options and ride-sharing apps such as Uber and Lyft. By 2024, car sharing is expected to exceed 23 million users globally.[277] Detroit's Big Three—GM, Ford, and Fiat Chrysler—and other auto manufacturers have invested significantly in the growth of these ventures. Look no further than GM's $250-million investment in Lyft in early 2016.[278] Similarly, Toyota invested $500 million in Uber as recently as August 2018 to form a "driverless car pact" to bridge the future of MaaS and autonomous vehicles.[279]

If we consider the size of these investments and the millions of miles of successful test drives, we see that these companies have the capital and capabilities to bring about a driverless future more quickly than many car owners may expect. According to *WIRED*, the general consensus in the automotive industry is that the development of level-four autonomous vehicles (i.e., one level below full automation) is rapidly accelerating (Table 5-1).[280]

TABLE 5-1

SIX LEVELS OF AUTONOMY

0	1	2	3	4	5
No automation	**Driver assistance**	**Partial automation**	**Conditional automation**	**High automation**	**Full automation**
The driver controls all aspects of driving, even with enhanced warning or intervention systems.	The driver controls the vehicle, but the vehicle design includes some driving assistance features. ·	The vehicle can steer and manage speed, but the driver must monitor the vehicle and maintain situational awareness.	The driver need not maintain situational awareness but must be ready to take control of the vehicle.	The vehicle can perform all driving tasks under certain conditions; the driver has the option of taking control of the vehicle.	The vehicle can perform all driving tasks under all conditions; the driver may have the option of taking control of the vehicle.

Source: Figure entitled, "SAE [Society of Automotive Engineers] Automation Levels," Preparing for the Future of Transportation: Automated Vehicle 3.0, letter by Sec. Elaine L. Chao, US Dept. of Transportation, 4 Oct. 2018, p. vi, accessed 28 July 2019. Adapted courtesy of the US Dept. of Transportation. Not copyrightable in the United States.

THE BLESSING AND CURSE OF AUTONOMY

Despite significant progress, the long-term consequences of such a seismic shift in transportation warrant our attention. Typically, the headlines on autonomous vehicles focus on the positive environmental effects and the technology's potential to alleviate road congestion. Nevertheless, at a June 2018 conference, "Meeting of the Minds Mobility Summit," not far from the Motor City in Michigan, the topic was serious: "How do we prevent autonomous vehicles from bringing American cities to financial ruin?"[281] The consensus of the attendees was that, while many may generally think of self-driving cars as a gold mine, the economic realities of the technology are quite different.

Nico Larco, a director of the Urbanism Next Center at the University of Oregon and a speaker at the event, centered his talk on the heavy dependence of many municipalities on the revenue accrued from motor vehicles. In the United States alone, these revenue streams account for between 15 and 50 percent of transportation revenue.[282] City leaders have several reasons for concern. First, many of the concepts for autonomous cars are for electric vehicles (EVs); GM has chosen its Chevrolet Bolt as its primary EV of the future.[283] While others such as Ford have emphasized hybrids more, this transition will still likely reduce gas taxes. Second, manufacturers will likely program autonomous vehicles to follow traffic laws, effectively eliminating revenues from public driving violations. Finally, rather than park-and-pay fees, autonomous cars will be able to move on and service other riders.

We need creative solutions to fund public infrastructure. Lord Wolfson positioned the 2017 Wolfson Economics Prize to address this concern. The joint bid from Jacobs and Volterra recognized that, through a pay-per-use system, blockchain technology could become a vital revenue component of networks of autonomous vehicles. The authors of the joint bid noted that utilizing the blockchain can allow for privacy protection, permissioned monetization of personal data, frictionless billing, and account transparency and auditability.

BLOCKCHAIN AS A TRANSPORTATION PLATFORM

Blockchain is an emerging network technology that functions as a globally distributed ledger of value enabling exchanges between peers without the need for a trusted intermediary. The nature of the distributed ledger makes it both easy and cost-efficient to create networks that do not require a central point of control, such as a vehicle-to-vehicle information grid. Blockchain's inherent ability to communicate and to issue, trade, and manage value in a secure and reliable manner makes it particularly appealing as the foundation for a new revolutionary kind of transportation economy. Ballinger of MOBI said, "Blockchain can enable the provision of services in many interesting ways."[284]

Blockchain and autonomous vehicles are relatively recent developments. Just as the big automakers took several years to pursue self-driving cars after Google's 2009 launch of Waymo, enterprise took years to begin piloting blockchain projects after Satoshi Nakamoto's 2009 release of the Bitcoin blockchain protocols.[285] Despite this brief history, start-ups have done much to understand how blockchain could support a network that enabled secure communication and even transactions of value among autonomous vehicles, human beings, and other entities.

TOLL ROADS: EARLY BLOCKCHAIN-BASED VEHICLE VALUE TRANSFER SYSTEM

Some of the earliest blockchain-based vehicle value transfer systems emerged to tackle issues associated with toll-road billing. Oaken Innovations is a Texas-based blockchain technology company that focuses on autonomous blockchain-based mobility and secure IoT applications for machine-to-machine (M2M) communication and value transfer. Oaken first made waves in February 2017 when it received the top prize of $100,000 at the World Government Summit, a conference focused on smart governance and building blockchain-based solutions for advancing smart city applications.[286] Its winning submission put a Tesla on the blockchain with the aim of building a P2P toll-road solution.

Oaken's platform grows what it likes to call *autonomous communication over redundant nodes* (ACORNS). It uses Ethereum, IPFS, and Node.js to power its decentralized system.[287] Because ACORNS run on top of Ethereum Virtual Machine (EVM), the platform is compatible with all blockchains that use EVM at their core.

Oaken's system works as follows. A tollbooth equipped with ACORN has a virtual tollgate signified by a red light and a green light. The Tesla's ACORN then communicates with the tollgate that it wants to pay the toll causing the tollbooth to trigger a smart contract transaction. The smart contract transaction takes the raw Tesla data and communicates it to the blockchain in the form of an IPFS hash. The Tesla then validates the blockchain transaction using the raw canvassed data and compares them to the global positioning system (GPS) data from the tollgate smart contract. The canvas data are stored on IPFS and trigger a pay-toll smart contract to pay the toll seamlessly with cryptocurrency. Finally, the tollbooth's ACORN receives the signal from the pay-toll contract, opens the gate, and permits the Tesla access to the toll road.[288]

Tolls are becoming more prevalent because they help to pay down significant levels of infrastructure debt. Examples include the US Interstate Highway System, a network initially planned to be funded through tolls. The network, which cost $132 billion to build, was eventually funded by a federal gas tax, which raised $119 billion.[289]

Significant research has touted the benefits of tolling, with Rhode Island as a proven benefactor.[290] Yet, tolling is not without its warts. Toll roads require expensive toll-road infrastructure to manage accounting, identity, and payments that come with expensive transaction fees of three percent or higher. One tolling solution is Kapsch TrafficCom's E-ZPass technology.[291] E-ZPass is an RFID system comprised of at least three things: in each vehicle is a transponder, which stores a unique identifier associated with a user account; in each toll lane is another transponder, which is associated with the location of the tolling station (and even the lane) and connected by a local area network to a third thing, a centralized server. It works like this: the booth transponder is continually emitting a signal in search of vehicle transponders. When a vehicle transponder enters the booth transponder's reading field, it broadcasts its unique identifier. The booth transponder receives the signal, routes the identifier, location, and possibly the lane data to the system's central server. The server associates the identifier with the user account and charges that account.[292] But the system isn't encrypted, and so hackers can extract an individual driver's information from the transponder or more data from the central database.[293]

A blockchain-based solution for tollbooths can provide several benefits. The use of blockchain has added a substantial amount of value to the process because it has eliminated the centralized server infrastructure of the database, identity, and credit card systems. Doing so can reduce the three percent charge between the two parties to 0.1 percent with the added benefit of instantaneous remittance. Randy Cole, executive director of the Ohio Turnpike and Infrastructure Commission, stressed the importance of the blockchain to manage this administration. He stated that current systems place high amounts of undue costs on the back end of managing transactions, which are then passed on to drivers.[294]

In truth, this is not so different from the declarations of many in enterprise blockchain to move archaic legacy banking systems onto a distributed ledger to help save millions in streamlined processes. From this perspective, the use case appears to fit quite well. It also begs the question of where else does blockchain provide a solution to transportation pain points.

MOBILE OPEN BLOCKCHAIN INITIATIVE

In May 2018, CEO Chris Ballinger announced the founding of MOBI, a consortium comprised of large manufacturers such as Toyota Research Institute, Ford, GM, and BMW. MOBI now encompasses more than 80 percent of global auto manufacturers.[295] Joining the automakers are Oaken and other blockchain and distributed ledger start-ups such as Gem, BigChainDB, and Commuterz as well as consulting and development firms like IBM, Accenture, and ConsenSys. These stakeholders seek to provide the initial auto platform that will power the ecosystem's automobile data exchange and mobility platform. MOBI's primary goal is to make transportation safer, more affordable, and more widely accessible using blockchain and other technologies.[296]

According to Ballinger, MOBI operates as a sort of neutral convener between these companies. As the R&D costs to produce viable blockchain solutions in independent labs would likely be too expensive for many of these operators, MOBI functions as a public good where multiple entities can give funding and all benefit from shared breakthroughs. The consortium represents the end isolated proof-of-concept (POC) pilots, secret research, and development projects. This open-innovation working group includes competitors, suppliers, regulators, and government agencies with common goals.[297] With so many impressive stakeholders present, it also allows for the creation and enforcement of common standards to which all members can agree so communication between vehicles is easier in the future. The collaboration afforded by a structure such as this has already produced several key products for the road map of the future.

Vehicle identity passport, history, and tracking

According to Ballinger of MOBI and John Gerryts, co-founder of start-up Oaken, digital identity is one of the most critical components of a blockchain and driverless vehicle platform. As a result, MOBI's first project is to develop an identity system, known as a "car passport," for vehicles that tracks mileage and all relevant data on the blockchain.[298] It is similar to the CARFAX model in that it reduces fraudulent sales in used cars, because buyers and sellers have access to the vehicle's untampered history. This transparency spotlights the "lemons" or overvalued assets from car sales.[299]

Insurance pricing

With vehicle identity figured out, insurance applications that run on the blockchain are also a target for development. With an immutable data feed characterizing a car's history, insurance providers can apply a dynamic pricing model specific to that vehicle and its driver's own history. The result is a tailored price for each individual, rather than pricing by the perceived riskiness of drivers or their vehicles based on age, gender, make, or model. This model is known as *usage-based mobility pricing*.

While accuracy and efficiency are definitely the drivers here, this technology should also deter reckless driving. But, to what level of detail should insurance companies track driving habits? Although insurers should reward cautious drivers, everyone is prone to the occasional mistake. Data privacy may become contentious.

Vehicle leasing, car sharing, and ride hailing

Digital identity once again fundamentally ties into inbound payments. Inbound payments will eventually manage most P2P services such as automobile leasing from peers and the vehicle-to-vehicle or M2M ride-sharing payments associated with them.

At Consensus 2017, MOBI debuted its blockchain-enabled P2P car lease application. This application allows for consumers to lease the vehicle from a car owner using a smart contract on the Ethereum blockchain, file storage on IPFS, and a mobile application to lease and control access to the vehicle.[300] These applications allow for instantaneous remittance between transacting parties and do so without the need for payment processors by using logic coded to a smart contract. The hyper-secure blockchain-based IoT controls add a level of security not currently available on the consumer market, all while reducing or eliminating the need for server infrastructure.

MOBI stated that blockchains could handle application logic and data storage, thereby replacing traditional server infrastructure. The application layer in the blockchain could store vehicle identity as well as GPS, road, and map data.[301] Trusted entities could update this decentralized data layer. Concurrently, smart road sensors could feed this database. It would give a complete view of all vehicles and infrastructure, including current construction and traffic conditions, and third parties could build applications on top of these data. Vehicle data could also be amended for lease or ride-sharing services to build consumer mobile apps using this blockchain services layer.

In a potential ride-share or lease transaction using blockchain technology, instant value transfer and microtransactions are now possible. Within one smart contract transaction is an immediate remittance to several parties:

- Vehicle owner
- Driver
- Insurance provider
- Toll-road authority
- Road tax entity (e.g., a state department of transportation)

All entities receive instantaneous and guaranteed payment of funds. In addition, a rider can pay for a microinsurance policy for the rider's lease transaction to an escrow contract and then remit to the insurance provider once the ride is complete, with the balance of that escrow going to the rider or the lessee. As we discussed, users can implement an escrow contract for autonomous toll payments, or even eliminate tollgates from the toll-road infrastructure as we can prove the location of the vehicle using GPS. We could even have smart toll-road infrastructure where roads charge tolls only during peak hours.

In addition, by tokenizing the car's identity, we could enable private GPS and time-stamped data to the data exchange, immediately allowing for route optimization and capacity modeling for other entities to consume. This system also allows other owners to lease their own vehicles by utilizing blockchain-based rider identity.

As consumer behavior moves away from purchasing fuel and begins to favor pay-per-ride mobility over vehicle ownership, road and infrastructure authorities will face a shortfall of tax revenue that currently funds the construction and maintenance of roads. MOBI hypothesizes a usage-based tax included in the mobility transaction to replace this lost revenue. It can accommodate even short trips with a fraction of a penny in taxes.

Through this system, asset owners and drivers, tax entities, toll roads, and insurance providers all receive the benefits of instantaneous remittance in a single transaction without payment processing intermediaries. The blockchain-based car-sharing platform works as follows:

- An authenticated driver or rider finds an available vehicle to rent and the prices for the car rental.

- The driver or rider selects the vehicle that the driver wants to rent and can now unlock the doors and use the car's push start button to operate the vehicle. In the background, an internal automobile key fob has turned on to grant that driver the ability to operate the vehicle.

This process is extremely valuable because automobile owners are immediately able to monetize their unused vehicle time to trusted drivers or riders. In preparation for the future of autonomous vehicles, this platform enables users to pay and get mobility on demand.

IMPLEMENTATION CONSIDERATIONS

While blockchains certainly possess the properties to underpin an autonomous vehicle MaaS-based network, the technology has significant hurdles to overcome, and we must address the personal, legal, and ethical concerns before we see large-scale adoption.

BLOCKCHAIN LATENCY AND SCALABILITY

Because of the number of users that would be using pay-per-use autonomous vehicle networks, these systems would inherently experience a high volume of transactions. Large public blockchain networks like Ethereum have struggled when faced with too many users.

Ethereum has slowed considerably when faced with high transaction volumes. In November 2017, Ethereum's most popular Dapp, CryptoKitties, made large headlines. CryptoKitties is a mobile game that allows players to buy and breed "crypto-pets" on Ethereum's underlying network.[302] The game's developers said that CryptoKitties provided a "key step" for bringing blockchains into the hands of everyday mobile users, something a blockchain-based MaaS service would certainly provide.[303] But the game was such a resounding success, it caused a reported sixfold increase in pending transactions and accounted for over 10 percent of total transactions on Ethereum.[304] Business users were concerned that the game transactions received the same priority as general business transactions on the network. Worse, all transaction times significantly slowed because of the increased traffic.

How blockchains process and come to consensus in verifying transactions contributed to the slowdown. When exchanges between peers occur on the network, all nodes must update their records to maintain the current state of the chain, a single source of "truth," but doing so fundamentally slows the processing capability of the technology as a whole.

These network issues then become problematic when we consider the number of trips that ride-hailing apps like Uber process daily. According to the *Business of Apps*, Uber serviced 40 million customers a month in 2017.[305] We can break this number down into roughly 900 transactions a second, not including similar service applications like Lyft. Those who believe that the future holds fewer vehicle owners and more users of MaaS-based ride-hailing apps also expect the number of users to grow. At present, Ethereum can handle only 15 or so transactions a second.[306] At first look, the difference between these two numbers seems like a chasm, but many creative efforts are underway to increase transaction capacity on Ethereum and other blockchains.

The first of these solutions is known as *state channel*. State channels are transactions that occur *off-chain*—not on a particular blockchain (*on-chain*) per se—and that significantly reduce the cost and improve the speed of transactions.[307] Consider a shared ride with multiple different stops, requiring many payments to be processed in a short period. We need record only the beginning and ending account balances on-chain, because we can reprocess all the in-between payments off-chain. This capability serves to reduce the volume of transactions recorded on the main ledger.

The *sidechain* is another advance that follows a similar logic, with transactions occurring off the main blockchain. The advantage here is, several uncoordinated parties can all take advantage of the same blockchain.[308] To illustrate, Uber often charges riders higher fees, known as *surge pricing*, when Uber is servicing more users at once.[309] Sidechains could operate as a structure to handle these additional transactions, to keep network fees reasonable and processing times manageable. Raiden Network and Plasma are applying these principles to scale services on the Ethereum blockchain.[310] According to Sam Cassatt, chief strategy officer at ConsenSys, these networks can already handle thousands of transactions safely in lower-value increments.[311]

Last, one of the most interesting solutions is known as *sharding*, an older data storage technique used by companies such as Google. Sharding partitions databases into small, easily digestible pieces known as *shards*, meaning *small pieces*.[312] When we view these shards in aggregate, we see the original data structure.[313]

While technical breakthroughs in the scalability of blockchains will undoubtedly improve autonomous vehicle Dapps, the future of blockchain-enabled autonomous vehicles may revolve around multiple stakeholders; a single network like Ethereum need not be the one protocol underlying any large system such as an autonomous vehicle data grid.

Matthew Spoke is the founder of AION (now known as the Open Application Network), a protocol that focuses on interoperability and communication among different blockchains. He is not alone in believing that the required infrastructure will consist of many different chains, just as the Internet consists of many networks.[314] With such an infrastructure, blockchains could communicate and transact with each other, sharing the heavy volume of transactions through a method called atomic cross-chain swaps.[315] Some projects operating in this space include AION, Cosmos, and ICON.[316]

John Gerryts, CEO of Oaken, is fond of another project called Polkadot, which functions similarly and could aid projects like MOBI. Polkadot allows for connectivity between these blockchains, essentially meshing their networks together.[317] Polkadot uses a sharding method known as *parachains*, in which multiple chains advance simultaneously in lockstep. However, these chains can also talk to different chains with different consensus algorithms. Thus, a blockchain using its native logic must determine the consensus of other chains. While complex, these kinds of breakthroughs lead us to believe that the tech will be ready for high volume in the near future.

Many projects are trying to bring blockchain up to speed, with great efforts and resources devoted to accomplishing this future. Just as autonomous vehicles require more development to be ubiquitous on our roads, blockchain requires innovation to support the demands of a large-scale MaaS network.

COMMUNICATIONS NETWORK LATENCY

Today 5G networks represent the next advance in connectivity. Improved communications infrastructure, advances in the latest research, and cutting-edge network technology stand to make connections exponentially faster.[318] Average download speeds are expected to reach one gigabyte per second.[319] A large reduction in latency is a critical component to help power a large rise in the IoT. This is an essential development for an autonomous vehicle network.

Ray Sharma is the co-founder and executive manager of Extreme Venture Partners and an avid investor in early-stage emerging tech companies. In a recent conversation at the Ivey Business School at the University of Western Ontario, Sharma stated, "The single biggest benefactor to 5G are autonomous vehicles."[320] In fact, in 2018, *Forbes* released a report supporting this statement stating that a world in which autonomous vehicles are commonplace is likely dependent upon a ubiquitous 5G network.[321] This is because driving is still about human cognition, reflexes, and reaction. The speed and data processing capabilities needed to mimic these actions are high. According to Dr. Joy Laskar, co-founder and CEO of Maja Systems, self-driving cars will produce two petabytes (two million gigabytes) of data a week. For clarity, he said, "With an advanced Wi-Fi connection, it will take 230 days to transfer a weeks-worth of data from a self-driving car and that is why we need much faster ASIC [application specific integrated circuits] processing technology and products."[322]

In truth, the Bitcoin community faced a similar issue. Mining, the process of validating blockchain transactions, largely depends on ASIC processing chips as well. Computational performance and efficiency is required to run these complex systems adequately, and therefore, innovation in these chips is very much a bottleneck for the next generation of technologies.[323] Nevertheless, large companies like Intel and Qualcomm that specialize in these semiconductors may be on the verge of breakthroughs in ASICs that will significantly improve processing capabilities.[324] These advances will combine current innovative antenna architectures and digital radio with larger bandwidth and 5G frequencies.[325] The result will essentially take connected vehicles and turn them into powerful "data-centers on wheels" with the ability to make accurate real-time decisions.[326]

Furthermore, a recent report by international law firm Holland & Knight (H&G) suggests that the incorporation of blockchain into 5G will yield a host of benefits. As 5G is expected to bring about a proliferation of IoT devices like autonomous vehicles, H&G stated that blockchain would help improve both the security and the validity of the data on these devices.[327] The sheer quantity of these devices will no doubt substantially increase the amount of information available. Considering how reliant some operational processes will be on this information, such as a GPS determining a car's whereabouts in coordination with other vehicles, it is imperative that the integrity of the data collected by them remain uncompromised.

While this future may seem distant, it may arrive sooner than anticipated. The Trump administration explored deploying 5G at an accelerated pace and estimated that 5G could help create three million new jobs, $275 billion in private investment, and $500 billion in new economic growth.[328] Larry Kudlow, then National Economic Council director, affirmed that the 5G race would be won "principally through the free enterprise, free market economy," with some support from such government institutions as the US Federal Communications Commission, which just recently voted to repeal regulatory barriers to implementation.[329]

Kudlow's sentiment spurred the creation of new consortia like the Telecom Infra Project, a partnership of over 450 telecom companies spearheaded by such giants as Intel and Facebook.[330] The goal of this consortium is to accelerate the pace of 5G infrastructure development around the world. We could see 5G ubiquity within two to five years.[331] It would remove one of the largest barriers to adoption of autonomous vehicles.

In summary, while the race to bring autonomous vehicles to market is intensifying, we need more pervasive 5G network infrastructure before these cars experience their highest performance and functionality. Despite this, several significant stakeholders, from government to large enterprise, have all shown their intention to back a similar push to develop this network over the next few years. The relationship among these technologies bears watching, as the adoption of 5G will likely precede the age of autonomous vehicles.

IMMUTABLE RECORDS VERSUS PRIVACY

In the world of technology, no issue has been more prevalent this year than data privacy. In early 2018, we learned that a UK-based data analytics firm, Cambridge Analytica, had obtained information from 50 million Facebook user accounts without consent.[332] This breach was associated with a US presidential election, under many a watchful eye. This incident put privacy infringement under the microscope, as people began asking who had access to or were monitoring their data and how were they using this information?

This issue deserves extra attention in autonomous vehicles and MaaS systems because the more that users utilize networked technologies to facilitate their transportation, the more vulnerable they are in theory to having this movement tracked and recorded. In 2014, Uber's management came under heavy criticism after the public learned of a feature in use known as "God's View."[333] God's View is a tool that enabled the corporate office of Uber to track the location and movements of any individual in real time.[334] While the office stated this information was used only for legitimate business purposes such as paying drivers, monitoring fraudulent activity, and troubleshooting user bugs, some reports from *Time*, among others, corroborated stories that suggested more nefarious and irresponsible practices.[335] But the purpose of this chapter is only to illustrate the prevalence of data in MaaS-based systems and transportation, and the dangerous ramifications, if data are handled improperly.

When the European Union passed the GDPR in 2018, it established significant laws on data and privacy protection for all individuals in the European Union, including the export of personal data beyond its jurisdiction.[336] These rules are important because, while any bad actor could use a new technology nefariously, we have an opportunity to use these innovations for an incredible amount of good. Data and analytics are shaping the future of transportation. The industry is leading the charge in creating the Internet of Everything.[337] Sensors embedded in transportation networks are collecting and providing information on vehicle locator systems, fare collection, and ticketing.[338]

Leaders in the space are using big data and advanced analytical and planning tools to design and construct more efficient, coordinated, and effective transport routes. Urban planners and transportation agencies are using these data to improve operations, reduce costs, and better serve travelers. They are examining the impact of vehicle accidents and transit maintenance on efficiency as well as the impact of late public transit or transit labor strikes on the economy, and they are modeling the relationship of new urban and commercial development to transit systems.[339]

While these uses of data present opportunities, we must be careful when incorporating a new technology such as blockchain into the conversation. Any individual who has heard of blockchain knows that one of its most highly touted virtues is its property of immutability, guaranteed by a ledger of transactions, all verified by consensus among network participants. Once a transaction has reached an appropriate level of validation, cryptography ensures that it cannot be altered, changed, or reversed.[340]

When it comes to our whereabouts, we may not want to use a system of immutable data. With any blockchain-based MaaS system, we must consider the collection and usage of self-identifying data. In 2014, the European Union introduced another progressive data law known as the "Right to be Forgotten," under which individuals may have any piece of personal data wiped from the Internet.[341] The law goes:

The correspondingly named rule primarily regulates erasure obligations. According to this, personal data must be erased immediately where the data are no longer needed for their original processing purpose, or the data subject has withdrawn his consent and there is no other legal ground for processing, the data subject has objected and there are no overriding legitimate grounds for the processing, or erasure is required to fulfil a statutory obligation under the EU law or the right of the Member States. In addition, data must naturally be erased if the processing itself was against the law in the first place.[342]

Under such legislation, the properties of blockchain may seem to exclude it from underpinning a MaaS-based service. Yet, its technical properties also enable users to claim ownership of or dissociate their identity with their own data.

First, users could incorporate zero-knowledge proofs in their transactions. Zero-knowledge proofs enable a "prover" to assure a "verifier" that the prover knows a secret or statement without revealing the secret itself.[343] While initially complex, these proofs allow for completely anonymous transactions with enhanced security and privacy: users would not be identifiable in their movements and mobility, at least not in their transaction history. Furthermore, we are seeing the implementation of this technology in blockchain through a slight variation known as zk-SNARKS. While the Electric Coin Company, the Dash Core Group, and the Monero Project—companies focused on enhanced privacy—were the first to adopt this standard for cryptocurrency, Ethereum has since added in this functionality through a system upgrade known as Byzantium.[344]

Second, users could establish what Joseph Lubin, CEO of ConsenSys, called a "persistent digital ID and persona," stored and managed on a blockchain.[345] The Tapscotts called this store of private data a "virtual black box":

> Your black box may include information such as a government-issued ID, Social Security number, medical information, service accounts, financial accounts, diplomas, practice licenses, birth certificate, various other credentials, and information so personal you don't want to reveal it but do want to monetize its value, such as sexual preference or medical condition, for a poll or a research study. You could license these data for specific purposes to specific entities for specific periods of time.[346]

For example, users could share their driver's licenses to qualify as drivers in blockchain-based transport system, or their digital wallet addresses to confirm that they could pay for transportation.

Brave is a blockchain-based browser developed by former Mozilla CEO Brendan Eich. Last year, Brave raised $35 million in 30 seconds in an ICO to fund the development of a browser that protects users' data and blocks advertisers from using it.[347] Simply for reading content on the browser, users receive Brave's native coin, Basic Attention Token.[348] Of an even greater magnitude, Facebook, in the midst of its data crisis, began talks with several cryptocurrency exchanges to list a Facebook coin, potentially as a reward for capitalizing on user data through what is known as a *data dividend*.[349]

In *Blockchain Revolution,* the Tapscotts discussed the ability of blockchain to license data for specific purposes to specific entities for specific periods of time.[350] Consider mobility: users could license their transportation history to the relevant transportation agencies, so that the agencies could make better-informed decisions while the users earn licensing revenue.

DOVU, a member of MOBI, is a blockchain project trying to provide data licensing capabilities. In April 2017, DOVU received seed funding from inMotion Ventures, Jaguar Land Rover's investment arm, and Creative England, a fund backed by the UK government. DOVU recognizes the value these data have to transportation authorities. Rather than procure this information illicitly, these parties can buy it from those users willing to exchange it for DOVU's native DOV token.[351] According to Ballinger, MOBI is working on establishing a similar system referred to as *data markets*.[352]

In this way, users receive tokens for the data they create and share. In turn, they can use these tokens to pay for transportation-related services such as using a leased autonomous vehicle, a ride-sharing service like Uber, or any other related public transport. This concept is powerful. John Gerryts, Oaken's co-founder, said, "You know when you think about it, it's almost like a form of universal basic income."[353] Ray Kurzweil, Google's chief futurist and director of engineering, is known for his accurate predictions of the future. At a 2018 TED Conference, he echoed Gerryts's thoughts when he said, "In the early 2030s, we'll have universal basic income in the developed world, and worldwide by the end of the 2030s. You'll be able to live very well on that. The primary concern will be meaning and purpose."[354] So the implications go far beyond blockchains, data, and autonomous vehicles with untold consequences.

In summary, while apprehension over data and privacy will likely intensify, incorporating blockchain into MaaS applications may provide a solution. The incorporation of zk-SNARKS, anonymous transactions, identity black boxes, and avatars may help users to feel safe about using their information in mobility applications and sharing personal data in exchange for tokens.

DEVICE SECURITY

Autonomous vehicles on our roads can guarantee one thing: a proliferation in the number of networked devices based on the IoT. This will involve the increased connectivity of not only the cars on the road but also the number of mobile devices needed to interact with them and the quantity of external devices also feeding these vehicles information. By 2025, as many as 7.5 billion devices will be connected to the Internet of Things.[355]

Yet, with such an increase in the number of IoT devices also comes a heightened level of security vulnerability. In early 2018, the University of Michigan released a paper concluding that the risks associated with autonomous vehicles are both unprecedented and undocumented.[356] Hackers have an increasing opportunity to infiltrate and leverage millions of devices. According to industry experts, much of the firmware running on these devices is both highly vulnerable and insecure, putting an indeterminate number of critical systems and devices at risk.[357]

While hackers have breached a few significant IoT systems to date, from cardiac devices at St. Jude Medical Center to the notorious Mirai Botnet attack, perhaps the most telling was a July 2015 incident known as the "Jeep Hack," which exposed a firmware update vulnerability.[358] While a single Jeep was traveling the freeway, hackers took control of it using the Sprint cellular network and discovered that they could make the Jeep accelerate, decelerate, and even drive off the road.[359]

According to *Forbes*, attacks using IoT jumped 280 percent this year.[360] Researchers at the University of Michigan said such attacks could involve denial-of-service or distributed denial-of-service attacks where cars would shut down in the middle of the road. Hackers could also take control of a vehicle and ransom it or its passengers for a specific amount of bitcoin.[361] Last, unmanned vehicles could be hacked and driven to a local chop shop without the thief's gaining physical access to the car.[362]

Faced with these threats, the team at Michigan developed a tool called the Mcity Threat Identification Model to enable researchers, academics, and industry workers to identify threats and their potential severity. The matrix covers five key areas: the attack scenario, the ability of a system to withstand the attack, the capability of the attacker, the motivation of the attacker, and the impact to stakeholders.[363] Researchers use the inputs to develop an encompassing vector stat and determine the total threat and impact level.

The need for common security standards and protocols is also growing. The US Department of Commerce has launched several initiatives, both educational and technical, to ensure that consumers know the security level of the products they are buying and that device makers adopt preventive security measures in device design and manufacturing.[364]

The use of a blockchain-based system integrated with IoT may provide additional security benefits. Some of the downfalls of IoT security include questions on the identity and authentication of devices and its centralized security model and infrastructure.[365] IoT operates using a distributed client/server model: for these networks to run, an administrator or central authority must manage the network (as with E-ZPass), thus creating a single point of attack and failure for the entire system.[366]

With blockchain, data are stored on ledgers distributed across many nodes, and so hackers must attack one specific node at a time. Once the other nodes in the network recognize a node's nefarious behavior, they can isolate it to prevent further harm. When IoT nodes are registered on-chain, they receive a unique transaction identifier and corresponding hash. All changes to the ledger require this signed authority; all nodes can trace a change back to the node that made it. Nodes will not verify unauthorized changes in consensus.[367]

While blockchain's properties may offer security enhancement, they are not immune from attacks. Blockchain's most commonly cited vulnerability is known as the "51 percent attack," where hackers take control of at least 51 percent of the nodes in the network, which amount to the majority of the network's hashing power. Yet, blockchains are just as susceptible to bugs and errors in code as other middleware. In fact, these bugs have led to significant losses: the notorious Mt. Gox, the DAO, Bitfinex, and NiceHash hacks cost users around $700 million in aggregate.[368] An additional $150 million became frozen after Parity's security breach in late 2017.[369]

If we expect blockchain and IoT to underpin a vast connected system of autonomous vehicles connected to thousands or millions of digital wallets, then we must take prudent measures to mitigate the substantial risk. Educating users and manufacturers of acceptable security standards and data handling practices is an important step. So is the enforcement of these standards and practices on hardware manufacturers. Worthwhile bounties can attract better testers to canvass the code for errors.

In summary, the coming proliferation of IoT devices and connected vehicles inherently opens up more opportunities for hackers and for security solutions that withstand attacks. High-profile hacks such as those directed at St. Jude's and the Jeep demonstrate that blockchain and IoT have significant ground to make up for enhancing security. In truth, as this technology becomes more ubiquitous, this problem may get worse before it gets better. Further technology development, sound risk-assessment tools, the education and enforcement of security standards, and software bounty programs may mitigate potential risk.

LEGAL AND ETHICAL IMPLICATIONS

The law and technology experience an interesting relationship. Common law is a legal standard practiced in Canada, the United States, the United Kingdom, Australia, and other countries. It is based on the principle of *stare decisis*, also known as legal precedent. Court decisions influence the outcomes of future cases. In this way, the law evolves by looking to the past to inform the future. This evolution is also painstakingly slow, and decisions can take weeks, with legislative processes spanning months or years. To be fair, such a considered process minimizes knee-jerk rules and reactive regulations.

In contrast is technological innovation. Innovation is interested in only speed and one direction: fast and forward. Kurzweil called this the "law of accelerating returns," a theory explaining the exponential growth of diverse forms of technological progress.[370] The law is frequently slow to develop frameworks that can adequately compensate for the speed of technological development.

On 19 March 2018, the autonomous vehicle industry suffered a devastating setback. In Tempe, Arizona, one of Uber's self-driving cars struck and killed a pedestrian while completing one of its countless miles in test drives.[371] Ryan Calo, a researcher of the legal implications of vehicle autonomy at the University of Washington, stated that while an investigation was launched, the accident is unlikely to set a legal precedent, because even if the person struck was partly responsible, Uber may also be liable and will move quickly to settle and avoid a test case.[372] Nevertheless, it calls into question who is responsible for incidents of this nature.

Uber's move to settle quickly may represent a changing of perspective on liability and autonomous vehicles. According to *VentureBeat*, companies like Google, Volvo, and Mercedes-Benz have already jumped to the forefront of companies willing to accept responsibility should one of their self-driving systems be found at fault for an accident.[373] This limits exposure to Ralph Nader–like consequences that may be harder to control. Tesla is even extending insurance to its customers.[374] Car insurance may even change in response to autonomous vehicle technology. Over time, we may see a reduction in the number of total accidents. In addition, as large resourceful auto manufacturers and tech companies with capital begin to accept this liability, we will likely see auto insurance premiums drop considerably.[375]

Even if accepting liability sorts out that issue, the ethics of accidents are still rather muddy. Consider the "trolley problem," where cars must choose between two potential victims in an accident and may not have the necessary cognition to assess such a situation.[376] The Uber accident follows another fatal crash in May 2016: a Tesla on autopilot mode failed to see an oncoming truck. In both situations, the vehicle sensors did not register the obstruction, or the algorithm did not understand what the sensors were communicating.[377]

Even if legislation regulating liability and autonomous vehicles is passed, and insurance complications are sorted out, these are not preventive measures; rather, they deal with consequences. Therefore, we must place the onus on developing the technology to avoid these situations altogether. Current methods of vehicle coordination involve a combination of onboard sensors, computer vision, and machine learning with third-party data sets.

The privately held company INRIX has developed an AV Road Rules platform for safe autonomous vehicle deployment that allows city officials and transportation authorities to integrate road and traffic laws into the cognition of autonomous vehicles operating on public roads.[378] These stakeholders can digitize their specific driving restrictions—stop signs, bus lanes, school zones, crosswalks, and speed limits—to ensure compliance with each locality.[379] INRIX has also introduced a communication channel from the vehicles to these same road authorities so the data can better inform asset maintenance and management.[380] By focusing on prevention, INRIX can help public stakeholders to handle challenging real-world road environments.

In summary, although vehicle manufacturers have accepted liability for accidents caused by software, the true legal implications of a future with autonomous vehicles remain unknown. The law will take the necessary time to come up with a proper legal framework. However, considering how quickly this industry is emerging, regulators must keep pace with innovation. Regardless, the technology must operate with high enough performance to mitigate the risk of accidents.

LOOKING TO THE FUTURE

While blockchains and autonomous vehicles may already push the boundaries of the imagination for many, the rapid acceleration of technological development continues on its path. Every day new advancements stand to enhance the capabilities of our existing technology and even pave the way for new ones once thought impossible.

A TRUE SHARING ECONOMY

When MaaS solutions such as Uber first hit the market, many pundits raced to declare the coming of a new age known as the sharing economy. Companies used technology to unlock the value of underutilized assets and make profit from their rent. Similarly, Airbnb allowed property owners to make additional revenue streams on unoccupied real estate.

Ballinger said this is one goal of incorporating blockchains into these systems. By enabling seamless value transfer, blockchains can significantly increase the number of profit functions inherent to the car. In addition to asset leasing, vehicle owners can now profit from tokenized energy and data. A blockchain platform applied in an autonomous driving world enables us to go beyond rider mobility.

Consider energy sharing. Solar energy production is highest during the day when the sun is shining the most. By comparison, energy demand typically spikes in the morning and then again in the evening—when solar energy production is weakest. During low mobility demand time, automated vehicles can store solar energy from peak production times and deliver that energy when and where it is needed.

Let's say we parked in a parking lot beside our friend's vehicle. We also needed to refuel. Through a Dapp, we determined that our friend's vehicle had excess fuel available for sale, and so we transferred this energy wirelessly between our cars. In exchange, we sent a tokenized electronic credit to our friend, who can use it to access fuel from another vehicle in the network. The effects of this capability become more pronounced in managing a fleet of vehicles, perhaps as a taxi service. Here, a taxi coordinator could manage energy efficiency among a portfolio of vehicles to optimize energy levels. While transformative, such a system will likely demand improvements in electric battery storage and performance. It is a concept that MOBI has begun to develop.

This sharing economy can extend beyond energy and into data capabilities. As ubiquitous autonomous vehicle networks would demand 5G connectivity, the opportunity is there to provide a self-healing mesh network across large areas and partitioned consumer Wi-Fi service. Similar to energy sharing, vehicles would receive microtransaction reimbursements for sharing their Internet connection; autonomous vehicle features reliant upon this level of connectivity could maintain peak performance.

In summary, while MaaS has undoubtedly allowed vehicle owners to earn additional revenue from their assets by participating in ridesharing, blockchain enhances this capability. Through a tokenized credit system, participants can share key resources such as energy fuel, mobile data, and Internet connectivity and reciprocate with remittances instantaneously and seamlessly, ushering in a new era of the sharing economy.

FLYING CARS

Perhaps no technology defines the future of mobility like the flying car. In October 2018, presales for the world's first flying car began. The vehicle was designed by Terrafugia, a manufacturer owned by German auto giant Volkswagen.[381] The model known as the TF-X can take off from regular roads without requiring an airport because of its equipped foldout wings. The car can also transition from car to mobile plane in under one minute with a top speed of 200 mph in the air and a 500-mile flight range.[382]

Multiple stakeholders are racing to develop viable solutions to personal flight. Most of it is centered on eVTOL vehicles. At the Consumer Electronics Show in Las Vegas in January 2019, several working prototypes were displayed, reminiscent of the early AV prototypes. Vibrant start-ups such as NFT (for New Future Transportation here) are making waves.[383] A Japanese crowdfunded solution known as Cartivator is slated to light the Olympic torch at the 2020 games in Tokyo.[384] Joby, Volocopter, and EHang have all received significant levels of funding. Meanwhile, larger players such as Airbus and Uber's "Elevate" have announced themselves, with Uber's cars expected to hit the market in cities like Los Angeles by 2020.[385] Last, Google has entered the fray, backing three separate start-ups (Cora, Flyer, and Opener) in the race to produce an eVTOL.

Many of these plans go beyond vehicle innovation; they are becoming large-scale infrastructure projects. While a coordinated autonomous vehicle network could address issues of traffic congestion, the effect of removing these cars altogether from roads would have a demonstrably greater impact. Here's perhaps the toughest question of all: should we use the instant remittances and cost allocation afforded by smart contracts on a blockchain protocol to repair and fund old highway infrastructure, or should we apply this funding to constructing an entirely new transportation network? In an October 2016 white paper, Uber revealed its plans for a rooftop-to-rooftop transportation system with launchpads (skyports) atop buildings.[386]

While the impact of such a development is likely hard to measure, some are more skeptical than others. Gartner listed several implementation challenges: high costs, safety concerns, and regulatory burdens.[387] Uber expanded on these concerns, with such barriers as market feasibility, certification process, and eVTOLs compliance with the US Federal Aviation Administration and the European Aviation Safety Agency, which regulate 80 percent of the world's aviation safety.[388] Pilot training is also crucial, and the quantity of qualified pilots could curtail adoption—although automation could mitigate the need for pilots. In a similar vein to EVs, battery technology must also improve, to power long-distance flight.[389]

With a much higher volume of vehicles in the air, air traffic control becomes paramount. On-demand flights have twice the fatality rate of privately operated cars; nevertheless, Uber maintains that a properly coordinated system that is autonomously facilitated could make these vehicles safer than driving on land. São Paulo, Brazil, already manages a large volume of helicopter travel.[390] Cost and affordability are another sticking point. If costs are not managed, these eVTOLs could become vehicles of the wealthy. However, Uber has stated it will not come to market if these services are not affordable—as predominantly urban vehicles, emissions, and noise must be kept under control.[391] Perhaps the most significant stumbling block is urban infrastructure: cities would need a variety of locations equipped with launchpads, veriports, and veristops, requiring a sizable scale and investment.

However, the adoption of autonomous road vehicles will likely clear the takeoff of autonomous eVTOLs because they both involve the development of mobility-as-a-service applications, they both strive to reduce traffic congestion and combustion vehicle emissions, and they both require significant level of capital and resources.

CONCLUSIONS

Although we began by looking at how blockchain could fund the repair and development of national transportation networks, we believe that blockchain will have a far greater impact on the transportation industry.

Affordable mobility-as-a-service is a growth market. The sheer level of intellectual and financial capital, technological development, prominent stakeholders, and other resources going into these efforts means this future is now much closer to reality. The swift rise of MaaS providers such as Uber and Lyft in this decade alone demonstrated how quickly new mass markets can emerge.

Autonomous vehicles offer new sources of revenue. Faced with these obstacles, next-generation technologies like blockchain and distributed ledger provide examples of innovative solutions to these complex problems. While blockchain is shown to have a demonstrable impact on tolling systems by reducing the need for heavy infrastructure, centralized servers and databases, identity, and credit card systems, it can also help to increase the profit functions of vehicles. We can capture and use these revenue streams to finance public state and federal roadway networks through instantaneous remittances.

Large-scale innovation requires mass collaboration. To understand how multiple stakeholders may benefit and prepare for such technological change, large consortia such as MOBI provide examples of how we should approach innovation. Gone are the days of siloed and secretive R&D undertaken by single entities. Rising tides lift all ships, and collaborative development among technology developers, automotive manufacturers, transportation authorities, and government demonstrate the outcome of this coordination.

Blockchain disrupts insurance and used car sales. Blockchain's integration with vehicles provides an answer to more than infrastructure funding. Apprehension over the liability of an accident and its legal recourse is proving innovative to insurance. Eliminating information asymmetry in used car markets, improving insurance claims headaches with verified time-stamped data and automated processing, and creating the underpinnings of a trusted P2P autonomous vehicle leasing system are just some examples of this innovation.

Innovation in transportation is fueling broader innovation. The challenges that these technologies face are pushing innovations in other industries. The need to be proactive rather than reactive to accidents is pushing sensor technology and machine learning to new heights. The need for high-frequency data input is necessitating the creation of national 5G networks. Demand for blockchain networks with high user volumes solves scalability such as state channels and side channels, sharding, and interoperable chains.

Ownership of personal data could drive social change. Concerns over data privacy have ignited such a fundamental change in the concept of information ownership that its solutions in data renting and dividends may one day provide an answer to one of humanity's greatest challenges by ushering in an age of universal basic income for anybody with a mobile phone. Rising fears over the security of these data on a growing number of interconnected devices is leading to the enforcement of higher security standards, consumer education, and even further integration of blockchain and connected IoT devices.

Income opportunities increase beyond car sharing. Vehicle operators may receive compensation for sharing basic resources like renewable energy and Internet connectivity. Perhaps the most forward-looking realization in this blockchain-based sharing economy may take place not only between grounded vehicles; it could also extend to eVTOLs and personal aircraft that facilitate transportation across the skies.

Transportation authorities must prepare for change.
Governments at all levels must prepare for disruption. Despite this progress, we must prepare for the consequences of technological innovation. If the beginning of a ubiquitous autonomous vehicle network becomes a reality sooner than we think, then government and relevant transportation and public authorities must be informed so that they can overcome the challenges faced in future infrastructure development.

On its face, this level of development seems stunning. Microsoft founder, Bill Gates, explained this phenomenon: "We always overestimate the amount of progress that will occur in the next ten years and underestimate the change that will occur in the next ten. Don't let yourself be lulled into inaction."[392]

CHAPTER 6

SLOCK.IT

Enabling IoT and the Universal Sharing Network

Alan Majer

 UNIVERSAL SHARING NETWORK IN BRIEF

- The history of Slock.it reads like a fast-paced science fiction novel: a brainy group of technologists breathes life into an autonomous system, frenzied cryptocurrency speculators try to cash in on this invention, and then an anonymous hacker puts in place a devious trap that seized over $50 million in one of the largest attempted heists in corporate history.

- These dramatic events have at times thrust Slock.it into an unwanted storm of controversy and media attention, but they have also positively influenced Slock.it's founders and their business approach. The company has emerged with a practical focus on building its business the old-fashioned way: becoming cash flow positive, acquiring customers and partners, and turning prototypes into products and profits.

- Slock.it's goal is straightforward: to create a blockchain-enabled platform for the sharing economy, a universal sharing network (USN). This USN will enable true P2P sharing and exchange via the blockchain and will integrate with real-world assets and devices.

- Users of the USN can share objects—bikes, washing machines, or apartments—directly with one another with the aid of *smart contracts*, a unique combination of cryptocurrency, Dapps, and IoT that brings cryptocurrency transactions into the real world.[393]

- While a bold vision of peer-based IoT sharing is at the heart of the company, it differentiates between the speculative hype surrounding blockchain and the practical challenges of building and implementing a blockchain business.

THE PROBLEM TO BE SOLVED

Around the world, companies such as Airbnb, Uber, GetAround, and Fon have created platforms for putting unused assets to work. Owners of cars, apartments, and even Wi-Fi hotspots can grant others access to these assets through such platforms. Some call it the "sharing economy," but it is really another form of matchmaking where a middleman aggregates all the offers to share something, takes fees for making matches, and captures everyone's data in the process, potentially monetizing its proprietary view of a particular market.

Large participants in the sharing economy aren't automatically generous. The challenge of these so-called sharing businesses is that they tend to operate in domains that have strong *network effects*—that is, as the network grows, it becomes more valuable. In business terms, it creates a winner-take-all environment where the dominant firms wield increasing influence. The same network effects that cause these firms to struggle in the beginning as they fight for critical mass (often enticing users with special benefits or cut-rate commissions), later cause them to do the opposite (sometimes raising rates and extracting higher commissions) once they've attained market dominance. Uber, for example, has pressured drivers by continuing to reduce the price per mile paid to them, while raising its own commission rates at the same time.[394]

Physical technologies such as IoT can help automation systems to improve efficiency and potentially alter that go-between role. Those overseeing a matchmaking system should consider all the elements of cost and friction in the system. That means streamlined payments, verifying identities, or providing physical access to an asset: any activity or process that contributes to making the system easier to use is a candidate for automation. So, embedding the sharing process itself into physical assets like cars, houses, and more is a potentially potent source of innovation and efficiency.

Using blockchain technologies, Slock.it can address both issues: supporting more P2P exchanges that depend less on a middleman and creating IoT technologies that automate a system via autonomous objects (like locks) connected to the blockchain.

SLOCK.IT'S SOLUTION

One of the unusual properties of a currency like bitcoin is that it enables software, not just people, to own money. Following bitcoin's invention, discussion began to circulate about this strange new possibility. In 2011, Gregory Maxwell speculated how a Dropbox-like system might be able to buy storage from the cloud and resell it at a profit.[395] It was a curious concept, "and it fascinated me," said Stephan Tual, who would later co-found Slock.it.[396] Mike Hearn, another prominent blockchain technologist, discussed a variation of this idea, that machines in the real world might use blockchain currency to support their autonomous livelihood. Imagine a self-driving car that could earn money with fares.[397] While interesting, these ideas seemed largely theoretical.

Moreover, the Bitcoin blockchain was promising for payments but difficult for building smart contracts: simply put, the money on Bitcoin was not "programmable," limiting its usefulness for an autonomous system. In 2013, the situation started to change when Stephan received an email from Vitalik Buterin, who had done his own thinking about the potential of autonomous systems. Vitalik wondered:

> What if, with the power of modern information technology we ... create an inviolable contract that generates revenue, pays people to perform some function, and finds hardware for itself to run on, all without any need for top-down human direction?[398]

By the end of 2013, Vitalik had laid out a vision for Ethereum, a new blockchain that could support smart contracts.[399] That convinced Stephan to do everything he could to join Ethereum, where he was exposed to research that indicated an interest and potential in the mixture of IoT and blockchain technologies.[400] Convinced that this was the future, Stephan left Ethereum in 2015 to pursue his entrepreneurial ideas.

Then Christoph Jentzsch reached out to him: "'Hey, come over to Berlin. I've got something to show you that you're going to love,'" Stephan recalled.[401] Christoph had built a working prototype of a physical lock linked to the blockchain—send it money and it opens. "Holy crap, that's it, you've built it!" Stephan told Christoph, and Slock.it was born, with Stephan as its chief operating officer.[402]

Christoph, Slock.it's CEO, described the company's vision as "connecting all kind of smart locks to the blockchain, enabling them to receive payments directly and be used to rent, sell, or share just about anything. We call this the 'universal sharing network.'"[403]

In these earliest days, the company took what would turn out to be a dramatic detour. Like many crypto- or blockchain-related businesses, Slock.it's founders weighed the idea of an ICO, to the point that they began coding some enabling smart contracts. The initial idea was to issue tokens with built-in voting rights so that token holders could guide how Slock.it spent money.[404]

The founders wondered whether they could take these ideas further. Christoph explained: "After further consideration, we gave token holders even more power, by giving them full control over the funds, which would be released only after a successful vote on detailed proposals backed by smart contracts."[405]

DAO: THE HOPE, THE HACK, AND THE HARD FORK

Could they go still further and create a radically decentralized and fully autonomous organization? Christoph believed so and detailed how they could achieve it in a provocative white paper, "Decentralized Autonomous Organization to Automate Governance."[406] The company took a daring decision that would hurl the blockchain itself into uncharted territory, and it began coding the framework for an autonomous organization that could solicit proposals and distribute funds to any entity, Slock.it or otherwise. Formally, this DAO would be out of Slock.it's hands, too. Stephan said, "We did not run the DAO, we did not launch the DAO," and that autonomy was what people loved about the DAO.[407] "A 'Slock.it dao' would actually be the antithesis of what a true DAO stands for—autonomy—and would have actually counterintuitively hindered its success rather than help[ed]," suggested Stephan—it was a distinction that would be pivotal.[408]

Operations went exceedingly well—at first. In May 2016, the DAO raised a record-breaking 12 million ether, worth more than $150 million at the time (and $22.4 billion today).[409] It was the largest crowdfunding event in history.[410] This unexpected growth was a mixed blessing for the innovative new entity. Christoph admitted, "The time for a project of its magnitude turned out to be too early."[411] On 6 June, *WIRED* labeled the DAO "very much a work in progress," and a "risk on an enormous scale."[412]

Then, on 17 June, the unthinkable happened: an attacker started draining millions from the DAO, eventually holding more than

$50 million in ether hostage.[413] The attack exploited a bug in the DAO's code—a recursive transaction call that allowed the attacker to dump a balance multiple times into an account before subtracting it—combined with a DAO feature involving splits.[414] It appears to have required advanced planning to lay the groundwork for the attack; the required split feature of the attack was realized when the attacker submitted proposal 59, titled "lonely, so lonely," on 8 June—a full nine days before launching the main attack.[415]

The aftermath was more complicated than the attempted heist itself. First, a group of "Robin Hoods" used the same attack vector to attempt to drain and store the remaining DAO funds, a gallant effort that created legal complications for them.[416] The magnitude of the attack itself was so great that the community decided to alter the previously inviolable blockchain with a something called a *hard fork*. The fork would keep the rest of the blockchain history intact but rewrite a single "tiny" historical fact: it would take back the attacker's funds and put them into a refund account, effectively making it look as if the attack never happened.[417] With the reversal of these funds, the bold experiment in autonomy ended.[418]

CULTURE REBOOT: GROUNDED IN PRACTICAL APPLICATIONS

The culture and attitudes at Slock.it today owe a lot to its experience with the DAO. While Slock.it shares the typical start-up's excitement about new blockchain possibilities, an atypical air of temperance, even conservativism, pervades the company's current business approach. "One thing that differentiates Slock.it from all other companies is that we have a ten-year plan," and that allows Slock.it to take a step back, said Stephan Tual. "We differentiate between the speculative aspect of this stuff where Ethereum is three times the entire market cap of Twitter, for example, but has zero users—which is also ridiculous—and the actual genuine benefits of this technology when it comes to integration with the IoT."[419]

While Stephan enjoys the open-ended possibilities of P2P sharing and autonomous contracts, he's quick to point out that the future of truly autonomous machines is more of a lifelong pursuit than a short-term aspiration. It will take 20 years to build this economy, said Stephan. "People say, 'Oh, it's like the Internet in 1993.' Well, I don't think so. I think it's more like the Internet in 1968 when Douglas Englebart was presenting the mouse, collaborative editing, hypertext—all that stuff was right in his head."[420] The culture and focus of Slock.it today is grounded in building practical IoT and blockchain applications with clients. The company focuses on three areas:

- Building blockchain applications in conjunction with its customers
- Developing a universal sharing network
- Enabling blockchain IoT via an "Ethereum computer"[421]

Siemens AG is working with Slock.it to implement a blockchain-based DAO that allows for voting on projects with a social purpose. An initiative with a Fortune 500 electronics firm is also in the works.[422] The Share&Charge service by MotionWerk is one of Slock.it's first customer deployments on the Ethereum blockchain.[423] The MotionWerk service is an ideal crossover between P2P blockchain transactions and IoT.

It's a perfect business case for P2P sharing. In Germany, there are just over 6,000 public charging stations for EVs, yet EV drivers themselves collectively own over 45,000 home charging stations; sharing just a small number of these chargers would more than double the publicly available infrastructure.[424]

That's where Slock.it comes in. In addition to MotionWerk's own stations and those provided by smaller utilities, private owners of charging stations could share or rent theirs to others. Each MotionWerk station communicates with a Share&Charge app to handle the blockchain-driven control of the charging station and accounting.[425] Slock.it would like to integrate blockchain directly into charging stations at the hardware level, as it did in one case using a Raspberry Pi.[426] The blockchain system consists of Ethereum smart contracts. Simon Jentzsch, Slock.it co-founder and chief technology officer, detailed the system's operation in "Share&Charge Contracts: The Technical Angle."[427] Three aspects of the system stand out:[428]

- All contracts are 100 percent updatable, giving full control for future adjustments or emergency situations.

- There is a clear separation in the system between data and logic, a common design principle consistent with "separation of concerns."

- There is a fully backed digital euro at the heart of the system to facilitate transaction settlement.

Because the system itself is deployed on a public blockchain, it is radically transparent, and allows third parties to engage directly with system operations via contracts, tokens, and accounts, should they choose to do so.

As of 5 October 2017, there were three core tokens viewable through Simon's JSON ABIs (JavaScript object notation application binary interfaces), *etherscan.io*, or similar tools.[429] Note the assignment of an identity to the charging pole:

```
Mobility Token: 0x8262a2a5c61A45Aa074cbeeDE42c808D15ea3ceD
Charging Pole: 0xb642a68bD622D015809bb9755d07EA3006b85843
Library Manager: 0xf4d9d65481352C3Afd0750B46FbE0462eb29206d
```

These open pieces of blockchain infrastructure are radical departures from traditional electronic commerce and business practices. They are far beyond an API, the vanilla way to achieve open interoperation. A traditional API is, in effect, an external *transaction interface* that allows us to get inside a proprietary system. Here, start-ups such as Slock.it are *taking the insides out* and allowing users to operate directly with these systems.

RADICAL TRANSPARENCY: THE UNIVERSAL SHARING NETWORK

This spirit of transparency is central to Slock.it's vision of its universal sharing network. The typical sharing economy systems tend to have central gatekeepers. Very rarely are they true P2P sharing systems. That intermediary—an Airbnb, Uber, or other large middleman—will usually control and manage the system in exchange for a slice of the action. Yet as these systems grow, network effects start to work in their favor. As their power grows, often their slice of the action does, too.

Consider Uber: in addition to raising its own fee structure while pressuring drivers to accept lower payment, it has obfuscated the model for how drivers get paid.[430] Vitalik Buterin, founder of Ethereum, said that corporations take this type of bait-and-switch approach to openness itself. A start-up might have an open philosophy to encourage system adoption in the beginning, but later locks things down to protect its ability to monetize, said Vitalik. "Building a decentralized service is the strongest way for an application developer to pre-commit not to be a jerk and not to shut down forever."[431]

However, for the USN model to succeed, it must overcome the basic liquidity concerns of every other matching or capacity-sharing system: *it must achieve critical mass*. That's where Slock.it's business model comes into play. Rather than bootstrapping each blockchain-based sharing application, Slock.it works with clients to bring their existing customers, products, or sharing networks onto the blockchain, onboarding the liquidity and flow of transactions with them. For Slock.it's clients, the value proposition is an inexpensive ready-made infrastructure suited to their sharing application.

So, while an Airbnb or an Uber could use Slock.it's platform to build its system, it would have to agree to transparency as a key condition of usage: any asset brought onto the network must be visible on the USN. It's open and designed for easy onboarding, too, and so entities don't necessarily need Slock.it's permission to use it.[432]

Launching the USN along with compact hardware to handle IoT and smart contract interactions, Slock.it has made it easy to control washing machines and door locks or even to rent a microwave for popping popcorn on the fly. Christoph demonstrated the latter two examples to a live audience at Devcon3.[433]

Slock.it's USN is a *platform* and *delivery network* that allows true P2P sharing in a radically open fashion.[434] By creating sharing systems that operate over Ethereum's public blockchain, business applications operate via a series of public smart contracts. Unlike an API, which creates access to functions held internally, the USN pulls the functionality onto the network, in the process turning it into a piece of public infrastructure. Others can use this infrastructure freely, or extend it in some cases, as if it were their own.

The result is an exceptionally robust public infrastructure capable of mission-critical security. Other features and benefits of the platform include scalable deployment, modular architecture (which accommodates extensions of the system), straightforward clearance and settlement, simple data synchronization, and clear governance that specifies the contractual terms in code.

POSTSCRIPT TO THE CASE

In 2018, Slock.it launched its Incubed client, "a minimal verification client suited for mobile applications as well as IoT devices," Christoph wrote. "By selling enterprise licenses and providing consulting services, we became profitable and grew to more than 30 people." In 2019, Blockchains LLC acquired Slock.it for its ecosystem of innovation.[435] Founded by consumer protection attorney Jeffrey Berns, Blockchains focuses on breakthroughs in digital identity, digital assets, stability in digital payment systems, and connected devices. It owns over 67,000 acres in northern Nevada that it plans to use as a real-world sandbox to experiment at the intersection of blockchain, IoT, autonomous machines, and other emerging technologies—all with the consumer's needs and rights in mind.[436]

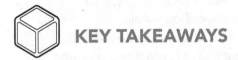

KEY TAKEAWAYS

While many organizations are exploring the business applications of blockchain, none can claim to have done so on the public blockchain to the extent that Slock.it has. The process has led to some spectacular successes and failures and has yielded immensely valuable insights for building public blockchain infrastructure and business applications.

Focus on genuine business value, not ICO hype. The ease with which many start-ups have raised funds through token sales has led to heady speculation. Some of the worst offenders are offering shares of businesses hastily cobbled together for investment. "It's ridiculous," said Stephan Tual.[437] Don't get caught up in ICO hype or the dramatic swings in cryptocurrency values. Blockchain firms are just like any other business: they must create genuine value via innovations and customer acquisition.

Prepare for extreme transparency. Operating an application on the public blockchain isn't for the faint of heart. Not only are your business events out on the blockchain for all to see but also your businesses and their processes potentially become bits of public infrastructure that anyone can use or reassemble as they see fit.[438] Businesses themselves can almost act as pieces of open-source software. It's incredibly powerful, but also daunting for many corporate executives and government officials.

Build in safety nets to handle unanticipated consequences. Whether you subscribe to the "code as law" philosophy doesn't matter. Once a smart contract is deployed, it is irrevocable.[439] If you want to change your mind, then you need to build that option into the contract. For complex or dynamic systems, any design must allow for future iteration. Share&Charge contracts are 100 percent updatable, for example.[440]

Look for business model innovation. Automating your business on the public blockchain is about turning real-world activities into digital code and smart contracts. Before doing that, inspect your current business practices, question management assumptions about the business model, and identify opportunities to do things differently. Blockchain is about business model innovation, not just business model automation.

Pursue applications that harness key blockchain features. Even Vitalik Buterin concedes that many apps are perfectly suited to traditional centralized systems.[441] The apps best suited to blockchain are those that embrace, and can benefit from, "trustless" technology features—accurate data storage that's widely distributed, globally accessible, and guaranteed forever with guaranteed execution of programs over long periods of time.[442]

Insure against the unthinkable. The Ethereum blockchain hosts digital assets with a market capitalization in excess of $305 billion and consummates tens of millions of transactions, but this industrial strength and scale do not come easily. For mission-critical systems, put in place bug bounties, time delays, and other measures.

Start cultivating talent. Creating a smart contract is hard. Solidity, a language for coding smart contracts, seems easy to use but is actually quite complex. Users must understand the nitty-gritty *anti-patterns*, that is, software design patterns that might be commonly used but can cause code to execute in unintended ways.[443] Competent blockchain developers are also exceedingly difficult to find; Stephan estimated there are as few as 500 in the world.[444] Organizations—both commercial and educational—should look to develop curricula and training programs to meet the need for this expertise.

Advocate for stewardship of the blockchain. True autonomy is incredibly difficult. The DAO was challenging not only technically but also because it involved the orchestration and governance of an autonomous system. Even a concept as simple as a Gregory Maxwell's hypothetical "autonomous Dropbox" turns out to be incredibly hard in practice because of difficulties such as humans gaming the system or dealing with falsified measures.[445] Complex systems are a delicate dynamic balancing act.

Significant short-term opportunities will come from traditional applications ported to the distributed versions on the blockchain, but others will be entirely new and disruptive applications: applications that only blockchain technologies themselves can *bring to life*.

CHAPTER 7

QUANTUM-PROOFING THE BLOCKCHAIN

Security in the Age of Quantum Supremacy

Vlad Gheorghiu, Sergey Gorbunov, Michele Mosca, and Bill Munson

QUANTUM THREAT AND DEFENSE IN BRIEF

- The arrival of powerful quantum computers will shatter currently deployed public key cryptography and weaken symmetric-key cryptography, thereby undermining the cybersecurity that protects our systems and infrastructure. The digital signature scheme used in blockchain technology to authenticate transactions is completely vulnerable.

- The problem of quantum-proofing the blockchain can be divided into two scenarios. The first scenario refers to quantum-proofing new blockchains, that is, designing quantum-resistant blockchains from scratch, whereas the second refers to quantum-proofing existing blockchains (such as the Bitcoin network).

- Perhaps the cost-effective way of making the blockchain resistant against quantum attacks is to replace the currently deployed digital signature schemes (based on RSA or EC-DSA) with post-quantum ones, which derive their security from the difficulty of certain mathematical problems; hence, they offer what is often called *computational security*.

- Quantum computation is highly susceptible to environmental noise, and so it needs quantum error correcting codes to function properly. Hence, such a realistic quantum implementation would not pose a threat unless we make significant progress in the fault tolerance quantum error correction or new quantum computing architectures come into play.

- Post-quantum digital signature schemes offer security against a quantum adversary, at the expense of much larger public/private key sizes or signature sizes, which may pose serious scalability challenges. Reducing both the signature sizes and the public/private key sizes is paramount to designing a robust and efficient quantum-resistant blockchain.

INTRODUCTION TO THE QUANTUM THREAT

We appear to be at the cusp of what some have called the *blockchain revolution*.[446] The blockchain is a permissionless decentralized distributed ledger of transactions (not necessarily financial) across a P2P computer network, in which the network collectively establishes trust without a central authority. This capability has profound implications, as society has always strived for distributed trust.

Soon enough, we will be at the cusp of what we might call the *quantum revolution*. Scientists and engineers around the world are working to build the first viable computer that uses quantum bits (or qubits) rather than conventional bits to solve exceedingly difficult mathematical problems astronomically faster than today's computers can. The arrival of phenomenally powerful quantum computing will shatter currently deployed public key cryptography and weaken symmetric-key cryptography, thereby undermining the cybersecurity that protects our infrastructure and systems.

Unfortunately, we cannot assume that blockchains, with their strong reliance on public key cryptography, are immune from this existential threat. The security of the blockchain is based on modern cryptographic protocols.[447] For instance, the authenticity of a transaction is based on public key cryptographic digital signatures, and the validation and further immutability of the data is based on symmetric-key cryptography (hash functions). The currently deployed public key infrastructure is vulnerable to quantum attacks, being based on the hardness of computational problems such as factoring or computing a discrete logarithm, which can all be broken by a quantum computer.

Therefore, the blockchain community must act to ensure that the technology can withstand quantum-powered cyberattacks. This means assessing the potential impact of quantum computing on the encryption that protects the elements of a blockchain system, and then designing and implementing the measures needed to mitigate the quantum threat by deploying cryptography designed to resist quantum attacks.

A STORY FROM THE YEAR 2030

It's the year 2030. A vast global company runs its entire operation on the blockchain. Its customers (and all its robots) participate in part of the blockchain network: they negotiate by smart contract for products and services and pay in cryptocurrency on the blockchain.[448] The level of trust in the company is significantly higher than it was back in 2017, because the integrity of each transaction is now intrinsic and guaranteed on the blockchain.

In another corner of the world, a group has assembled and is about to deploy the first fault-tolerant universal quantum computer.[449] For the first time outside the lab, a computer will be able to factor 2048-bit RSA numbers.[450] The first prototype is expected to hit the markets in less than six months. Unfortunately, our massive global company has never considered quantum computing as a serious risk; its CEO dismissed warnings as scientific mumbo-jumbo with no real implications for business operations any time soon—if ever.

Now imagine that some of the nodes (i.e., participants, be they human or thing) in the company's blockchain are on the list of customers waiting for access to quantum computers, and ready to be using them in less than a year. Some of these nodes will not let moral—or even legal—code prevent them from making a great deal of money very quickly. Maybe these ne'er-do-wells will use the quantum computer to alter, whenever possible, the transactions sent for validation and misdirect funds by replacing the intended destination address with their own.

Mounting such an attack is impossible without a quantum computer, as digital signatures—unforgeable using classical (non-quantum) computers—protect the authenticity of the data. However, the universal fault-tolerant quantum machine will enable our ne'er-do-well nodes to forge the digital signature in a matter of minutes, in less than the 10 minutes needed on average for the network to validate a block. The attacking nodes then broadcast the altered transaction, which looks perfectly valid to other nodes; they will not know that some of the money went straight into the attackers' digital wallets instead of returning to the original sender's.

Blockchain is meant to be public and immutable and should maintain its integrity and security features for many decades. However, with a quantum computer, one can potentially rewrite history: forge a transaction that happened 10 years ago, and efficiently compute a new longest-path chain to overwrite entire history for last 10 years. We will analyze the severity of such an attack later.

Returning to our story, as time passes, more and more attacks of the sort just described take place. Public trust in the company is at an all-time low. Clients are already re-investing their assets in more secure companies that employ quantum-resistant blockchains as their underlying business model.[451] Within a year, the company goes bankrupt.

Does this scenario seem far-fetched? Sixty years ago, most people believed that the automated computing machine would never be useful outside big corporations, and a personal computer was totally unimaginable. Nowadays we each have more processing power in our smartphone than the total computing power available in the world fifty years ago.

Quantum computers are a real threat to modern cryptography. Even if one is not available today, the chance that a quantum computer will be available by 2026 is estimated to be one in seven, and the chance of one's being available by 2031 increases to an ominous one in two.[452] Given that cryptography underpins our cybersecurity, we think even one in seven is too large a chance to ignore.

Let's return to 2030, where an organization (say, a foreign government or large corporation) has access to the first general purpose quantum computer, and no one else in the world is aware of it. The computer is powerful enough to break RSA or elliptic curve cryptography (ECC) keys in a matter of seconds or a few minutes by running Shor's algorithm. For the current blockchain technology, such a scenario is catastrophic. Why?

Suppose that the above organization maliciously targets a bank that uses the Bitcoin blockchain as its underlying payment system. Each client of the bank has a wallet, which consists of pairs of public keys/secret keys, where the public key is derived from the secret key, but the secret key is impossible to recover from the public key alone.[453] Similarly, the bank has a wallet that consists of many such public key/secret (or private) key pairs. Each time the bank wants to send money (in this case, bitcoin) to a client, the bank uses the hash of the public key of the respective client as the address of the wallet the money will go to, then signs a transaction of the form "I, the Bank of X, sent 10 bitcoins to the client Y identified by the address Z." The bank signs the transaction with one of its secret keys, then broadcasts to the blockchain network, which will validate it within 10 minutes.[454]

However, the private key of the bank is broken within seconds or a few minutes by the malicious organization using a quantum computer. Then the latter can install a new wallet, load the compromised key in it, and then make payments pretending to be the bank. Since this new wallet is identical to the wallet of the original bank, no one will be able to see the difference in transactions and will assume transactions are valid and should be included in the blockchain. The malicious organization now can tap into and redirect all the bank's payments to its own wallet(s).

This is only one example of how the security of the current Bitcoin blockchain becomes obsolete against a quantum adversary. We mentioned before that quantum computers can not only break the current public key cryptography based on RSA or ECC using Shor's algorithm but also speed up attacks against hash functions by running the Grover's search algorithm. The speedup of the latter is less dramatic, being only quadratically faster than any brute-force classical algorithm. Nevertheless, such an attack can still create havoc in the blockchain.

For example, let's suppose that a whole chain of transactions was already validated and added to the blockchain. Suppose, too, that our malicious organization goes "back in time" to a certain point on the blockchain and forks the chain at that point in time, then starts modifying all the transactions in the chain sequentially and validating them on the fly so that the funds (bitcoin) are redirected to its wallet. The malicious organization will most likely be able to validate each transaction faster than some other mining pools because it can perform the PoW significantly faster.

Eventually, the malicious organization is able to "catch up" with the current honest fork in the blockchain and then extend its malicious fork further. Ultimately, the network agrees that the new malicious fork is longer than the existing honest fork and collectively agrees to switch to the new fork—and a whole long chain of transactions is compromised at once.

The above examples only scratch the surface of how malicious users can use quantum computers against unaware public blockchain networks.[455] There will probably be even more clever attacks, which we will only become aware of when or after they have happened, as cybersecurity history shows us. Endangered will be many applications, ranging from financial institutions that use blockchain as a ledger to validate transactions among themselves, to IoT systems that use the blockchain for micropayments or to record state information such as users' health to the blockchain.[456]

THE ISSUE: BLOCKCHAIN IS NOT ENTIRELY QUANTUM SAFE

Today's blockchain is not quantum safe, at least not entirely. A blockchain transaction consists of two steps: the transaction *per se*, followed by a validation of multiple transactions grouped together in a block by the blockchain network. The transaction itself can be anything. For simplicity, let's assume it is a financial transaction where Alice agrees to pay Bob 100 units. Such a transaction is time-stamped and digitally signed by Alice, who broadcasts it to the network, which collectively agrees that indeed Alice agreed to pay Bob 100 units. How can the network guarantee that it was Alice herself who sent the message to Bob, and not Bob trying to get rich quick?

Here's where public key cryptography comes into play. Alice's digital wallet consists of one or more so-called public key/private key pairs. Each private key directly corresponds to the public key; the public key and the private key are mathematically linked. However, recovering the private key from the public key alone is computationally infeasible with today's technology.[457] Alice uses her private key (known only to her) to digitally sign a transaction and then broadcasts the corresponding public key to the network. The network can verify that it was indeed Alice who used her public key to send the transaction. No one else could have signed the message.

What kind of digital signature schemes do we use in practice? The most popular are RSA-based signatures (Rivest-Shamir-Adelman), the DSA (digital signature algorithm), and EC-DSA (elliptic-curve digital signature algorithm), which is the scheme used in the Bitcoin blockchain today.[458]

RSA-based signatures derive their security from the difficulty of factoring a product of two very large primes, each in the range of hundreds to thousands of bits long, depending on the particular scheme. If we're given such a large number, then extracting its factors seems like an exponentially difficult computational problem.

The latter two schemes are based on a completely different difficult problem: solving the discrete logarithm problem in a large Abelian group (i.e., a group where the result of applying the group operation to two group elements does not depend on the order in which they appear).[459] Simply put, if we're given an element of a group—let's call it g, of the form $g=b^k$, where b is another known element of the same group and k is an unknown integer—the problem is to find k.

With EC-DSA, the group itself consists of points on an elliptic curve, and the group operations follow some rules.[460] Both the factoring and the discrete-log problem are instances of a more general class of problems called the *hidden subgroup problem* (HSP) over a finitely generated (Abelian) group. Classical computers find the HSP problem intractable, and its intractability underpins our current public key infrastructure.

In 1994, Peter Shor realized that a universal quantum computer could factor and find discrete logarithms in polynomial time, that is, could solve those problems efficiently.[461] Hence, any public key cryptosystem based on these problems (or the HSP) is not secure against a quantum adversary. In our case, the digital signature scheme used in the blockchain to authenticate transactions is completely vulnerable: anyone with a powerful enough quantum computer can impersonate Alice and redirect some of the assets from a transaction to his/her own pocket (digital wallet) without the network realizing that an attack took place. This is because the attacker can recover the private key from the public key with the help of the quantum computer and then alter the transaction and forge the signature using the respective private key, which will appear to the network as a perfectly legitimate transaction, because only Alice could have been able to sign the transaction correctly.

Therefore, quantum computers pose a very serious threat to the blockchain: a user's wallet would be safe only as long as the user did not spend from it. In other words, as long as users only collect assets into their wallets and never broadcast their public keys, an adversary has no way of learning about their private keys.[462] Users broadcast their public keys only when they need to sign a transaction, that is, when they want to spend. If someone impersonates the user at that stage, then the user can irreversibly lose the money associated with that public/private key pair.

What about the second stage, the validation by the network? After transactions are grouped into a block, the block must be validated by the entire network. Only when the majority of network nodes agrees on the block, is it added to the blockchain, that is, linked to the previous block via a hash of the latter. Often the validation scheme is based on a proof-of-work principle (although other schemes exist), which requires the nodes of the network to solve a hard computational problem or a puzzle, such as inverting a hash function on a subdomain. The node that first solves the puzzle often receives some reward (such as newly minted bitcoins according to the Bitcoin protocol), and so nodes have an incentive to participate in the validation process.

Could an attacker try to double spend some assets by broadcasting two transactions in which the attacker spent the same asset with both Bob and Charlie? Only if the attacker could take over the network and attempt to validate both transactions. However, to do so, the attacker would have to solve the proof-of-work problem faster than the rest of the combined network. Otherwise, the rest of the network will come up with a solution before the attacker, and the blockchain validates the transactions that belong to the longest chain, which in this case will belong to the honest users.

Fortunately, quantum computers pose a less serious threat to hash functions and symmetric-key cryptography in general.[463] The best-known attack against hash functions is based on brute force, that is, the attacker searches for preimages of the hash until the required validation condition is achieved. Because such a search is completely unstructured, all a quantum computer can offer over a classical computer is a quadratic speedup.[464]

Therefore, quantum computers indeed threaten hash functions, but we could easily make the proof-of-work puzzle harder so that even a quantum computer could not solve it fast enough. However, users with more computational power (which may include quantum computers) in the network have higher chances of winning the puzzle and, hence, always concentrate power. Therefore, an asymmetric distribution of fast computational machines (i.e., fast machines such as quantum computers available only to a restricted number of users) pose a significant threat to the network. We should take this into account when designing quantum-resistant blockchains.

ANALYSIS OF OUR OPTIONS

AN ABSTRACT MODEL OF THE BLOCKCHAIN

The blockchain is a distributed ledger of trust in which consensus is obtained collectively by the network without any need for a centralized authority. The blockchain consists of blocks of transactions, each linked to its parent via some linking mechanism such as a hash of the previous block header. Only when the network validates a block is it appended to the blockchain (Figure 7-1).

FIGURE 7-1

BLOCKCHAIN SCHEMATIC MODEL

Each block is "linked" to the previous block via the hash of the latter, i.e., each block contains a hash of the previous block (depicted here by the arrow pointing back to the previous block).

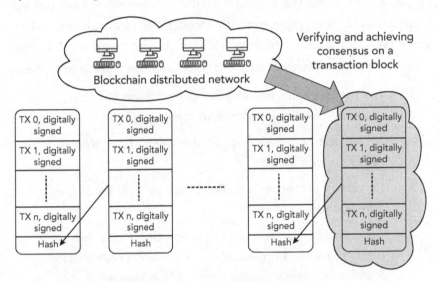

Created by Vlad Gheorghiu, Sergey Gorbunov, Michele Mosca, and Bill Munson, 2017.

The best-known consensus mechanisms are:

1. Proof of work, in which only the network node that first solves a computationally hard problem can validate the transaction

2. Proof of stake, in which the nodes with more at stake (e.g., holding more cryptocurrency) are more likely to be chosen as validators

3. Proof of storage or proof of time, in which the nodes that have more computational resources available to the network, such as disk space or central processing unit time, are more likely to be chosen as validators

All the consensus mechanisms above prevent the problem of double spending. Whereas PoW is considered cryptographically secure, it has a major disadvantage, namely, that it requires significant thermodynamic work and time.[465] The other consensus mechanisms, such as fault-tolerant Byzantine agreement (e.g., Algorand, Tendermint, and Hyperledger), avoid the PoW problem.[466] However, we are not yet entirely clear how cryptographically secure those protocols are, and we know even less about whether we can make them quantum resistant.

From a higher level, we can see the blockchain as consisting of layers:

1. The cryptographic building blocks (e.g., hash functions, public key exchange, symmetric cryptography)

2. Algorithmic primitives (e.g., Merkle trees, cryptographic puzzles, global clocks)

3. Consensus protocols (e.g., PoW, fault-tolerant Byzantine agreement)

4. Additional non-default security properties (e.g., Zcash blockchains use a variant of zero-knowledge proofs called SNARKs—zero knowledge Succinct Non-interactive ARguments of Knowledge—to provide transaction anonymity. SNARKs are not quantum safe, and so 30 years of blockchain data could suddenly become de-anonymized once a quantum computer appears)

Here we focus on the cryptographic building blocks only, and mostly on the PoW-based blockchains. At this stage, we cannot assume that the more advanced algorithms or protocols within the blockchain are quantum safe.

WAYS OF PATCHING THE BLOCKCHAIN

Given the importance of the information and relationships protected by blockchains, and the consequent certainty that blockchains will frequently be targeted for cyberattack by malicious actors, we would be prudent to introduce quantum resistance by design and ensure the most reliable forms are utilized for the most critical and vulnerable assets.

The most important security objectives of the blockchain are unforgeability and the impossibility of double spending. Currently, the problem of quantum-proofing the blockchain can be divided into two scenarios. The first scenario refers to quantum-proofing new blockchains, that is, designing quantum-resistant blockchains from scratch, whereas the second refers to quantum-proofing existing blockchains (such as the Bitcoin network). The first scenario is considerably simpler than the second.

In the analysis below, we will consider that quantum computers are either available to everyone (which we will call *symmetric adversaries*) or available to only a very few (which we will call *asymmetric quantum adversaries*). Table 7-1 depicts the possible combinations of types of blockchains and flavors of quantum adversaries.

TABLE 7-1

POSSIBLE COMBINATIONS OF QUANTUM ADVERSARIES

Symmetric quantum adversaries / existing blockchains	Symmetric quantum adversaries / new blockchains
Asymmetric quantum adversaries / existing blockchains	Asymmetric quantum adversaries / new blockchains

DESIGNING QUANTUM-RESISTANT BLOCKCHAINS FROM SCRATCH

Designing quantum-resistant blockchains from scratch is relatively straightforward: we can apply post-quantum cryptographic schemes and quantum cryptography.

Using post-quantum cryptographic schemes

The most obvious, and perhaps cost-effective, way of making the blockchain resistant against quantum attacks is to replace the currently deployed digital signature schemes, which are based on RSA or EC-DSA, with post-quantum ones. Post-quantum cryptographic schemes derive their security from the difficulty of certain mathematical problems; hence, they offer what is often called *computational security*.

Examples of post-quantum schemes are lattice-based schemes (learning with errors, LWE), supersingular isogenies schemes, multivariate-polynomial schemes, code-based schemes, or Merkle tree-based signatures.[467] All these protocols are designed to be resistant to quantum attacks; and until now, no one has been able to find an attack that destroys any of these schemes. However, such robust schemes come with a performance cost because of their slightly (or sometimes considerably) larger key sizes and significant decrease in computational speed, necessitating a trade-off of efficiency for security.

Unfortunately, industry and government have been slow to act on widespread awareness of the quantum threat until recently. At the present time, cryptographic researchers around the world are increasing their focus on studying quantum-resistant algorithms; but, in the absence of international standards, the result may be a confusing plethora of competing, under-tested proprietary cryptosystems.

Fortunately, in 2016, the US NIST began a multiyear standardization project to identify candidate quantum-resistant cryptosystems.[468] This calls for submissions due November 2017, followed by a three- to five-year public review, followed by a one- to two-year standardization phase—leading to NIST standards between 2021 and 2024. These standardized algorithms will provide a more focused and manageable suite of alternatives for organizations to consider incorporating into their systems. However, it will likely be too soon to pick an ultimate winner (or winners), and so cryptographic agility remains critical.

Blockchains using quantum cryptography

In principle, we may use numerous quantum cryptographic tools to make blockchains more secure. Quantum random number generators

(QNRGs) are likely the most practical tools in the short term.[469] They avoid the cryptanalytic risks associated with pseudo-random number generators, and promise a more fundamental and more reliable source of randomness than conventional entropy-based random number generators.[470]

Also, quantum key distribution (QKD) systems are increasingly commercially available (though still in their early days).[471] QKD is a method for using an untrusted quantum channel to establish symmetric keys through an untrusted, but authenticated, communication channel. This is what is often achieved today using public key-based key agreement authenticated by public key signatures and can be achieved in the future using post-quantum public key schemes.

The advantage of establishing keys using QKD compared to post-quantum schemes for key establishment is that QKD's security does not rely on computational assumptions (i.e., it is "information theoretically" secure), and thus is resilient to cryptanalysis. Post-quantum schemes, in contrast, are based on computational assumptions, and thus come with some risk of future cryptanalysis. However, QKD requires specialized hardware (such as lasers, fiber optics, etc.) to run, and we are many years away from a global QKD network.

In practice, we don't know for sure how helpful QKD will be in improving the security of blockchains in the future. In a recent proposal for a QKD-based blockchain, the authors described a blockchain scheme in which the authentication is achieved via a QKD network among the participants, and the consensus is obtained via a Byzantine agreement-like protocol.[472] The practical usefulness of such a scheme is not yet clear.

There are also various quantum tools, such as quantum authentication, quantum money, and quantum fingerprints, that may someday help further to reduce the threat of cryptanalysis.[473] We might also consider a fully quantum blockchain, that is, based on a distributed architecture in which the nodes are quantum computers, all linked via quantum communication channels.[474] For our purposes here, we note simply that these schemes generally require quantum computation and communication tools that will not be available, especially not for practical use, for many years to come.

FLAVORS OF QUANTUM ADVERSARIES

Asymmetric quantum adversaries

As with the development of classical computers, we expect that quantum computers to be available initially to very few entities such as governments, large research institutions, and large corporations— in other words, we expect an asymmetric distribution of quantum adversaries.

Let's consider the impact that such a quantum computer will have on a PoW-based blockchain in which hash functions are used to enforce the immutability of transactions. We assume that the system uses quantum-resistant digital signatures to ensure the authenticity of transactions. The question is, how much damage can an isolated quantum computer (or a small number of quantum computers) do to such a network?

First, we note that the only vulnerability may be in the PoW component of the blockchain and not in the digital signature itself (if a quantum-safe signature scheme is used). Therefore, a quantum adversary cannot impersonate someone else and try to spend his or her money. The only viable attack is against the PoW system based on hash functions, where the quantum adversary may try to validate transactions faster than the rest of the combined blockchain network. If it succeeds on average, then it can double spend without the network's awareness.

To make this example more concrete, let's look at the current Bitcoin network. The combined difficulty of the PoW is continuously adjusted (on average, increased) over time so that, on average, a solution (hence, a validation) is found every 10 minutes. This adjustment is needed because new and improved hardware is injected into the network as time passes. Between September 2016 and August 2017, the combined hash rate of the entire Bitcoin network increased from under two million terahashes per second (TH/s) to over eight million. In August 2017, the network performed approximately 7×10^{18} hashes per second, which means approximately 4.2×10^{21} hashes on average every 10 minutes.[475] As of 9 March 2021, the rate had reached 156.53 million terahashes per second, almost 20 times greater than in this original study.[476]

Therefore, to succeed, a quantum adversary must search a space of 4.2×10^{21} hash preimages in a time that is significantly smaller than 10 minutes.[477] The best such attack is via Grover's algorithm, which can potentially offer a quadratic speedup in terms of time. An ideal quantum computer (i.e., with no need for error correction) will therefore be able to perform such a search in $\sqrt{4.2 \times 10^{21}} \approx 6.5 \times 10^{10}$ time steps. Assuming, very optimistically, a 1GHz quantum machine (i.e., a quantum computer that performs 10^9 operations per second), this search will be performed in about a minute.

Thus, the PoW system is highly vulnerable to such idealized quantum machines, as the latter can not only validate much faster than the rest of the network but also rewrite history by creating a fork in time, adding new bogus transactions to the chain, and validating each block fast enough that the new chain eventually becomes the valid one that all network participants accept.

However, in reality, quantum computation is highly susceptible to environmental noise and it needs quantum error correcting codes to function properly. Quantum error correction introduces significant computational overhead because of the need for redundant encoding of information.[478] Optimistically, we assumed a quantum computer operating at a 1GHz frequency and physical components with error rates smaller than 10^{-5} (which is again a very optimistic approach). With those numbers, we computed that approximately 2.2×10^{14}

steps would be required to perform the attack, all of which would take approximately two and a half days.

Hence, such a realistic quantum implementation would not pose a threat unless we make significant progress in the fault tolerance quantum error correction or new quantum computing architectures come into play. We do not know yet what the future holds, including the potential of new cryptanalytic attacks.

Note that searching via Grover's algorithm cannot be parallelized efficiently.[479] In other words, the best we can do is to split the searching space in chunks and use a separate quantum computer for every chunk. Hence, if K quantum computers are used in parallel to search a space of size N, the running time will be proportional to

$$\sqrt{\frac{N}{K}} \text{ and not } \frac{\sqrt{N}}{K}$$

as one may have expected. In the fault tolerant example above, an adversary will need approximately 33,000 ($\approx 2^{15}$) fully fault tolerant quantum computers to reduce the searching time to 10 minutes.

Symmetric quantum adversaries

In this case, the whole protocol can assume the existence of widespread quantum computation, including the availability of such quantum machines to the majority of computing nodes (or mining farms). Hence, on average, there will be no outside computing power that can be significantly faster than the rest of the network. Therefore, we conclude here that the blockchain is secure against generic quantum attacks on the hash function.

QUANTUM-PROOFING EXISTING BLOCKCHAINS

Patching existing blockchains against quantum attacks may be significantly harder than designing quantum-safe blockchains from scratch.

The first step is to replace the vulnerable cryptographic primitives with quantum-resistant ones. For example, in the Bitcoin network, we would need to replace the digital signature scheme with a quantum-resistant scheme and use the latter to sign new transactions. This approach would provide security for future transactions.

The problem, however, is what would happen with old transactions? Let's assume that a wallet spent some cryptocurrency from an address. Because the address is a hash of the public key associated with that wallet, the public key has been publicly revealed and a quantum adversary can recover the corresponding secret key. If the wallet still has some cryptocurrency associated with that address, a quantum adversary can impersonate the wallet's owner and spend the rest of the funds.

A solution to this problem: never reuse a public key or make sure that there are absolutely no more funds available to an address for which the public key has been revealed. If quantum-safe digital signatures are introduced into the blockchain before quantum computers become a reality, then the network can ask every user to perform a *self-transfer* transaction in which the user transfers all funds associated with his or her old (non-quantum safe) public key to an address that corresponds to the user's quantum-safe public key.

The discussion of symmetric versus asymmetric quantum adversaries follows the same line as our flavors of quantum adversaries. In the worst-case scenario, an asymmetric quantum adversary is able to solve the cryptographic puzzle significantly faster than the rest of the network. Although this scenario is highly unlikely based on current assumptions, we cannot rule it out as impossible. Therefore, we need to take precautions.

For example, we could consider transactions longer than a fixed number L of blocks to be completely immutable and modify the blockchain protocol such that blocks longer than L are not allowed to be forked and mined anymore. Although this option somewhat fixes the problem of rewriting history older than L blocks, it does not address the quantum adversary's ability to validate pending transactions much faster than the entire network and, therefore, to take control over the network. There is no obvious solution to this last problem, and we need significantly more research. We could design variable-difficulty cryptographic puzzles that a quantum computer could not solve faster. Of course, no one should be able to solve such puzzles by searching, because Grover's algorithm would provide a speedup.

PERFORMANCE ANALYSIS

According to one acknowledged expert, one of the main technical difficulties in implementing a post-quantum blockchain resides in the overhead introduced by the post-quantum digital signature schemes to be used (Table 7-2).[480] For example, the Bitcoin protocol uses EC-DSA for transaction authentication, the average size of which is equal to 71 bytes.

In contrast, post-quantum digital signature schemes are at least six times larger or much worse and significantly slower computationally than the current ones deployed, such as EC-DSA. The constraints introduced by post-quantum digital signature schemes may pose serious scalability challenges for quantum-resistant blockchains. For example, supersingular isogenies post-quantum schemes, which are very promising for public key encryption in terms of the shortness of their key sizes (about half a kilobyte), are currently inadequate as digital signature schemes in space-constrained environments such as blockchains, because the corresponding signature size is around 140 kilobytes (in contrast to 71 bytes for EC-DSA).[481]

On the other hand, code-based and multivariate-based digital signatures have short sizes, but their corresponding public/private keys used for signature generation and verification are relatively large. Hence, for those two schemes, the size of a hypothetical block in a PoW blockchain will probably be around seven times larger than the current size of the Bitcoin blockchain. However, the required

PKI will require significant more storage since the corresponding public/private keys are significantly larger than the current EC-DSA keys. Moreover, multivariate-based schemes have a relatively large number of opponents because their security is less convincing than other schemes.

TABLE 7-2

POST-QUANTUM KEY SIZES AND SIGNATURE SIZES AT 128-BIT SECURITY LEVEL

All sizes are in bytes.

POST-QUANTUM SCHEME	PUBLIC-KEY SIZE	PRIVATE-KEY SIZE	SIGNATURE SIZE
Hash based	1,056	1,088	41,000
Code based	192,192	1,400,288	370
Lattice based	7,168	2,048	5,120
Ring LWE based	7,168	4,608	3,488
Multivariate based	99,100	74,000	424
Isogeny based	768	48	141,312
Isogeny based (compressed)	336	48	122,880

See Y. Yoo, R. Azarderakhsh, A. Jalali, D. Jao and V. Soukharev, "A Post-Quantum Digital Signature Scheme Based on Supersingular Isogenies," Cryptology ePrint Archive, 2017, p. 186. eprint.iacr.org/2017/186.pdf.

The next candidate on the list is the LWE-based digital signature scheme, which suffers from a slightly larger key (3–5 kilobytes). The schemes are provably secure asymptotically via hard-problem reduction arguments.[482] There are no such tight security proofs for real-world parameters, but the cryptographic community has not yet found any flaws or security issues with the scheme. The public/private key sizes are also reasonable in size; hence, LWE seems to be a viable candidate for quantum-resistant blockchains.

The hash-based schemes are the most trusted ones in terms of security and have relatively small public/private keys. However, the corresponding signature size is over 40 kilobytes long, which is problematic in a very space-constrained environment such as the blockchain.

Lamport one-time based signatures are another potential candidate.[483] Their public key size is 16 kilobytes, the corresponding secret key size is 16 kilobytes as well, and their signature size is eight kilobytes. Slightly more efficient schemes (in terms of signature size) such as the Winternitz one-time signature scheme are also viable.[484] Winternitz signature compression reduces the size of the private key and public key by slightly less than a factor of two times the chunk size (in bits) and half that factor for the signature. The computation time increases by slightly more than a factor of two times the chunk size (in bits). Those schemes are *one time*, that is, they are secure as long as keys are not reused when signing new transactions.

In conclusion, post-quantum digital signature schemes offer security against a quantum adversary at the cost of much larger public/private key sizes or signature sizes. We need significantly more research in the area of post-quantum digital signatures.[485] Reducing *both* the signature sizes *and* the public/private key sizes is paramount in a robust and efficient quantum-resistant blockchain.

WHAT THE EXPERTS SAY ABOUT BLOCKCHAIN SECURITY

During our research, we interviewed several blockchain experts on the security of current and future blockchain protocols against quantum adversaries. We asked them about the challenges and defects that organizations may need to address when implementing quantum-resistant ledgers.

Dr. Manfred Lochter, Federal Office for Information, Germany

Question. *How do you see breaking EC-DSA within 10 minutes?*

Answer. Do not use EC-DSA if quantum computers exist! If not, look at what kind of attack it is and how it scales, perhaps increase the security parameter.[486]

Q. *Do you believe that quantum computers will affect the security proof-of-work systems based on hash inversion?*

A. Hashes are the least of the problem in a proof-of-work system, but it depends on the type of blockchain. For example, there may be serious issues with time-stamping blockchains, in which collision resistance is of paramount importance. If a quantum computer finds a collision, it can attack the system.

Q. *How often do current wallets reuse keys?*

A. Wallets are indeed an issue. There are wallets out there that use deterministic algorithms for generating key sequences. Moreover, the number of public key collisions out there is larger than expected, mainly because of poor wallet implementations.[487]

Dr. Ghassan Karame, Chief Security Researcher, NEC Labs, Germany

Question. *How do you see quantum threat affecting the blockchain? How serious is this threat perceived?*

Answer. The threat is not only particular to the blockchain—it applies to all systems. I do not see blockchain as an exception. ... What we know is that there are lots of inactive addresses currently in the blockchain, in the sense that if in 10 years someone can break those keys, then he or she can get lots of money. There is currently also a considerable number of coins that are dormant [Satoshi's coins].[488]

Q. *What is the most vulnerable part of the blockchain implementations as of today?*

A. Many attacks are on the network layer implementation. It is very weak in most blockchains [because of the attempt] to optimize for scalability and losing security features in the process. ... This is one of the weakest links of the existing implementations. ... When there are users involved, the user becomes the bottleneck in security, for example, the private keys are not always properly managed.

Q. *How often do wallets reuse keys or use a deterministic algorithm to generate a key sequence? Can you comment on current wallet security issues?*

A. Bitcoin should give you a new address by default when collecting change (unless one manually alters the code). The issue is that this is not good enough. There are implementation issues as well.

Q. *Do you think a quantum-safe blockchain is useful as of today?*
A. Yes, it may make sense. Hashes are quantum resistant, but currently the standard dilemma in the community is how to come up with a proper key-management solution for the digital signature part of the blockchain. This is a problem even for the current ECDSA key management infrastructure. ... I think we should have quantum-safe blockchains in mind.

Dr. Nadia Diakun-Thibault, North Carolina State University

Question. *What is your opinion about quantum computing attacks on the blockchain infrastructure?*

Answer. Currently, blockchain notwithstanding, we may have some quantum capabilities today, is safe at SHA-256, which is what Bitcoin blockchain uses. ... The problem is humans are involved, and they may not secure the system well, may not follow all security rules, or may inject human error. ... More research is needed in areas in which the blockchain is indeed vulnerable, such as digital signatures, smart contracts, or security rules and security applications in cloud computing.[489]

Q. *How common is it for wallets to have implementation security problems/major software flaws? Major catastrophes?*

A. That is where the problem really is. Wallets, exchanges, accounts may be in the cloud; they are not necessarily secure. Cloud providers don't know all that goes on in the cloud. Mining can be done in the cloud. What assurance can the cloud provider give that security measures are fully applied? Most security problems are at the provider's/user's/wallet's end.

Q. *Is there any Canadian government official position or advice regarding quantum threats to the blockchain or regulating the blockchain?*

A. At this time, none that I know of. In my view, it's an area many will be very reluctant to comment on. Government can regulate use, but not with respect to blockchain itself—there are no standards. I do not think we can "regulate" blockchain; one could say it would be akin to regulating a "database." Government can stipulate where it would be appropriate to use blockchain, whether it would be permissioned or permissionless, who the participants are, security requirements, compliance measures, et cetera. These are reasonable expectations.

Dr. David Jao, Centre for Applied Cryptographic Research, University of Waterloo

Question. *What is the most challenging part in building a quantum-resistant ledger?*

Answer. Definitely the digital signatures. Post-quantum signature schemes are still way larger than EC-DSA, and simply plugging a post-quantum replacement may work fine for relatively small blockchains, but will create major scalability issues for large blockchains such as the Bitcoin. The cryptographic community needs more research in the area of post-quantum digital signatures.[490]

CONCLUSIONS AND RECOMMENDATIONS

Post-quantum solutions are not yet fully standardized, so making a strong recommendation at this time is exceedingly difficult. However, what we can definitely recommend now is to build agile blockchain protocols, in which the digital signature scheme is modular so that it can easily be switched out and replaced by a quantum-resistant one. While stateful hash-based signatures are attractive from a security perspective, there are also practical advantages for stateless schemes (which also include stateless hash-based signatures), for example, digital signatures based on the hardness of lattice problems, such as LWE, or code-based digital signature schemes.[491] Remember, there is currently no quantum-resistant digital signature scheme that offers *both* short signatures *and* short key sizes.

Our recommendation is to be agile and design a quantum-resistant blockchain in which changing the digital signature scheme should be a fully integrated part of the code base. For example, assume a common API for digital signatures, and design the protocol with the ability to change the signature on the fly, whenever needed.

We also highly recommend a careful design of the end-user blockchain architecture, such as the digital wallet infrastructure. Remember, the end-user infrastructure is the most vulnerable link in the cryptographic chain. Making it secure is therefore of paramount importance.

A far more difficult problem is how to patch a blockchain system based on PoW. If quantum computers are widely available, then we can modify the network protocol so that it assumes everyone is using quantum searching to find the preimages of hash functions. However, if only a small minority of users has access to quantum computers, then how to avoid an attack is unclear, when all transactions in a chain are modified sequentially. Likely, there will always be an asymmetry in the blockchain network, and those very few users with access to quantum computers will eventually be able to compromise long chains.

One brute-force solution is simply to modify the blockchain protocol such that forks longer than a specified length should not be accepted for mining anymore. This solution only partially addresses the issue: while it guarantees the integrity of past transactions beyond a specified number of steps, it does not prevent malicious users from validating transactions faster than everyone else and basically taking over the network.

We hope these issues raise awareness in the blockchain research community so that it can develop novel protection schemes. Currently, we do not see hash inversion as a very serious security issue, at least not in the near term and medium term. The first generations of quantum computers will most likely suffer from significant overhead because of error correction. Remember, in this case, Grover will not really speed things up enough so that hash inversion becomes a security issue. However, 25 years from now, we may have powerful enough asymmetric quantum adversaries who will be able to find hash preimages much faster than a large majority of the network. Currently, we lack a full solution to this problem, except for the aforementioned brute-force patch.

To conclude, the most stringent requirement in designing a quantum-resistant blockchain is the authentication part. Current digital signature schemes are vulnerable and must be either replaced in current blockchains or implemented from the very beginning in new quantum-resistant ledgers designed from scratch.

None of the existing post-quantum digital signature schemes satisfies all the requirements of a distributed ledger system, namely small size and efficiency. We hope that future research in the area will bring smaller and more efficient schemes. Until then, we recommend maintaining agility in the architectural design and building ledgers in which changing the digital signature scheme should be relatively easy (i.e., built into the protocol or via straightforward update patches).[492]

The Open Quantum Safe project is a collaborative open source effort that developers can leverage for testing and benchmarking various quantum-resistant key exchange and signature schemes in blockchain applications.[493] We hope our research will motivate fruitful collaborations among blockchain experts, cryptographers, and software developers in designing the quantum-resistant ledger of the future.

CHAPTER 8

STANDARDIZED AND DECENTRALIZED?

Rethinking the Blockchain Technology Stack

Christian Keil

STANDARDIZATION IMPERATIVE IN BRIEF

- Standardization is powerful because of the power of network effects and the outsized economic gains that flow to winners of standards wars. To discuss the decentralized world of blockchain technology in practical terms, we need to distinguish between two types of standardization: semantic and technological.

- Semantic standardization is alignment on how to talk about blockchain technology—defining a "stack" that resembles the open systems interconnection (OSI) stack for the Internet. We should pursue this kind of standardization in all cases, as it can help us contextualize innovations, find new opportunities for innovation, and ask powerful questions about the blockchain ecosystem as it currently exists.

- Technological standardization is alignment on how to build blockchain technologies, like that of the Internet protocol, and is significantly more difficult than semantic standardization. We can surely achieve it in the decentralized context, evidenced by the acceptance of

ERC-20 as a token standard in Ethereum, provided that we follow the golden rule, "Don't roll your own crypto."

- The ideological wars and corresponding forks within the biggest blockchain ecosystems Bitcoin, and Ethereum, reveal the difficulty of defining and aligning on technological standards, especially in light of evidence that blockchain protocol splits can be value-creative.

- Ultimately, the rules of the standardization game differ in the decentralized context. Technologists and academics alike would be wise to consider the different prospects of semantic and technological standardization and to resist consensus for consensus' sake.

AN ORIGIN STORY

In the beginning, there was a white paper. Today, nearly 10 years later, Satoshi Nakamoto's technological breakthrough—bitcoin and the blockchain technology behind it—has generated hundreds of billions of dollars of economic value:

- Global cryptocurrency markets are worth around $1.8 trillion as of 9 March 2021.[494]

- 299 separate organizations have raised $5.03 billion in non-dilutive capital funding through ICOs.[495]

- The world's largest corporations—Alibaba, American Express, AT&T, Cisco, Comcast, Goldman Sachs, A.P. Møller–Mærsk, Microsoft, JetBlue, J.P.Morgan, Sprint, Toyota, Verizon, Visa, Walmart, and many others—have invested untold billions in the space.[496]

In the parlance of Marc Andreessen, blockchain technology is eating the world—something Satoshi hardly could have imagined when he published a short paper to a niche cryptography mailing list in 2008.[497]

But has this new world emerged *too* quickly? Even after such a significant influx of capital, we have yet to see a game-changing (nonfinancial) consumer blockchain application.

Joichi "Joi" Ito, former director of the MIT Media Lab, explained his perspective on the maturity of blockchain technology:

> Looking at many [blockchain] businesses, they look like start-ups during that period, but instead of pets.com, we have blockchain for X. I don't think today's blockchain is the Internet in 1996—it's probably more like the Internet in 1990 or the late [1980s]—we haven't agreed on the [Internet] protocol and there is no Cisco or PSINet. Many of the application layer companies are building on an infrastructure that isn't ready from a stability or a scalability perspective and they are either bad idea or good idea [sic] too early. ... There are start-ups and academics working on these basic layers, but I wish there were more.[498]

In that frame, the dearth of world-changing applications makes sense, for application-layer teams are still building their houses on ever-shifting sands.

How, then, can we—as blockchain technologists and academics—help solidify the deep foundations of blockchain technology, the scaffolding on which future consumer-facing applications can rely?

The answer Ito implies is to align on standardized protocols—but is that the right solution for blockchain, an inherently decentralized technology? Put more directly, is there a contradiction between standardization and decentralization?

In this chapter, we explore the origins of standardization, whether we should use that framework to guide the development of blockchain tech, and if yes, then how. In doing so, we'll discover the difference between semantic and technological standardization, create a Rosetta stone for unifying different dialects of blockchain-speak, survey the most bitter internecine blockchain battles, and conclude with tactical advice for organizations, academics, and technologists hoping to navigate the emerging blockchain ecosystem successfully.

WHY STANDARDIZE?

In the age of the Internet, the technology stack reigns supreme. As Joi Ito proclaimed, "The Internet works because we have clear layers of open standards."

Those "layers" are technologies that fill a particular function in an end-to-end solution—like "network" (IP), "transport" (TCP), or "application" (HTTP, SMTP)—and together, they define the *lingua franca* of the Internet. Because those protocols have been well-defined and universally adopted, everything that makes up the Internet—from Wi-Fi routers to your browser of choice—knows precisely how to receive data and how to pass it on.

The positive effects of standardization are many; two are most worth discussing here.

NETWORK EFFECTS

First, standardized technology can help players benefit from *network effects*. The obvious example here is the App Store, debatably the iPhone ecosystem's most influential feature. Now that the iPhone has become the most profitable product in history, many forget that, immediately after its launch in 2007, developers scoffed at the product and their inability to create applications within its new operating system.[499] In early 2008, however, Apple released a software development kit and the App Store, and everyone quickly forgot its initial reticence. By May 2013, the App Store had supported 50 billion downloads and delivered $9 billion to app developers.[500]

By all external signals, Apple appears to have tapped into a force of nature with its App Store, and perhaps it did in Metcalfe's law, the proposition that the value of a network is proportional to the square of its number of users.

Apple's iPhone, because it was in the hands of every consumer, gave the best developers strong incentives to spend time making apps for the iOS platform. Consumers, in turn, had even stronger reasons to buy an iPhone after those apps went live, and the virtuous cycle of compounding network effects was set in motion.

OUTSIZED ECONOMIC GAINS

Second, and perhaps more obviously, *outsized economic gains* often flow to those who win "standards wars." This is most directly true for API companies: their products are effected standards for common types of data transactions—from Stripe and Twilio to cloud computing giant Salesforce, which makes more than half its revenue through APIs.[501]

Other more traditional industries have also felt the dramatic effects of standards wars. In telecom, for example, a battle was waged to determine the industry standard for fourth generation (4G) wireless technology. Two suitors, WiMAX (Worldwide Interoperability for Microwave Access) and LTE (Long-Term Evolution), threw their hats into the ring—and it wasn't clear which standard would win as both boasted of speeds four times faster than that of the existing 3G service.[502]

Considering you've probably never heard of WiMAX before the preceding paragraph, it isn't too much of a spoiler to reveal that LTE won the day and remains the global standard for 4G. Its victory gave companies like AT&T and Verizon that invested in LTE in the *antebellum* and *in bello* years a significant head start on a trillion-dollar market.[503] The equal and opposite reaction was seen at Sprint, which invested tens of billions of dollars in WiMAX only to find it incompatible with the iPhone.[504]

HOW DOES THE "STANDARDIZATION" MODEL APPLY TO BLOCKCHAIN?

The benefits to standardization in a normal technological context are undeniable, but blockchain is no normal context. What, exactly, would it mean for an explicitly decentralized technology to be standardized? To guide the rest of our exploration of this seeming conflict, let's distinguish between *semantic* and *technological* standardization.

Semantic standards are those that resemble OSI—or the *open systems interconnection* model of the Internet that gained popularity the 1980s. Semantic standards unify how we *talk* about technology. The OSI standard itself isn't a way to transmit network traffic; rather, it codifies how people should describe the architecture of the Internet. Whenever you talk about a part of the Internet, then you ought to use one (and only one) of the seven words that label OSI's layers—in my native consulting jargon, they are mutually exclusive but collectively exhaustive (MECE) categories.

Technological standards, conversely, describe a particular way to *build* end-to-end solutions. TCP/IP is a technological standard because it defines one totalizing architecture for the Internet. If you want to integrate with TCP/IP applications, then you ought to construct your lower-layer tech using this (and only this) technological specification.[505] In the remainder of this chapter, we'll explore how these two flavors of standardization manifest in the world of blockchain technology.

SEMANTIC STANDARDIZATION: DEFINING THE BLOCKCHAIN STACK

The first and most influential attempt to define the layers of blockchain technology was created by venture capitalist Joel Monegro and popularized in his 2014 article, "The Blockchain Application Stack." Monegro's stack is fairly simple, with just five layers: the bitcoin blockchain, overlay networks, decentralized protocols, open source and commercial APIs, and applications.[506]

Monegro's diagram is commendable and certainly sparked considerable discussion—by my read, it's still the most-referenced "stack" to date. That said, it was created in 2014 (i.e., the Monolithic Era, measuring time in blockchain years). Accordingly, it's in need of a refresh, and we will turn to three alternative stacks—those proposed by David Xiao, Vitalik Buterin, and Arun Devan—to better capture the advances, both technological, cultural, and otherwise, in our attempt at semantic standardization (Figure 8-1).[507] In the following sections, we'll discuss five new semantic choices that can enhance Monegro's stack and update it for the modern day.

FIGURE 8-1
FOUR ILLUSTRATIVE BLOCKCHAIN TECHNOLOGY STACKS

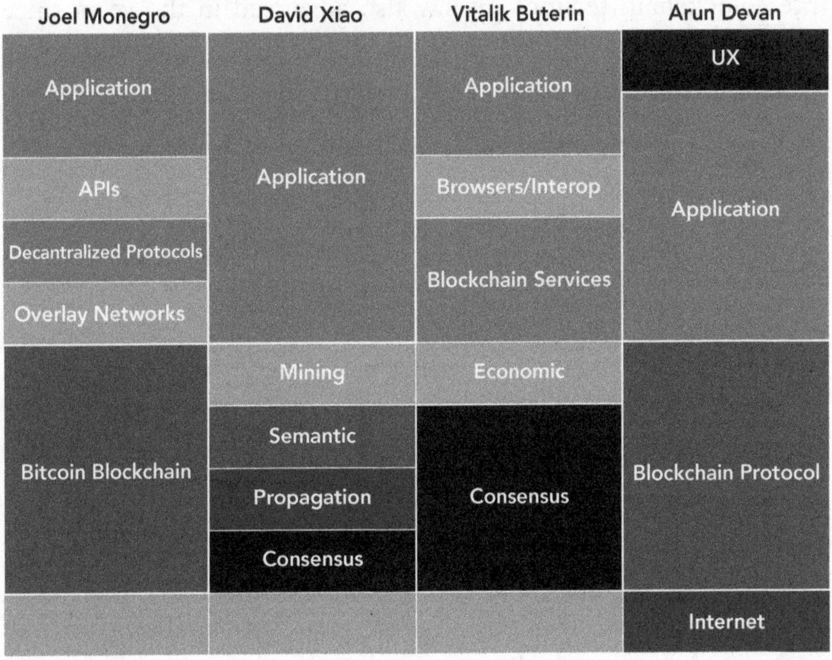

Joel Monegro	David Xiao	Vitalik Buterin	Arun Devan
Application	Application	Application	UX
APIs		Browsers/Interop	Application
Decentralized Protocols		Blockchain Services	
Overlay Networks			
Bitcoin Blockchain	Mining	Economic	Blockchain Protocol
	Semantic	Consensus	
	Propagation		
	Consensus		
			Internet

Summary graphic and comparative mappings by Christian Keil, 2018.

BEYOND BITCOIN

A modern blockchain stack should generalize beyond Bitcoin. In 2014, it may have seemed like a great majority of blockchain transactions would always run through Bitcoin's blockchain—it represented over 90 percent of the total market capitalization of all cryptocurrencies combined at the time. In February 2018, however, that same number was less than 35 percent. The emergence of Ethereum (~20 percent), Ripple (~10 percent), and numerous altcoins gave credence to the belief at the time that the future of blockchain technology wouldn't be dominated by any single blockchain.[508] But by March 2021, Bitcoin had regained much ground, with a market dominance around 60 percent compared to Ethereum's 12 percent and Ripple's 1.34 percent.[509]

SUBDIVISION OF THE BLOCKCHAIN LAYER

Inter-blockchain technology has also advanced in the years since Monegro's stack was initially defined, as captured by David Xiao's stack. Xiao advocates subdivision of a blockchain into four layers:

- *Consensus*, which determines which version of the ledger is valid
- *Propagation*, which determines how blocks and ledgers are sent from node to node in the network
- *Semantic*, which determines how new blocks relate to existing ones
- *Mining*, which determines the incentive structure for driving the addition of blocks to the chain

That specificity is helpful, but a quick observation of where the energy lies in blockchain R&D today leads us to a simpler (but still subdivided) picture like that proposed by Vitalik Buterin, the founder of Ethereum. Recent debates over *consensus* mechanisms (i.e., PoW vs. PoS) have been an incredibly hot topic of late, and similarly, Vitalik's *economic* sub-layer—which corresponds to Xiao's *mining*—is a crucial piece of the "token economy."

REDEFINING OVERLAY NETWORKS

Monegro defines his *overlay networks* layer by using the example of sidechains. That particular structure, however, has fallen out of favor in recent years as blockchain technologists have grown to prefer forks or tokens to achieve similar goals. Here's our explanation of a sidechain:

> A sidechain is a type of fork that uses the underlying unit of a large protocol like Bitcoin like collateral: they "freeze" bitcoins in escrow accounts, and award new tokens on other blockchains in return. While my ten bitcoins are frozen, for example, I am given access to ten tokens in another network that can do certain types of computation that Bitcoin cannot.

Even so, some types of overlay networks have become crucially important to the future of blockchain technology—most notably, off-chain scaling solutions like the Lightning Network and Raiden. These technologies offer extremely fast transactions at little to no cost by creating off-chain "payment channels," basically decentralized (and still cryptographically secured) escrows, where the only on-chain transactions occur when users open or close payment channels.[510]

These overlay networks are not unique blockchains, nor do they directly alter blockchain data—rather, they are best understood as a new layer above both the *blockchain data* layers and the *core protocols* that edit them.

CONNECTING APPLICATIONS TO PROTOCOLS

The layer that Monegro called *APIs* has also evolved in the intervening years. Here we'll use the word *interconnection* to describe this layer of technologies that connect applications to blockchain protocols. Examples include projects like 0x, a protocol for exchanging ERC-20 tokens via liquidity pools, or MetaMask.[511] Ashley Lannquist, consulting manager for Blockchain at Berkeley, explains the importance of the latter example and its correct place in the stack:

> MetaMask is the crucial layer connecting the Ethereum-based app to the Ethereum blockchain without the user needing to run a full Ethereum node on her computer; and it holds a digital currency wallet, so that when the user interfaces with various applications, they can connect to Ethereum and use a single identity and wallet hosted in MetaMask. The user engages directly with the application, and MetaMask allows the app, via its browser, to connect to the blockchain lower in the stack.[512]

ADDING END-TO-END COMPLETENESS

Finally, Arun Devan's stack offers two unique layers, which he calls *UX* and *Internet*—both of which we believe to be worthy additions for the sake of completeness.

User (B2C, business to consumer) or corporate (B2B) *experience* is only very rarely discussed today, but we expect it to grow in popularity as competitive differentiation (and therefore developer energy) work up the stack. IBM, of all companies, recently wrote a particularly great article about designing blockchain products, "Blockchain Design Principles," a must-read for blockchain technologists.[513] It's easy to forget that, as Jonny Howle said, "Just because blockchain technology is built to eliminate the reliance on trust doesn't mean users will trust [it]."[514]

The *Internet* is a similarly underappreciated part of end-to-end blockchain solutions. We prefer the broader term, *infrastructure*, which can encompass both the connectivity *and* hardware solutions (e.g., Thales's secured hardware for Chain and Gem) that are needed to support blockchain technologies.[515]

THE MODERN BLOCKCHAIN STACK

In the end, these considerations lead to the following view of block-chain technology—an attempt at aggregating the wisdom of the aforementioned sources (and three years of additional development, post-Monegro) into semantic standardization (Figure 8-2).[516]

FIGURE 8-2

AN UPDATED BLOCKCHAIN STACK

Layer		FUNCTION	EXAMPLES
Experience		Facilitate easy, trusted interaction with blockchain solutions	Users; Businesses
Application		Connect blockchain technology and the outside (digital or analog) world	Augur; Gnosis
Interconnection		Connect user applications (whether blockchain-native or traditional internet) to blockchain protocols	MetaMask; Ox
Blockchain Protocol	Overlay	Build functionality on top of core protocol	Lightning Network; IPFS
	Core	Define language for interaction with blockchain	Solidity (Ethereum)
Blockchain Data	Economic	Incentivize the execution of a consensus mechanism to validate a blockchain	Mining/Staking; Tokens
	Consensus	Determine which blockchain history is correct	Proof of Work; Proof of Stake
Infrastructure		Support the blockchain software and enable communication	Internet Hardware

Graphic, descriptions, and examples by Christian Keil, 2018.

We hope that this updated semantic structure can help us contextualize technological solutions, find new opportunities for innovation, and ask powerful questions about the blockchain ecosystem as it currently exists.

For example, future research could focus on the amount of investment at each layer—do we find similar investment by venture capital, corporate investment, and ICO dollars at every level of the stack, or are certain investors only investing in particular layers? Similarly, we could build on the great analysis completed by Justine and Olivia Moore of CRV, and see whether similar equity or disparity across layers exists in the number of GitHub commits, Telegram group memberships, subreddit subscriber counts, Google search scores, and so forth.[517] The possibilities are many, and all rely on the existence of a semantic standard.

TECHNOLOGICAL STANDARDIZATION: DECENTRALIZED UNANIMITY

Those who believe that the paradox of decentralized standardization is too much to overcome may be doomed to repeat the mistakes of the past. In September 2017, IOTA—then the eighth largest cryptocurrency, with over $1.9 billion market capitalization—was discovered to have a serious vulnerability: an error in its code made it possible to forge signatures and therefore create fraudulent transactions.[518] This mistake was entirely avoidable had IOTA simply followed the technological standard for "hashing," SHA-256. Instead, it broke the "golden rule of cryptographic systems," according to Neha Narula, director of the Digital Currency Initiative at the MIT Media Lab: "Don't roll your own crypto."[519] The existence of such a rule indicates the feasibility of—and importance of understanding—technological standardization in a decentralized world. In the sections to follow, we'll cover some examples of technological standardization (or lack thereof) to uncover why, and how, these standards arise.

CORE PROTOCOL LAYER: ETHEREUM CLASSIC AND BITCOIN CASH

One new competitive dynamic in the blockchain world, one almost entirely absent in the relatively centralized world of the modern Internet, is the *fork*. A fork is a blockchain divergence where one unified history turns into two parallel ones. A "hard fork" is one in which the new chain is not backwards-compatible, and a "soft fork" is one in which the new chain is backwards-compatible. They sound benign enough, and they can be. In the early days of Ethereum, for example, two hard forks occurred—one just days after launch, and one to release a new set of code called "Homestead." Both were simple upgrades of the system; they went off without much fanfare, and the legacy, pre-upgrade chains simply died off as planned.

At times, however, forks are *much* more dramatic. Recently, we've seen bitter ideological disagreements over *core protocol* architectures in which threatened forks made the future of billions of dollars of economic value hang in the balance.

Bitcoin block size

In the early years of Bitcoin development, Satoshi Nakamoto wrote a simple piece of code to limit the size of each block to a maximum of one megabyte.[520] His decision was inconsequential at the time—the average block was less than one kilobyte in early 2010—and the code passed into the core client without fanfare.[521] That inconsequential decision has recently threatened to tear the Bitcoin community in two.

One group of combatants believes that the block size should be increased to help Bitcoin scale up its transaction throughput—today, the network can only handle about three transactions per second, which is far, far fewer than the 65,000 transactions-per-second maximum capacity of Visa.[522]

Another group, however, *vehemently* disagrees. The opponents contend that increasing the block size would be a temporary fix, make running a full node (i.e., mining Bitcoin and processing transactions) prohibitively expensive, and thereby sacrifice the decentralization of mining power (and thereby Bitcoin as a whole).[523] In their words, this technical disagreement has escalated into a "constitutional crisis."[524]

Many attempts have been made over the years to forge a compromise between the two sides. But, in the words of Daniel Morgan, author of an oft-cited piece on the Bitcoin scaling debate, these efforts have failed because:

> The culture, technology, and governing development team is resistant to what has been deemed "contentious." A "contentious" proposal is something that doesn't yet have complete support from the Bitcoin community. Bitcoin Classic, Bitcoin XT, Bitcoin Unlimited, and Segwit2x are all examples of alternative clients that have sought to build a consensus in larger block sizes.[525]

In April 2017, the Digital Currency Group attempted to reconcile this contentious proposal by publishing the "New York Agreement," a plan to implement a 2MB block size via hard fork. "Fifty-eight companies located in 22 countries, 83.28 percent of hashing power, [and] $5.1 billion monthly on chain transaction volume" signed the agreement—and it still failed. The political challenge of instituting a cooperative hard fork in general *and* a block size upgrade in particular proved too challenging, even given what the authors claimed to be consensus from a supermajority of the community. According to Morgan, lingering dissidents called the New York Agreement a "corporate takeover" of Bitcoin by a few individuals, and their criticisms prevented a peaceful, unanimous resolution to the crisis.[526]

Ultimately, the ideological gap between the two camps proved unbridgeable and a controversial hard fork occurred on 1 August 2017. The big-block-size proponents created a Bitcoin fork now commonly known as bitcoin cash (BCH), including a shiny, new, eight-megabyte block size. The legacy chain remained bitcoin (BTC).

This debate is still playing out to this day as BTC and BCH vie for the moral high ground (and hash power), but the troubled history of this change has already taught the community a key lesson of technological standardization: sometimes, differences can truly be irresolvable, and one size cannot always fit all in a world as decentralized as blockchain.

Ethereum and the DAO

Bitcoin Cash did not introduce the blockchain world to controversial hard forks. In fact, Ethereum found itself on the verge of such a fork over an entire year earlier—in the aftermath of the hack of the DAO, then the world's largest ever crowdfunding project. The hack itself was massive—a hacker siphoned off more than $50 million in ether—but the real story comes from the Ethereum community's response to it.[527]

Hard fork advocates, like Ethereum founder Vitalik Buterin and Consensus Systems founder Joe Lubin, argued that the community should intentionally branch off a new blockchain in which the hack never took place. Lubin said such a measure was necessary because the hack was an existential threat: "If the hacker's goal was to destroy Ethereum, then the hacker could have staged denial-of-service attacks for many years, messing up the network's ability to process transactions efficiently. We would have been chasing this person in and out of different smart contracts, in a sort of a cat and mouse game."[528]

To others, however, a hard fork felt like sacrilege. It was wrong to allow "extra-protocol" politicking to change the supposedly immutable ledger of the blockchain, they claimed, and the community ought to recognize the crypto-maxim that "code is law."

As the date of the proposed hard fork approached, nobody was quite sure how it would turn out. An informal vote showed seven-to-one support *for* the fork, but it was unclear what would happen to the original Ethereum blockchain—would the minority community still have enough firepower to mine and maintain the blockchain?

The eventual result surprised even Vitalik. In an interview with venture capital (VC) firm Andreessen Horowitz (also called a16z), he explained how the eventual split was—against all odds—value *additive*. One plus one equaled three after ether (ETH) forked from Ethereum Classic (ETC).

> [The value of] ETH plus ETC is above ETC before the fork, which is actually interesting. I feel like this is one of the great political debates ... [people like] network effects, people working together. But doing the opposite of that is sometimes perceived as either weakness or confusion or chaos ...
>
> In this case, it definitely does seem like it's been positive value on net. The question, of course, is why. The answer here is interesting because the general viewpoint in cryptocurrency land before this was Metcalfe's Law ... you want to have all the users on a single network to maximize value, but here we've basically learned that there are some cases where it actually goes the other direction.[529]

That an event so destructive (i.e., invalidating a blockchain history) or at the very most distributive (i.e., dividing a whole into parts) can *create* economic value is a radical development, and one worth exploring in more detail in the future.

Could this be evidence that too much technological standardization is a bad thing in the distributed world of blockchain? Or is this a false signal, produced by speculation-driven trading? Only time will tell, but for whatever reason, a clear lesson emerges from the ETC/ETH fork: sometimes, divergences in opinion about core protocols—even those that subdivide communities—can be value-creative.

CONSENSUS LAYER: PROOF OF WORK AND PROOF OF STAKE

Another technological standardization question in blockchain today concerns PoW and PoS, rival technologies within the *consensus* sub-layer of the blockchain stack. This debate is much discussed, and those looking for a technical introduction to the topic can find a more in-depth resource than this chapter; but the "one-sentence philosophy," courtesy of Vitalik Buterin, is that PoS security comes from "putting up economic value at loss," where in PoW, "security comes from burning energy."[530] Even more simply, PoW is difficult to break because it takes a lot of computing power, where PoS is costly to break because you would lose your "damage deposit" if you did so.

The debate between these two standards has centered around what many see as a fatal flaw of PoW: energy consumption. Definitionally, PoW mandates miners to waste energy on useless computation to make faking transactions costly—but it may be *too* good at achieving that goal. According to the Bitcoin Energy Consumption Index, the Bitcoin network currently consumes 729 kilowatt hours of electricity for every transaction, which equates to 50.4 terawatt hours of electricity annually.[531] The latter is enough to power the country of Portugal for an entire year.[532] That's problematic, considering that nearly all blockchain protocols today use PoW.[533]

Vitalik is actively working to develop PoS today, but the challenges in his way are immense. There's the technical challenge, of course, which has led to a delay of nearly two years in the release of the new consensus mechanism.[534] But perhaps even greater is the political challenge—people have a lot of money tied up in the system, and recent vulnerabilities have left them skeptical of a change as large as a new consensus mechanism. In fact, the first planned upgrade to PoS in Ethereum won't (can't) even be a full rollout; at the end of this year, the "Constantinople" update will still keep Ethereum 99 percent PoW, with one out of every 100 blocks validated by PoS.[535]

In a sense, proposing and executing technological updates is less a decision of which technology is better and more a choice of how to allocate the time and brainpower of core developers—it's like budgeting, not judging, because these challenges are so immense and the technical knowledge so concentrated in the hands of a few. A change as large as PoS likely could never take hold in Ethereum if Vitalik himself were not brought in—consider how difficult it has been to change something as simple as the block size in Bitcoin without Satohi's leadership. Knowing that, another lesson of technical standardization follows: standardization in the decentralized world looks more like politics than business.

ECONOMIC LAYER: THE ERC-20 TOKEN STANDARD

Perhaps no standardization effort to date has generated as much value as the ERC-20 token standard interface (Figure 8-3).[536] It's deceptively simple, as are most blockchain innovations: just six functions and two events enabled over 367,000 independent projects to raise their own capital, and the top 100 of them have a combined market cap of $232.6 billion.[537]

FIGURE 8-3

THE ERC-20 STANDARD SPECIFICATION

```
contract ERC20Interface {
function totalSupply() public constant returns (uint);
function balanceOf(address tokenOwner) public constant returns (uint
balance);
function allowance(address tokenOwner, address spender) public constant
returns (uint remaining);
function transfer(address to, uint tokens) public returns (bool success);
function approve(address spender, uint tokens) public returns (bool
success);
function transferFrom(address from, address to, uint tokens) public
returns (bool success);
event Transfer(address indexed from, address indexed to, uint tokens);
event Approval(address indexed tokenOwner, address indexed spender, uint
tokens);
}
```

Source: "ERC-20 Token Standard," TheEthereum.Wiki, accessed 12 Feb. 2018, used under CC0 1.0.

Ethereum's token standard was introduced in November 2015 in an Ethereum improvement proposal (EIP) for solving a pressing problem—the "token" was perhaps the most common type of Ethereum smart contract, but because no two were made alike, third-party applications (e.g., wallets and exchanges) could not promise universal token support. The proposed standard, in the words of Ethereum Foundation member Alex van de Sande, would be the "bare minimum" to ensure token interoperability, more or less a token API.[538] The Ethereum core developers approved the standard in May 2017, and it was officially merged into the Ethereum master code in September of that year.[539]

The EIP approval process, however, is more challenging than the above may let on. It's process that is notoriously opaque; perhaps the process for Ethereum standardization has itself never been standardized explicitly. The closest that the core developers have to codification is the following, found in the core developer meeting minutes: "[Standards] are approved/finalized once the community members who benefit from the [standard] and thought leaders come together, agree on [a spec], and implement the spec."[540]

To assess the difficulty of passing through this black box, however, we need look no further than its output: As of March 2021, the community had officially formalized only 69 EIPs and 18 ERCs that seek to define a specific standard of Ethereum usage.[541] Technology standards exist within the blockchain world, but they're very hard to come by. It takes a lot to win—which implies the question: how are winners chosen?

RECOMMENDATIONS FOR STANDARDIZING DECENTRALIZED TECHNOLOGY

If we've learned anything from following the checkered history of technological standards development and the ever-shifting sands of semantic standardization, it's that the old rules don't always work to help us navigate in this new, decentralized world.

So, in the spirit of our search for standards, here are some recommendations for blockchain technologists, academics, and organizations alike. They are bound to have exceptions but may assist in the paradigmatic shift that now seems necessary: away from the centralized mainland and into the decentralized frontier.

RELENTLESSLY PURSUE *SEMANTIC* STANDARDIZATION

The correct time and place to drive toward technological standardization is anyone's guess—but for semantic standardization, the answer is clearly "here and now." The blockchain community needs a standard like OSI, with which cataloging, organizing, and communicating advances in this new technology might be made significantly easier.

Why aren't such communicative advancements more popular today? Perhaps because of the conflation of technological and semantic standardization. When I reached out to several blockchain technologists asking them to comment on a piece about the blockchain stack, they scoffed. "There isn't just one," one (who wished to remain anonymous) argued, "so defining a stack would be meaningless."

That answer is entirely fair in the technological world—there are too many architectural variations and too many use cases to suggest that one particular blockchain protocol will triumph over all comers in all cases—but it's misguided to equate that fact with the effort to make sure those protocols all use the same words.

The community needs a semantic standard, which is why Joel Monegro's article was so influential; we hope that our analysis above can serve as the next step in our definition of the blockchain *lingua franca*.

MAKE BETTER STUFF THAN ANYONE ELSE

That's what you need to do if you still want to win a technological standards war. The blockchain community is ideologically decentralized enough that the system works more or less democratically—remember, before Ethereum's hard fork after the DAO, a vote was held. Yes, some animals (e.g., Vitalik Buterin) are more equal than others. For the most part, the blockchain ecosystem feels more purely meritocratic than how winners are chosen in today's corporate world of back-alley dealings and handshakes among the elite. (As some may remember from the New York Agreement, those strong-arm strategies don't always work in the cypherpunk-influenced, decentralized world.)[542]

Want to win a standards war? Make technology that solves a real problem (and avoids the ideological land mines that litter the blockchain community today), demonstrate to the community that it works—technologically, politically, economically, historically, cryptographically, etc.—get the community's buy-in, and roll it out to the world. Much easier said than done.

It is the hope of every serious technologist and the strong belief of many that, over time, the Bitcoin hype will die out and the truly world-changing blockchain solutions will be here to stay. If you want to be a winner, play the long game.

RECONSIDER WAGING A DECENTRALIZED STANDARDS WAR

Hal Varian, chief economist of Google, and Carl Shapiro, former deputy assistant attorney general for economics in the antitrust division of the US Department of Justice, wrote that standards war winners were those who had "intellectual-property rights, control over an installed base of users, ability to innovate, first-mover advantages, manufacturing abilities, strength in complements, and brand name and reputation."[543]

In the early days of the Internet, foundational standards were established because there was not yet a massive installed base of nontechnical consumers to weigh in—just patient, usually government or university-housed actors developing in (relative) peace.

In the decentralized world, however, so much attention—and so many dollars—flowed into the system before technological standards were able to take hold, which massively complicated technical decisions as economics, politics, and morality became as important as technology in determining the best path forward.

In the end, blockchain is radically different from the modern corporate world in numerous ways:

- Everything is open source and intellectual property is, at best, very difficult to protect.
- Tokens allow upstarts to bypass adverse small-network effects.
- Innovative first movers who "move fast and break things" may risk billions of dollars of capital to technological vulnerabilities.
- Everything is digital and relies more on brainpower than sheer pocketbook depth.
- There have been no killer apps (other than perhaps bitcoin) that we could or should complement.
- Trying to win points by branding is generally a transparent announcement that a token is a technological nightmare and/or outright scam.

Blockchain is a protocol-level disruption, which means we're not in Kansas anymore. Even the most tried-and-true rules of the old world, like Metcalfe's law, may not apply—and so players would be wise to reconsider trying to win a standards war just because that's what's always worked to generate outsized economic returns.

RESIST CONSENSUS FOR CONSENSUS' SAKE

We will conclude this section with an evergreen tale from the old world—one to drive home the message that consensus for consensus' sake isn't always a good idea. In the early days of the Internet, a fierce battle raged between the Internet protocol and asynchronous transfer mode (ATM) technology. Just as with WiMAX before, the fact that you've never heard of the latter is evidence of how this story will end—but it's important to understand why one became the technological standard for a new era and the other faded away into obscurity.

The full answer undoubtedly includes a more complex analysis of cost and interoperability, but we'd contend that one major reason for the downfall of ATM technology was its blind pursuit of compromise: that's how ATM packets ended up with a *prime number* of bits—53.[544] Eric Fair, a software engineer and developer at The NetBSD Foundation, explains:

> The Computer Networking People involved in the specification of ATM wanted to use 64-byte cells, to move data with low overhead. The Telephony People wanted to use 32-byte cells, to be able to subdivide their network bandwidth on a very fine grain. Naturally, they split the difference (48 bytes) and then added the five-byte header, resulting in a cell size that pleases no one.[545]

As blockchain technology moves toward technological standardization—or at least engages in very intense arguments about block size, scaling, and more—let's not repeat this mistake of the past.

 ## CONCLUSIONS

What began as a white paper has—in fewer than ten years—become a massive ecosystem complete with futuristic technology, vicious politics, and previously inconceivable amounts of financial wealth and economic activity.

The next ten years of blockchain technology promise to have higher stakes and greater challenges. We'll see the rise of scaling solutions in the *consensus* layer like PoS and in the *overlay protocols* like the Lightning Network. We'll face governance challenges as more contentious ideas like the DAO fork force themselves into the mainstream. And we'll continue to clarify the language we use to describe a class of technologies that could soon be worth collectively trillions of dollars.

At the risk of sounding trite, a short-term answer to these challenges may just be good, old-fashioned humility. As Brian Behlendorf said, "This stuff is ready to leave the lab as the Web was in 1993 or 1994. Let's make sure we don't encumber it with too much legacy and too much commitment."[546] In other words, we shouldn't rush into standardization—or worry about developing killer apps—until we have enough time to find great solutions to the hairy, lower-layer problems that we face.

We are still in the early innings of blockchain technology, and success in the years to come will largely depend on how well we handle the challenges—and the opportunities—of technological and semantic standardization.

ACRONYMS AND ABBREVIATIONS

4G, fourth generation wireless

5G, fifth generation network

ACORNS, autonomous communication over redundant nodes

AI, artificial intelligence

API, application programming interface

App, application

ARPANET, Advanced Research Projects Agency Network

ASIC, application specific integrated circuits

ATM, asynchronous transfer mode

B2B, business to business

B2C, business to consumer

BCH, bitcoin cash

BMW, Bayerische Motoren Werke

BTC, bitcoin

CAGR, compound annual growth rate

CAV, connected and autonomous vehicle

CDC, Centers for Disease Control and Prevention

CERN, Conseil Européen pour la Recherche Nucléaire (European Organization for Nuclear Research)

CoAP, Constrained Application Protocol

DAG, directed acyclic graph

DAI, decentralized artificial intelligence

DAO, decentralized autonomous organization

Dapp, distributed application

DARPA, Defense Advanced Research Projects Agency

DDoS, distributed denial of service

DLT, distributed ledger technology

DNS, domain name system

DPoS, delegated proof of stake

DSA, digital signature algorithm

ECC, elliptic curve cryptography

EC-DSA, elliptic-curve digital signature algorithm

EIP, Ethereum improvement proposal

ERC, Ethereum request for comments

ETC, Ethereum classic

ETH, ether

ETSI, European Telecommunications Standards Institute

EV, electric vehicle

EVM, Ethereum Virtual Machine

eVTOL, electric vertical takeoff and landing

FTC, Federal Trade Commission

GDPR, European Union's General Data Protection Regulation

GM, General Motors

GPS, global positioning system

HSP, hidden subgroup problem

HTTP, hypertext transfer protocol

ICO, initial coin offering

IEEE, Institute of Electrical and Electronics Engineers

IEN, Internet Engineering Note

IoT, Internet of Things

IOTA, Internet of Things asset

IPFS, InterPlanetary File System

JSON ABI, JavaScript object notation application binary interface

KSI, keyless signature infrastructure

LPWAN, low power wide area network

LTE, Long-Term Evolution

LWE, learning with errors

M2M, machine to machine

MaaS, mobility as a service

MARCO, Microsoft Machine Reading Comprehension

MECE, mutually exclusive but collectively exhaustive

MIT, Massachusetts Institute of Technology, Cambridge, MA

ML, machine learning

MOBI, Mobile Open Blockchain Initiative

MQTT, message queuing telemetry transport

NGO, nongovernmental organization

NIST, National Institute of Standards and Technology

OSI, open systems interconnection

P2P, peer to peer

PKI, public key infrastructure

PoA, proof of authority

POC, proof of concept

Pod, personal online data

PoS, proof of stake

PoW, proof of work

QKD, quantum key distribution

QNRG, quantum random number generator

QR code, quick response code

Qubits, quantum bits

R&D, research and development

RFC, request for comment

RFID, radio frequency identification tag

RSA, the public-key encryption technology developed by Rivest, Shamir, and Adleman of RSA Data Security

SMTP, simple mail transfer protocol

Solid, social linked data

SSL, secure sockets layer

STEM, science, technology, engineering, and mathematics

TCP/IP, transmission control protocol/Internet protocol

UDP, user datagram protocol

URL, uniform resource locator (aka universal resource locator)

USN, universal sharing network

VC, venture capital

VPN, virtual private network

Wi-Fi, wireless fidelity

WiMAX, Worldwide Interoperability for Microwave Access

ABOUT THE BLOCKCHAIN RESEARCH INSTITUTE

Co-founded in 2017 by Don and Alex Tapscott, the Blockchain Research Institute is an independent, global think tank established to help realize the new promise of the digital economy. For five years now, we have been investigating the transformative and disruptive potential of distributed ledger technologies on business, government, and society.

Our syndicated research program, funded by major corporations and government agencies, aims to fill a large gap in the global understanding of blockchain protocols, applications, and ecosystems. We look at their strategic and operational implications for enterprise executives, supply chains, and industry verticals—including financial services, manufacturing, retail, energy and the climate crisis, technology, media and education, telecommunications, healthcare and the pandemic, public services and the institutions of democracy.

Our global team of blockchain experts focus on informing leaders of the economic opportunities and challenges of this nascent technology. Research areas include the transformation of industries, the enterprise, and government; the regulation of innovation and the use of data, digital currencies, and self-sovereign identities; and the convergence of blockchain, artificial intelligence, and the Internet of Things.

Deliverables include lighthouse cases, big idea white papers, research briefs, roundtable reports, infographics, videos, and webinars. Our findings are initially proprietary to our members, then released under a Creative Commons license to help achieve our mission. To find out more, please visit

blockchainresearchinstitute.org

ABOUT THE CONTRIBUTORS

VLAD GHEORGHIU

Vlad Gheorghiu is CEO, president, and co-founder of softwareQ Inc., which designs quantum software. He is also a research associate at the Institute for Quantum Computing at the University of Waterloo, working with Michele Mosca on theoretical aspects of quantum computation and post-quantum cryptography. He also collaborates on quantum risk assessments with evolutionQ Inc. Vlad is involved in the CryptoWorks21 Quantum-Safe Cryptographic Infrastructure Program and is a member of the ETSI Quantum-Safe Cryptography Standardization Group. He graduated from Carnegie Mellon University with a PhD in theoretical physics.

SERGEY GORBUNOV

Sergey Gorbunov is an assistant professor in the Cheriton School of Computer Science at the University of Waterloo. He is interested in building cryptographic primitives, protocols, and systems that enable new applications in untrusted and distributed environments. He received a PhD from MIT, where he was a Microsoft PhD fellow, and MSc and BSc from University of Toronto. His PhD dissertation, "Cryptographic Tools for the Cloud," won the 2015 George M. Sprowls Award for outstanding PhD thesis in computer science at MIT. Sergey was on the founding team of Algorand, where he led the cryptography group. He also spent time at IBM T.J. Watson Research Centre.

DOMINIQUE D. GUINARD

Dominique D. Guinard is co-founder and chief technology officer of EVRYTHNG, an IoT platform-as-a-service helping companies to run their business differently with real-time data from each product, from the factory to the consumer and beyond. He is also an advisory representative at W3C working group on IoT-related topics. Before that, Dom worked for SAP, taking an active role in their IoT strategy. Dom was also pioneering Web of Things research at ETH Zurich and MIT where he worked on his PhD. He has more than a decade of IoT experience working on projects for Oracle, the Auto-ID Labs, Nokia, and SAP. Dom authored two IoT books, *Building the Web of Things* and *Using the Web to Build the IoT*, as well as many scientific articles and book chapters. In 2011 and 2016, Dom was listed in the top 10 IoT thinkers by Postscapes. His PhD on the Web of Things received the ETH Medal in 2012.

CHRISTIAN KEIL

Christian Keil is chief of staff at Astranis Space Technologies Corporation, a start-up building next-generation Internet satellites. He also writes the *Silicon Valley Outsider*, a weekly newsletter for prospective entrepreneurs who live outside the San Francisco Bay Area. Previously, he founded and was CEO of drect.ly, an award-winning start-up that developed blockchain-native software for the telecom industry. Before drect.ly, Christian specialized in telecom strategy as a management consultant at Deloitte. He worked with numerous top telecoms in the United States, and his analytics and modeling work helped guide multi-billion-dollar spectrum-purchasing decisions in the spectrum incentive auction. Christian also worked with Deloitte's chief strategy officer to publish "Ecosystems Come of Age," Deloitte's flagship report that generated over 100 million media impressions in 2015. He earned his MBA at University of California-Berkeley.

ALAN MAJER

Alan Majer is founder and CEO of Good Robot. For the first half of his career, Alan worked as a technology researcher and writer, helping to identify cutting-edge technology and business innovations.

Today, Alan also works with new technologies hands on, exploring the potential of connected sensors and the Internet of Things, new display technologies, machine intelligence, robotics, and interactive interfaces. The result is exciting new opportunities to innovate and transform client experiences, and the ability to combine strategy and research activities with a real-world approach to their implementation. Alan is an active member of the local maker scene, frequenting spaces like HackLab.to and InterAccess, and he holds an MBA from McGill University.

DAVID MIRYNECH

David Mirynech is co-founder and chief executive officer of FanClub Sports Capital, a sports team investment platform that gives teams and minority limited partnerships access to liquidity and provides fans and investors a chance to own their favorite teams. Previously, he was the director of research at Exponential Capital & Markets, a global advisory firm and digital asset platform with broker dealer and secondary trading capabilities. Prior to ExC&M, Dave worked at Charlesway Corporation, a private equity firm based in Southern Ontario. He was the first employee and director of research at MLG Blockchain, a global venture creation and advisory firm with block-chain technology development and broker dealer capabilities. Dave founded the Blockchain Education Network at the University of Western Ontario and served as the president of the Ivey Business School Fintech Club. He now sits on the board of advisers of the Scotiabank Digital Banking Lab and attended the master's program at the Catlica Lisbon School of Business and Economics.

MICHELE MOSCA

Michele Mosca is CEO of evolutionQ Inc., which provides products and services for helping organizations to evolve their quantum-vulnerable systems and practices into quantum-safe ones.

He is a founder and professor at the Institute for Quantum Computing at the University of Waterloo, where he is also a professor of mathematics in the Department of Combinatorics and Optimization. He is a founding member of the Perimeter Institute for Theoretical Physics and the Canadian Institute for Advanced Research. To develop global standards in this domain, Michele helped to initiate the ETSI-IQC workshop series in quantum-safe cryptography. He leads research in quantum algorithms and quantum circuit synthesis and optimization as well.

BILL MUNSON

Bill Munson is director of research and policy analysis of Quantum-Safe Canada at the University of Waterloo, with a focus on cybersecurity. He works as part of a small team to undertake research into the quantum threat to Canada's critical digital systems and to drive timely and effective responses. He is also a research associate at the Institute for Quantum Computing.

DON TAPSCOTT

Don Tapscott is chief executive officer of the Tapscott Group, executive chairman of the Blockchain Research Institute, and one of the world's leading authorities on the impact of technology on business and society. He has authored more than 16 books, including *Wikinomics: How Mass Collaboration Changes Everything* (with Anthony Williams), which has been translated into over 25 languages. He coined the term, "The Digital Economy," in his 1994 book of that title, and many of his big ideas are part of the business vernacular today. In 2016, he co-authored *Blockchain Revolution: How the Technology Behind Bitcoin and Other Cryptocurrencies Is Changing the World* with Alex Tapscott. His new book, *Supply Chain Revolution: How Blockchain Technology Is Transforming the Digital Flow of Assets*, debuted as the "#1 New Release" in the commerce category on

Amazon.com in June 2020. In 2019, then-ranked as the #2 living business thinker, Don was inducted into the Thinkers50 Hall of Fame. He is an adjunct professor at INSEAD and former two-term chancellor of Trent University in Ontario.

MARK VAN RIJMENAM

Mark van Rijmenam is founder of Datafloq and Mavin. He is a highly sought-after international public speaker, a big data and blockchain strategist, and author of the bestselling book, *Think Bigger: Developing a Successful Big Data Strategy for Your Business* (AMACOM, 2014), as well as the books *Blockchain: Transforming Your Business and Our World* with Philippa Ryan (Routledge, 2018) and *The Organization of Tomorrow: How AI, Blockchain, and Analytics Turn Your Business into a Data Organization* (Routledge, 2019). He was named a global top 10 big data influencer and one of the most influential people working with blockchain. He holds a PhD in management from the University of Technology Sydney on how organizations should deal with big data, blockchain, and responsible artificial intelligence; and he is the publisher of the *f(x) = ex* newsletter read by thousands of executives.

ANJAN VINOD

Anjan Vinod is an investment analyst at ParaFi Capital, a former consultant at Blockchain at Berkeley, and a graduate of the Haas School of Business. He also worked at OPEN Platform, a blockchain infrastructure for applications, where he led product development and operations. OPEN raised a private round of financing from some of the top venture capital firms in the space including Draper Dragon and NEO Global Capital. Anjan's previous experiences include hedge funds, investment banking, and AT&T where he was involved with its IoT division.

ACKNOWLEDGMENTS

Special thanks to Ethan Buchman, Ian Jacobs, Rouven Heck, Shane Greenstein, Joe Lubin, Yvon Audette, Paritosh Gambhir, and Sir Tim Berners-Lee for shaping our thinking on saving the Web; to Andrew Tobin of Europe Evernym, David Knight of Terbine, Daniel Gasteiger of the Global Blockchain Business Council, and David Birch of Hyperion for their comments on big data and identity; to Lofred Madzou, Christos Oikonomou, Bob Tapscott, Henry Kim, George Polzer, and Toufi Saliba for their conversations about and generous feedback on distributed AI; to Dr. Joel Vogt for his review of the IoT material; to John Gerryts, Randy Cole, Chris Ballinger, Thomas A. Gardner, Karna Patel, Ashkay Sood, Kiran Malik, Noah Chait, and Samuel Zhang for their contributions to our autonomous vehicle research; to Stephan Tual for his candid discussion of Slock.it; and to John Schanck for very useful discussions regarding blockchain and quantum-resistant cryptography.

We thank the Blockchain Research Institute's members for their engagement in our programs: Accenture, Aon, Bank of Canada, Bell Canada, BPC Banking Technologies, Brightline (a Project Management Institute initiative), Canada Health Infoway, Canadian Imperial Bank of Commerce, Capgemini, Centrica, Cimcorp, Cisco Systems Inc., City of Toronto, the Coca-Cola Company, Deloitte, Delta Air Lines Inc., Depository Trust & Clearing Corporation, ExxonMobil Global Service Company, FedEx Corporate Services, Fidelity Investments Canada ULC, Government of Ontario, Gowling WLG, IBM, ICICI Bank, INSEAD, Interac, Intuit, ISED Canada, JumpStart, KPMG, Loblaw Companies, Manulife, Microsoft, MKS (Switzerland) SA, Moog, Nasdaq, Navigator, Ontario Ministry of Health and Long-Term Care, Orange, Philip Morris International Management, Procter & Gamble, PepsiCo, PNC Bank, Prophecy DeFi, Raymond Chabot Grant Thornton,

Reliance Industries, Revenu Québec, Salesforce, SAP SE, Standard Bank, Sun Life Financial, Tata Consultancy Services, Teck Resources, TELUS, Tencent, Thomson Reuters, TMX Group, University of Arkansas, University Health Network, University of Texas-Dallas, and WISeKey.

We are grateful for our pioneer members: Access Copyright, Attest Inc., Ava Labs, Blockchain Guru, Blockchain Technology Partners, Bloq, CarbonX, Cityzeen, Collider-X, Cosmos, Decentral Inc., EVRYTHNG, Huobi, Icon, Jumpstart, Liechtenstein Cryptoassets Exchange, LongHash, Matic, Medicalchain, Navigator Ltd., NEM Foundation, Numeracle, Ownum, Paycase Financial, PermianChain Technologies Inc., Polymath, SGInnovate, Shyft, Slant AG, Solve.Care, SpaceChain, Stride Africa, Sweetbridge, Telos Foundation, Veriphi, and YouBase.

Thanks, too, to our affiliate organizations and global partners: Alastria, BeinCrypto, Blockchain in Transport Alliance, Blockchain Industry Group, Blockchain Research Institute Nanjing, Blockwall Management (BRI Europe), BOSAGORA Foundation (BRI Korea), BRI Brazil, Chamber of Digital Commerce, Coalition of Automated Legal Applications, Enterprise Ethereum Alliance, Healthcare Information and Management Systems Society, Hyperledger hosted by The Linux Foundation, and InterWork Alliance, Konnect & Co (BRI Middle East), and the Standard Bank Group (BRI Africa).

Finally, we thank our Editor-in-Chief Kirsten Sandberg for creating a manuscript of all these research projects so that the whole is much greater than the sum of its parts.

NOTES

1. John Perry Barlow, "A Declaration of the Independence of Cyberspace," *Electronic Frontier Foundation*, Davos, Switzerland, 8 Feb. 1996. www.eff. org/cyberspace-independence, accessed 13 Nov. 2018.

2. Adrian Shahbaz, interviewed by CBC Radio, "Internet Freedom iIs Declining for 8th Straight Year, Says NGO Report," *CBC Radio*, CBC/ Radio-Canada, 9 Nov. 2018. www.cbc.ca/radio/spark/internet-freedom-is-declining-for-eighth-straight-year-report-says-1.4897623, accessed 14 Nov. 2018.

3. Solid, "Welcome to Solid," Inrupt Inc., n.d. solid.inrupt.com, accessed 14 Nov. 2018.

4. Guy Zyskind, Oz Nathan, and Alex "Sandy" Pentland, "Enigma: Decentralized Computation Platform with Guaranteed Privacy," White Paper, Massachusetts Institute of Technology, 10 June 2015. www. enigma.co/enigma_full.pdf, accessed 6 Dec. 2017.

5. Guy Zyskind, Oz Nathan, and Sandy Pentland, "Enigma."

6. Elizabeth M. Pierce, "Designing a Data Governance Framework to Enable and Influence IQ Strategy," Presentation, Proceedings of the MIT 2007 Information Quality Industry Symposium, Cambridge, MA, 19 July 2007. mitiq.mit.edu/IQIS/Documents/CDOIQS_200777/ Papers/01_08_1C.pdf, accessed 7 Dec. 2017.

7. Elizabeth M. Pierce, "Designing a Data Governance Framework."

8. Andrew J. Hawkins, "Uber and Lyft Drivers in California Sue to Overturn Prop 22 Ballot Measure," *The Verge*, Vox Media LLC, 12 Jan. 2021. www.theverge.com/2021/1/12/22227042/uber-lyft-prop-22-lawsuit-overturn-drivers-california, accessed 2 March 2021.

9. "Who Is Eva?" *Eva.coop*, Eva Global, 2019. eva.coop/index.php#about_us, accessed 29 July 2019.

10. Andrew J. Hawkins, "Uber and Lyft Are Getting Less Unprofitable, but COVID-19 Is Still a Drag on Their Business," *The Verge*, Vox Media Inc., 11 Feb. 2021. www.theverge.com/2021/2/11/22277043/uber-lyft-earnings-q4-2020-profit-loss-covid, accessed 2 March 2021.

11. Division of Viral Diseases, "What Rideshare, Taxi, Limo, and Other Passenger Drivers-for-Hire Need to Know about COVID-19," *CDC.gov*, National Center for Immunization and Respiratory Diseases, Centers for Disease Control and Prevention, updated 30 Jan. 2021. www.cdc.gov/ coronavirus/2019-ncov/community/organizations/rideshare-drivers-for-hire.html, accessed 2 March 2021.

12. Eugene Demaitre, "Four Robotics Applications Accelerated by COVID-19," *Robot Report*, WTWH Media LLC, 29 Dec. 2020. www. therobotreport.com/4-robotics-applications-accelerated-by-covid-19, accessed 2 March 2021.

13. Shannon Bauer, "Does UV Light Actually Disinfect and Kill Viruses?" *Beckman Laser Institute and Medical Clinic News*, University of California Irvine, 23 Sept. 2020. www.bli.uci.edu/does-uv-light-actually-disinfect-and-kill-viruses, accessed 2 March 2021.

14. Macy Bayern, "Autonomous Vehicles: How Seven Countries Are Handling the Regulatory Landscape," *Tech Republic*, ZDNet, a Red Ventures Co., 5 Feb. 2020. www.techrepublic.com/article/autonomous-vehicles-how-7-countries-are-handling-the-regulatory-landscape; and Harsha Vardhan, "Autonomous Robots Aid in Patrolling and Disinfecting COVID-19 Hit China," *Geospatial World*, Geospatial Media and Communications, 6 March 2020. www.geospatialworld.net/blogs/autonomous-robots-aid-in-patrolling-and-disinfecting-covid-19-hit-china, both accessed 3 March 2021.

15. Don Tapscott and Alex Tapscott, *Blockchain Revolution: How the Technology Behind Bitcoin and Other Cryptocurrencies Is Changing the World* (New York: Penguin Portfolio, 2018): 277. www.amazon.com/Blockchain-Revolution-Technology-Cryptocurrencies-Changing-dp-1101980141/dp/1101980141, accessed 6 Sept. 2020.

16. Steve Omohundro, interviewed by Don Tapscott and Kirsten Sandberg, 28 May 2015.

17. Masoud Mohseni, Peter Read, Hartmut Neven et al., Google's Quantum AI Laboratory, "Commercialize Quantum Technologies in Five Years," *Nature.com*, Macmillan Publishers Ltd., 3 March 2017. www.nature.com/news/commercialize-quantum-technologies-in-five-years-1.21583, accessed 18 Nov. 2017.

18. Jason Palmer, "Quantum technology Is Beginning to Come into Its Own," *The Economist*, Economist Newspaper Ltd., 9 March 2017. www.economist.com/news/essays/21717782-quantum-technology-beginning-come-its-own, accessed 18 Nov. 2017.

19. "The STEM Gap: Women and Girls in Science, Technology, Engineering and Math," *AAUW.org*, American Association of University Women, 2021. www.aauw.org/resources/research/the-stem-gap, accessed 8 March 2021.

20. Barry M. Leiner et al., "Brief History of the Internet," Internet Society, 1997. www.internetsociety.org/internet/history-internet/brief-history-internet, accessed 13 Nov. 2018.

21. Walter Isaacson, "The Two Original Sins of the Internet—and Why We Must Fix Them," Blog, Aspen Institute, 4 March 2016. www.aspeninstitute.org/blog-posts/the-two-original-sins-of-the-internet-and-why-we-must-fix-them, accessed 14 Nov. 2018.

22. Walter Isaacson, "The Two Original Sins of the Internet."

23. Kevin Featherly, "ARPANET," *Encyclopædia Britannica*, Encyclopædia Britannica Inc., 28 Nov. 2016. www.britannica.com/topic/ARPANET, accessed 13 Nov. 2018.

24. Vint Cerf and Robert Kahn, "A Protocol for Packet Network Intercommunication," *IEEE Transactions on Communications* 22, no. 5 (May 1974): 637–648. www.cs.princeton.edu/courses/archive/fall06/cos561/papers/cerf74.pdf; Information Sciences Institute, "Transmission Control Protocol," RFC-793, Protocol Specification, DARPA Internet Program, DARPA, Sept. 1981. www.rfc-editor.org/rfc/rfc793.html; Vint Cerf, "The Catenet Model for Internetworking," Information Processing Techniques Office, Defense Advanced Research Projects Agency, IEN 48, July 1978. www.rfc-editor.org/ien/ien48.txt; and Information Sciences Institute, "Internet Protocol," RFC-791, Protocol Specification, DARPA Internet Program, DARPA, Sept. 1981. www.rfc-editor.org/rfc/rfc791, all accessed 2 March 2021.

25. Mae Anderson, "How 'Net Neutrality' Became a Hot-Button Issue," *AP News*, Associated Press, 5 Nov. 2018. apnews.com/article/2ceb089790944682bfda0e40f4a1424c; and Jerome H. Saltzer, David D. Clark, and David P. Reed, "End-to-End Arguments in System Design," *Second International Conference on Distributed Computing Systems*, IEEE, Paris, France, 8–10 April 1981, pp. 509–512. web.mit.edu/Saltzer/www/publications/endtoend/endtoend.pdf, both accessed 2 March 2021.

26. Barry M. Leiner et al., "Brief History of the Internet." Mockapetris was at the University of Southern California Information Sciences Institute.

27. Tim Berners-Lee, Roy Fielding, and Henrik Frystyk, "Hypertext Transfer Protocol (HTTP/1.0)," RFC-1945, Network Working Group, Internet Engineering Task Force, May 1996. tools.ietf.org/html/rfc1945, accessed 2 March 2021.

28. "History: Tim Berners Lee," *BBC*, British Broadcasting Corp., n.d. www.bbc.co.uk/history/historic_figures/berners_lee_tim.shtml, accessed 14 Nov. 2018.

29. "Our Story," Mosaic Communications Corp., 1994. home.mcom.com/MCOM/mcom_docs/backgrounder_docs/index.html; David Shedden, "The First Commercial Web Browser, Netscape Navigator, Is Released in 1994," *Today in Media History*, Poynter Institute, 13 Oct. 2014. www.

poynter.org/reporting-editing/2014/today-in-media-history-the-first-commercial-web-browser-netscape-navigator-is-released-in-1994, both accessed 2 March 2021.

30. Shane Greenstein, interviewed via telephone by Christian Keil, 8 Sept. 2018.

31. Olivia Solon, "Tim Berners-Lee on the Future of the Web: 'The System Is Failing,'" *The Guardian*, Guardian News & Media Ltd., 15 Nov. 2017. www.theguardian.com/technology/2017/nov/15/tim-berners-lee-world-wide-web-net-neutrality, accessed 14 Nov. 2018.

32. "What Is Solid?" The Solid Project, Massachusetts Institute of Technology, n.d. solid.mit.edu, accessed 14 Nov. 2018.

33. "Data Protection and Online Privacy," *Your Europe*, European Union, modified 6 July 2018. europa.eu/youreurope/citizens/consumers/internet-telecoms/data-protection-online-privacy/index_en.htm, accessed 14 Nov. 2018.

34. André Staltz, "A Plan to Rescue the Web from the Internet," *Stalz.com*, Andre 'Staltz' Medeiros, 18 Dec. 2017. staltz.com/a-plan-to-rescue-the-web-from-the-internet.html; LastPass, LogMeIn Inc., n.d. www.lastpass.com; and RSA, "Secure Access Transformed," RSA Security LLC, n.d. www.rsa.com/en-us/products/rsa-securid-suite, both accessed 14 Nov. 2018.

35. Tim Berners-Lee, "WorldWideWeb—Summary," *W3.org*, World Wide Web Consortium, n.d. www.w3.org/History/19921103-hypertext/hypertext/WWW/Summary.html, accessed 14 Nov. 2018.

36. Shane Greenstein, interviewed via telephone by Christian Keil, 8 Sept. 2018.

37. Shane Greenstein, interviewed via telephone by Christian Keil, 8 Sept. 2018.

38. Martyn Williams, "How the Internet Works in North Korea," *Slate*, Slate Group, 28 Nov. 2016. www.slate.com/articles/technology/future_tense/2016/11/how_the_internet_works_in_north_korea.html; "Freedom on the Net 2017," *FreedomHouse.org*, Freedom House Inc., n.d. freedomhouse.org/report/freedom-net/freedom-net-2017; and Beina Xu and Eleanor Albert, "Media Censorship in China," *CFR.org*, Council on Foreign Relations, updated 17 Feb. 2017. www.cfr.org/backgrounder/media-censorship-china, all accessed 14 Nov. 2018.

39. Amar Toor, "Two-Thirds of the World's Internet Users Live Under Government Censorship: Report," *The Verge*, Vox Media Inc., 14 Nov. 2016. www.theverge.com/2016/11/14/13596974/internet-freedom-decline-global-censorship-facebook-whatsapp; John Mason, "VPN

Usage, Data Privacy & Internet Penetration Statistics," *TheBestVPN.com*, Godmode OÜ, updated 29 March 2018. thebestvpn.com/vpn-usage-statistics, both accessed 14 Nov. 2018.

40. Adrian Shahbaz, "Freedom on the Net 2018: The Rise of Digital Authoritarianism," *FreedomHouse.org*, Freedom House Inc., 9 Nov. 2018. freedomhouse.org/report/freedom-net/freedom-net-2018/rise-digital-authoritarianism, accessed 14 Nov. 2018.

41. World Wide Web Foundation, "Women's Rights Online Digital Gender Gap Audit," *WebFoundation.org*, 9 Sept. 2016. webfoundation.org/research/digital-gender-gap-audit, accessed 14 Nov. 2018.

42. Yana Watson Kakar et al., "Women and the Web," *Intel.com*, Intel Corp., 2012. www.intel.com/content/dam/www/public/us/en/documents/pdf/women-and-the-web.pdf, accessed 14 Nov. 2018.

43. "Our Mission," *Internet.org* by Facebook, n.d. info.internet.org/en/mission, accessed 14 Nov. 2018.

44. Olivia Solon, "'It's Digital Colonialism': How Facebook's Free Internet Service Has Failed Its Users," *The Guardian*, Guardian News & Media Ltd., 27 July 2017. www.theguardian.com/technology/2017/jul/27/facebook-free-basics-developing-markets, accessed 14 Nov. 2018.

45. "Vitalik Buterin about Ethereum, Smart Contracts, and Himself," *ForkLog.net*, 17 May 2016. forklog.net/vitalik-buterin-about-ethereum-smart-contracts-and-himself, accessed 14 Nov. 2018.

46. J. Weston Phippen, "Why Turkey Blocked Access to Wikipedia," *The Atlantic*, Atlantic Monthly Group, 29 April 2017. www.theatlantic.com/news/archive/2017/04/turkey-blocks-wikipedia/524859, accessed 14 Nov. 2018.

47. IPFS Team, "Uncensorable Wikipedia on IPFS," *IPFS Starlog Blog*, Protocol Labs, 5 April 2017. blog.ipfs.io/24-uncensorable-wikipedia, accessed 24 Feb. 2021.

48. David Foster Wallace, "This Is Water," Commencement Speech, Kenyon College, Gambier, Ohio, 2005. bulletin-archive.kenyon.edu/x4280.html, accessed 14 Nov. 2018.

49. Tim Berners-Lee, "Frequently Asked Questions," World Wide Web Consortium, n.d. www.w3.org/People/Berners-Lee/FAQ.html, accessed 14 Nov. 2018.

50. Kevin Kelly, "We Are the Web," *WIRED*, Condé Nast, 1 Aug. 2005. www.wired.com/2005/08/tech, accessed 14 Nov. 2018.

51. Ethan Buchman, interviewed via telephone by Christian Keil, 24 July 2018.

52. Adam Rosenberg, "Facebook's App Has Been Collecting Android Phone Data for Years on Some Devices," *Mashable*, Mashable Inc., 25 March 2018. mashable.com/2018/03/25/facebook-android-phone-call-data-gathering/#Q82epN8NasqM, accessed 14 Nov. 2018.

53. Max A. Cherney, "Facebook Stock Drops Roughly 20%, Loses $120 Billion in Value after Warning that Revenue Growth Will Take a Hit," *MarketWatch*, MarketWatch Inc., 26 July 2018. www.marketwatch.com/story/facebook-stock-crushed-after-revenue-user-growth-miss-2018-07-25, accessed 14 Nov. 2018.

54. Tim Berners-Lee, interviewed by Don Tapscott, from transcript created 1 Aug. 2013.

55. Imgur, "A Peek into Your Future. This Is Mexico, No Net Neutrality," Imgur Inc., 31 Aug. 2017. imgur.com/yYobj7x, accessed 14 Nov. 2018.

56. Stratecast, "Net Neutrality: Impact on the Consumer and Economic Growth," *Consumer Communication Services* 4, no. 13, Frost & Sullivan, May 2010. internetinnovation.org/files/special-reports/Impact_of_Net_Neutrality_on_Consumers_and_Economic_Growth.pdf, accessed 14 Nov. 2018.

57. "Web Inventor Sir Tim Berners-Lee Responds to US Net Neutrality Threat," *WebFoundation.org*, World Wide Web Foundation, 26 April 2017. webfoundation.org/2017/04/sir-tim-berners-lee-responds-to-us-net-neutrality-threat, accessed 14 Nov. 2018.

58. "Web Inventor Sir Tim Berners-Lee Responds to US Net Neutrality Threat."

59. Ethan Buchman, interviewed via telephone by Christian Keil, 24 July 2018.

60. "Online Casinos—Price and Transparency," Edgeless, n.d. www.edgeless.io/company, accessed 14 Nov. 2018.

61. "The adChain Registry," *MetaX*, MetaXchain, n.d. metax.io/products/adchain_registry, accessed 14 Nov. 2018.

62. NYIAX, NYIAX Inc., n.d. www.nyiax.com; MAD, "Privacy Is the New Frontier," MAD Network, n.d. madnetwork.io; and John Shinal, "By One Measure, Facebook just Made Alphabet CFO Ruth Porat Look like a Spendthrift," *CNBC.com*, NBCUniversal, updated 27 July 2017. www.cnbc.com/2017/07/27/facebook-vs-alphabet-operating-margin.html, all accessed 14 Nov. 2018.

63. Jessica Stillman, "Seven Jeff Bezos Quotes that Outline the Secret to Success," *Inc.com*, Manuseto Ventures, 7 May 2014. www.inc.com/jessica-

stillman/7-jeff-bezos-quotes-that-will-make-you-rethink-success.html, accessed 14 Nov. 2018.

64. Olaf Carlson-Wee, "The Future Is a Decentralized Internet," *TechCrunch*, Verizon Media, 8 Jan. 2017. techcrunch.com/2017/01/08/the-future-is-a-decentralized-internet, accessed 14 Nov. 2018.

65. "Token Tracker," *Etherscan.io*, n.d. etherscan.io/tokens, accessed 5 June 2021.

66. Don Tapscott and Imogen Heap, "Blockchain Could Be Music's Next Disruption," *HuffPost*, BuzzFeed Inc., 26 Sept. 2016, updated 6 Dec. 2017. www.huffingtonpost.com/don-tapscott/blockchain-could-be-music_b_12199748.html, accessed 15 Nov. 2018. Schwartz was speaking to members of the International Literary and Artistic Association in 2015.

67. Joel Monegro, "Fat Protocols," *USV.com*, Union Square Ventures, 8 Aug. 2016. www.usv.com/blog/fat-protocols, accessed 14 Nov. 2018.

68. Don Tapscott and Alex Tapscott, "Preface to the Paperback Edition," *Blockchain Revolution: How the Technology Behind Bitcoin and Other Cryptocurrencies Is Changing the World* (New York: Portfolio Penguin, 2018): xliv–lii.

69. Rouven Heck, interviewed via telephone by Christian Keil, 12 Oct. 2018.

70. Irving Wladawsky-Berger, "Blockchain and the Promise of an Open, Decentralized Internet," *Wall Street Journal*, Dow Jones & Co., 23 Feb. 2018. blogs.wsj.com/cio/2018/02/23/blockchain-and-the-promise-of-an-open-decentralized-internet, accessed 13 Nov. 2018.

71. Joseph Lubin, interviewed via telephone by Don Tapscott and Christian Keil, 9 Oct. 2018.

72. The thief was an employee of Anthem's Medicare insurance coordinator, LaunchPoint Ventures. Brendan Pierson, "Anthem to Pay Record $115 Million to Settle US Lawsuits over Data Breach," *Reuters*, Thomson Reuters, 23 June 2017. www.reuters.com/article/us-anthem-cyber-settlement/anthem-to-pay-record-115-million-to-settle-u-s-lawsuits-over-data-breach-idUSKBN19E2ML; Jessica Davis, "Anthem: Insider Theft Exposes Data of 18,000 Medicare Members," *Healthcare IT News*, HIMSS Media, 26 Oct. 2017. www.healthcareitnews.com/news/anthem-insider-theft-exposes-data-18000-medicare-members, both accessed 22 Feb. 2018; and Tapscott and Tapscott, *Blockchain Revolution*, pp. xliv–lii.

73. "The World's Most Valuable Resource Is No Longer Oil, but Data," *The Economist*, Economist Newspaper Ltd., 6 May 2017. www.economist.com/news/leaders/21721656-data-economy-demands-new-approach-antitrust-rules-worlds-most-valuable-resource, accessed 14 Nov. 2018.

74. Tony Bradley, "Security Experts Weigh in on Massive Data Breach of 150 Million MyFitnessPal Accounts," *Forbes.com*, Forbes Media LLC, 30 March 2018. www.forbes.com/sites/tonybradley/2018/03/30/security-experts-weigh-in-on-massive-data-breach-of-150-million-myfitnesspal-accounts/#6012b4cf3bba; "The Equifax Data Breach," *FTC.gov*, Federal Trade Commission, n.d. www.ftc.gov/equifax-data-breach; and Taylor Armerding, "The 17 Biggest Data Breaches of the 21st Century," *CSO*, IDG Communications Inc., 26 Jan. 2018. www.csoonline.com/article/2130877/data-breach/the-biggest-data-breaches-of-the-21st-century.html, all accessed 14 Nov. 2018.

75. Josh Keller, K.K. Rebecca Lai, and Nicole Perlroth, "How Many Times Has Your Personal Information Been Exposed to Hackers?" *New York Times*, New York Times Co., updated 3 Oct. 2017. www.nytimes.com/interactive/2015/07/29/technology/personaltech/what-parts-of-your-information-have-been-exposed-to-hackers-quiz.html, accessed 14 Nov. 2018.

76. Yuval Noah Harari, "Why Technology Favors Tyranny," *The Atlantic*, Atlantic Media Co., 13 Sept. 2018. www.theatlantic.com/magazine/archive/2018/10/yuval-noah-harari-technology-tyranny/568330, accessed 13 Nov. 2018. The piece was adapted from Harari's *21 Lessons for the 21st Century*.

77. Sean Gallagher, "Turkish Government Agency Spoofed Google Certificate 'Accidentally,'" *Ars Technica*, Condé Nast, 4 Jan. 2013. arstechnica.com/information-technology/2013/01/turkish-government-agency-spoofed-google-certificate-accidentally, accessed 14 Nov. 2018.

78. Eric Hughes, "A Cypherpunk's Manifesto," *Activism.net*, 3 March 1993. www.activism.net/cypherpunk/manifesto.html, accessed 13 Nov. 2018.

79. Samuel Falkon, "Cypherpunks and the Rise of Cryptocurrencies," *The Start-Up Blog*, A Medium Corp., 25 Nov. 2017. medium.com/swlh/cypherpunks-and-the-rise-of-cryptocurrencies-899011538907, accessed 13 Nov. 2018.

80. "Unmasked: What 10 Million Passwords Reveal about the People Who Choose Them," WP Engine, n.d. wpengine.com/unmasked, accessed 14 Nov. 2018.

81. Chris McCann, "12 Graphs that Show just How Early the Cryptocurrency Market Is," *Medium Economy*, A Medium Corp., 7 May 2018. medium.com/@mccannatron/12-graphs-that-show-just-how-early-the-cryptocurrency-market-is-653a4b8b2720, accessed 13 Nov. 2018.

82. Ethan Buchman, interviewed via telephone by Christian Keil, 24 July 2018.

83. Brian Forde, "Using Blockchain to Keep Public Data Public," *Harvard Business Review*, Harvard Business School Publishing Co., 31 March 2017. hbr.org/2017/03/using-blockchain-to-keep-public-data-public, accessed 14 Nov. 2018.

84. *Blockchain for Government Blog*, IBM Corp., n.d. www.ibm.com/blogs/blockchain/category/blockchain-for-government, accessed 14 Nov. 2018.

85. "Open Data Blockchains: The Missing Link for Opening Up Governments?" *European Data Portal*, European Union, 10 Oct. 2017. www.europeandataportal.eu/en/news/open-data-blockchains-missing-link-opening-governments, accessed 14 Nov. 2018.

86. Joseph Lubin, interviewed via telephone by Don Tapscott and Christian Keil, 9 Oct. 2018.

87. Brandon Goldman, "Why I'm Bullish on BAT and the Brave Browser in 2018," *Hacker Noon*, Artmap Inc., 19 Jan. 2018. hackernoon.com/why-im-bullish-on-bat-and-the-brave-browser-in-2018-8e2cbc0ce420, accessed 14 Nov. 2018.

88. Stephen Shankland, "Ad-blocking Brave Browser to Give Crypto-payment Tokens to Everyone," *CNET*, CBS Interactive Inc., 19 April 2018. www.cnet.com/news/ad-blocking-brave-browser-to-give-crypto-payment-tokens-to-everyone, accessed 14 Nov. 2018.

89. Mihai Alisie, email to Hilary Carter, 11 April 2018.

90. Solid is an acronym for "socially linked data." Sir Tim Berners-Lee serves as Inrupt's CTO. David Weinberger, "How the Father of the World Wide Web Plans to Reclaim It from Facebook and Google," *Digital Trends*, Designtechnica Corporation, 10 Aug. 2016. www.digitaltrends.com/web/ways-to-decentralize-the-web; Solid, "Get a Pod and a WebID"; and "About," *Inrupt*, Inrupt Inc., n.d. inrupt.com/about, all accessed 17 Jan. 2021.

91. "About Solid," Solid Project, n.d. solidproject.org/about; "Get a Pod and a WebID," Solid Project, n.d. solidproject.org/users/get-a-pod, both accessed 19 Jan. 2021.

92. Steve Lohr, "He Created the Web. Now He's Out to Remake the Digital World," *The New York Times*, New York Times Co., 10 Jan. 2021. www.nytimes.com/2021/01/10/technology/tim-berners-lee-privacy-internet.html, accessed 19 Jan. 2021.

93. Katrina Brooker, "Exclusive: Tim Berners-Lee Tells Us His Radical New Plan to Upend the World Wide Web," *Fast Company*, Mansueto Ventures, 29 Sept. 2018. www.fastcompany.com/90243936/exclusive-tim-berners-lee-tells-us-his-radical-new-plan-to-upend-the-world-wide-web, accessed 13 Nov. 2018.

94. Rouven Heck, interviewed via telephone by Christian Keil, 12 Oct. 2018.

95. Joseph Lubin, interviewed via telephone by Don Tapscott and Christian Keil, 9 Oct. 2018.

96. Christian Keil, "Standardized and Decentralized? Rethinking the Blockchain Technology Stack," foreword by Don Tapscott, Blockchain Research Institute, 28 Feb. 2018.

97. Madison Malone Kircher, "Who Knows Me Best: Google or Facebook?" *New York*, Vox Media LLC, 13 Dec. 2017. nymag.com/selectall/2017/12/how-to-see-what-data-facebook-and-google-have-about-you.html, accessed 14 Nov. 2018.

98. Ethan Buchman, interviewed via telephone by Christian Keil, 24 July 2018.

99. Yvon A. Audette, email to Paritosh Gambhir, Hilary Carter, and Kirsten Sandberg, 26 Sept. 2018.

100. Howard Shrobe, "It Is Possible to Design a Computer System that Can't Be Hacked: MIT Researcher," *CNBC.com*, NBCUniversal, 30 Sept. 2016. www.cnbc.com/2016/09/30/it-is-possible-to-design-a-computer-system-that-cant-be-hacked-commentary.html, accessed 13 Nov. 2018.

101. Doug Laney, "3D Data Management: Controlling Data Volume, Velocity, and Variety," File 949, *Application Delivery Strategies*, META Group Inc., 6 Feb. 2001, p. 70. blogs.gartner.com/doug-laney/files/2012/01/ad949-3D-Data-Management-Controlling-Data-Volume-Velocity-and-Variety.pdf, accessed 1 Dec. 2017.

102. "Cisco Visual Networking Index Forecast Projects 13-Fold Growth in Global Mobile Internet Data Traffic from 2012–2017," Press Release, Cisco Systems Inc., 5 Feb. 2013. newsroom.cisco.com/press-release-content?articleId=1135354; "Cisco Visual Networking Index 2017," Cisco Systems Inc., 7 Feb. 2017. www.cisco.com/c/en/us/solutions/service-provider/visual-networking-index-vni/vni-infographic.html; "Cisco Visual Networking Index: Global Mobile Data Traffic Forecast Update, 2016–2021," Cisco Systems Inc., 7 Feb. 2017, updated 28 March 2017. www.cisco.com/c/en/us/solutions/collateral/service-provider/visual-networking-index-vni/mobile-white-paper-c11-520862.html; and "The Zettabyte Era: Trends and Analysis," Cisco Systems Inc., 7 June 2017. www.cisco.com/c/en/us/solutions/collateral/service-provider/visual-networking-index-vni/vni-hyperconnectivity-wp.html, all accessed 1 Dec. 2017.

103. David Reinsel, John Gantz, and John Rydning, "Data Age 2025: The Evolution of Data to Life-Critical," White Paper, International Data

Corp., Sponsored by Seagate, April 2017. www.seagate.com/files/www-content/our-story/trends/files/Seagate-WP-DataAge2025-March-2017.pdf, accessed 5 Dec. 2017.

104. David Reinsel, John Gantz, and John Rydning, "Data Age 2025: The Evolution of Data to Life-Critical," p. 2.

105. Tim Brown, "Design Thinking," *Harvard Business Review*, Harvard Business School Publishing Co., June 2008, pp. 84–92. hbr.org/2008/06/design-thinking; Gerard George, Martin R. Haas, and Alex Pentland, "From the Editors: Big Data and Management," *Academy of Management Journal* 57, no. 2 (2014): 321–326. Academy of Management, aom.org/uploadedFiles/Publications/AMJ/Apr_2014_FTE.pdf, both accessed 6 Dec. 2017.

106. Dominic Barton and David Court, "Making Advanced Analytics Work for You," *Harvard Business Review*, Harvard Business School Publishing Co., Oct. 2012, pp. 78–83. hbr.org/2012/10/making-advanced-analytics-work-for-you, accessed 5 Dec. 2017.

107. Randy Bean, "Just Using Big Data Isn't Enough Anymore," *Harvard Business Review*, Harvard Business School Publishing Co., 9 Feb. 2016. hbr.org/2016/02/just-using-big-data-isnt-enough-anymore; and Phillip Long and George Siemens, "Penetrating the Fog: Analytics in Learning and Education," *EDUCAUSE Review* 46, no. 5 (12 Sept. 2011): 30. er.educause.edu/articles/2011/9/penetrating-the-fog-analytics-in-learning-and-education, both accessed 5 Dec. 2017.

108. Jay R. Galbraith, "Organizational Design Challenges Resulting from Big Data," *Journal of Organization Design* 3, no. 1 (10 April 2014): 2–13. papers.ssrn.com/sol3/papers.cfm?abstract_id=2458899; Robert L. Grossman and Kevin P. Siegel, "Organizational Models for Big Data and Analytics," *Journal of Organization Design* 3, no. 1 (2014): 20–25. www.jorgdesign.net/article/viewFile/9799/14689; Martin Berner, Enrico Graupner, and Alexander Maedche, "The Information Panopticon in the Big Data Era," *Journal of Organization Design* 3, no. 1 (2014): 14–19. www.jorgdesign.net/article/view/9736; and Michael E. Porter and James E. Heppelmann, "How Smart, Connected Products Are Transforming Companies," *Harvard Business Review*, Harvard Business School Publishing Co., Oct. 2015, pp. 53–71. hbr.org/2015/10/how-smart-connected-products-are-transforming-companies, all accessed 5 Dec. 2017.

109. Jessica Davis, "Big Data, Analytics Sales Will Reach $187 Billion by 2019," *InformationWeek*, Informa PLC, 24 May 2016. www.informationweek.com/big-data/big-data-analytics/big-data-analytics-sales-will-reach-$187-billion-by-2019/d/d-id/1325631, accessed 24 Aug. 2017.

110. Avita Katal, Mohammad Wazid, and R.H. Goudar, "Big Data: Issues, Challenges, Tools and Good Practices," *Contemporary Computing (IC3),* 2013 Sixth International Conference, IEEE, Noida, India, IEEE *Xplore* (13797966), 8–10 Aug. 2013. ieeexplore.ieee.org/document/6612229, accessed 6 Dec. 2017.

111. Anne Cleven and Felix Wortmann, "Uncovering Four Strategies to Approach Master Data Management," *System Sciences (HICSS),* 2010 43rd Hawaii International Conference, IEEE, Honolulu, HI, IEEE *Xplore* (112058910), 5–8 Jan. 2010; and Vijay Khatri and Carol V. Brown, "Designing Data Governance," *Communications of the ACM* 53, no. 1 (Jan. 2010): 148–152. cacm.acm.org/magazines/2010/1/55771-designing -data-governance/abstract, accessed 6 Dec. 2017.

112. Paul J. Lim, "Equifax's Massive Data Breach Has Cost the Company $4 Billion So Far," *Time*, TIME USA LLC, 12 Sept. 2017. time.com/ money/4936732/equifaxs-massive-data-breach-has-cost-the-company-4- billion-so-far, accessed 8 Dec. 2017.

113. Jennifer Surane and Anders Melin, "Equifax CEO Richard Smith Resigns after Uproar over Massive Hack," *Bloomberg News,* Bloomberg Finance LP, 26 Sept. 2017. www.bloomberg.com/news/ articles/2017-09-26/equifax-ceo-smith-resigns-barros-named-interim- chief-after-hack, accessed 8 Dec. 2017.

114. Anders Melin, "Three Equifax Managers Sold Stock before Cyber Hack Revealed," *Bloomberg News,* Bloomberg Finance LP, 7 Sept. 2017, updated 8 Sept. 2017. www.bloomberg.com/news/articles/2017-09-07/ three-equifax-executives-sold-stock-before-revealing-cyber-hack; and Stacy Cowley, "Equifax Faces Mounting Costs and Investigations from Breach," *New York Times*, New York Times Co., 9 Nov. 2017. www. nytimes.com/2017/11/09/business/equifax-data-breach.html, both accessed 8 Dec. 2017.

115. Stephen Cobb, "10 Things to Know about the October 21 IoT DDoS Attacks," *We Live Security*, 24 Oct. 2016. www.welivesecurity. com/2016/10/24/10-things-know-october-21-iot-ddos-attacks, accessed 4 July 2017.

116. Mikko Hyppönen and Linus Nyman, "The Internet of (Vulnerable) Things: On Hypponen's Law, Security Engineering, and IoT Legislation," *Technology Innovation Management Review* 7, no. 4 (April 2017): 5. helda.helsinki.fi/dhanken/bitstream/handle/123456789/168083/ HypponenNyman_TIMReview_April2017.pdf, accessed 6 Dec. 2017.

117. Mikko Hyppönen and Linus Nyman, "The Internet of (Vulnerable) Things," p. 5.

118. Prabaharan Poornachandran et al., "Internet of Vulnerable Things: Detecting Vulnerable SOHO Routers," *Information Technology*, 2015 International Conference, IEEE, Bhubaneswar, India, IEEE *Xplore* (15886578), 21–23 Dec. 2015.

119. "Retailer Sees Actionable Insights in First Week," Skullcandy Case Study, Sisense, 2017. www.sisense.com/case-studies/skullcandy, accessed 25 Aug. 2017.

120. Bernard Marr, "IoT and Big Data at Caterpillar: How Predictive Maintenance Saves Millions of Dollars," *Forbes.com*, Forbes Media LLC, 7 Feb. 2017. www.forbes.com/sites/bernardmarr/2017/02/07/iot-and-big-data-at-caterpillar-how-predictive-maintenance-saves-millions-of-dollars, accessed 25 Aug. 2017.

121. Avi Dan, "How Avis Budget Group Uses Data to Drive Its Marketing," *Forbes.com*, Forbes Media LLC, 26 March 2014. www.forbes.com/sites/avidan/2014/03/26/how-avis-budget-group-uses-data-to-drive-its-marketing, accessed 1 Dec. 2017.

122. Jonathan Taplin, *Move Fast and Break Things: How Facebook, Google, and Amazon Cornered Culture and Undermined Democracy* (New York: Little, Brown and Co., 2017).

123. Volker Benndorf and Hans-Theo Normann, "The Willingness to Sell Personal Sell Personal Data," *The Scandinavian Journal of Economics*, 2017. onlinelibrary.wiley.com/doi/10.1111/sjoe.12247/abstract; Alexander Tsesis, "The Right to Erasure: Privacy, Data Brokers, and the Indefinite Retention of Data," *Wake Forest Law Review* 49 (2014): 433. lawecommons.luc.edu/cgi/viewcontent.cgi?article=1502&context=facpubs, both accessed 6 Dec. 2017.

124. Rick O. Gilmore, "From Big Data to Deep Insight in Developmental Science," *Wiley Interdisciplinary Reviews: Cognitive Science* 7, no. 2 (24 Jan. 2016): 112–126. onlinelibrary.wiley.com/doi/10.1002/wcs.1379/abstract, accessed 6 Dec. 2017. See also Charles Arthur, "Facebook Emotion Study Breached Ethical Guidelines, Researchers Say," *The Guardian*, Guardian News & Media Ltd., 30 June 2014. www.theguardian.com/technology/2014/jun/30/facebook-emotion-study-breached-ethical-guidelines-researchers-say, accessed 1 Dec. 2017.

125. Jonathan Taplin, *Move Fast and Break Things*.

126. Don Tapscott, "Blockchain: The Ledger that Will Record Everything of Value to Humankind," *WEForum.org*, World Economic Forum, 5 July 2017. www.weforum.org/agenda/2017/07/blockchain-the-ledger-that-will-record-everything-of-value, accessed 1 Dec. 2017.

127. Corinne Reichert, "Telstra Launches Smart Home Devices and Pricing," *ZDNet*, Red Ventures, 15 Nov. 2016. www.zdnet.com/article/telstra-launches-smart-home-devices-and-pricing, accessed 7 Sept. 2017.

128. Ben Dickson, "How Blockchain Can Change the Future of IoT," *VentureBeat*, 20 Nov. 2016. venturebeat.com/2016/11/20/how-blockchain-can-change-the-future-of-iot, accessed 7 Sept. 2017.

129. David Swan, "Telstra Revs Up Start-Up Batch," *Australian Business Review*, 9 Feb. 2017. www.theaustralian.com.au/business/technology/telstra-revs-up-fresh-startup-batch/news-story/fd50c65e35f3ff2b2a6c719f0fdd9da0, accessed 7 Sept. 2017.

130. Corinne Reichert, "Telstra Launches Smart Home Devices and Pricing."

131. Corinne Reichert, "Telstra Explores Blockchain, Biometrics to Secure Smart Home IoT Devices," *ZDNet*, Red Ventures, 22 Sept. 2016. www.zdnet.com/article/telstra-explores-blockchain-biometrics-to-secure-smart-home-iot-devices, accessed 7 Sept. 2017.

132. Stephanie Weagle, "Financial Impact of Mirai DDoS Attack on Dyn Revealed in New Data," Corero Network Security, 21 Feb. 2017. www.corero.com/blog/797-financial-impact-of-mirai-ddos-attack-on-dyn-revealed-in-new-data.html, accessed 1 Dec. 2017.

133. Corinne Reichert, "Telstra Explores Blockchain, Biometrics to Secure Smart Home IoT Devices."

134. Justin Lee, "Telstra Testing Blockchain, Biometrics to Secure IoT Smart Home Devices," *Biometric Update*, 26 Sept. 2016. www.biometricupdate.com/201609/telstra-testing-blockchain-biometrics-to-secure-iot-smart-home-devices, accessed 7 Sept. 2017.

135. Corinne Reichert, "Telstra Explores Blockchain, Biometrics to Secure Smart Home IoT Devices"; Justin Lee, "Telstra Testing Blockchain, Biometrics to Secure IoT Smart Home Devices"; and Reenita Das, "Does Blockchain Have a Place in Healthcare?" *Forbes.com*, Forbes Media LLC, 8 May 2017. www.forbes.com/sites/reenitadas/2017/05/08/does-blockchain-have-a-place-in-healthcare, accessed 7 Sept. 2017.

136. National Research Council et al., ed. Stephen E. Fienberg, Margaret E. Martin, and Miron L. Straf, *Sharing Research Data* (Washington, DC: National Academy Press, 1985).

137. Mark van Rijmenam, *Think Bigger: Developing a Successful Big Data Strategy for Your Business* (New York: AMACOM, 2014).

138. Ryan Joe, "Coming in 2018: Comcast Hopes to Spur Data Sharing with Blockchain Technology," *AdExchanger*, 20 June 2017. adexchanger.

com/data-exchanges/coming-2018-comcast-hopes-spur-data-sharing-blockchain-technology, accessed 31 Aug. 2017.

139. "Comcast Collaborates with Industry Partners on Blockgraph Software to Jumpstart the Use of Secure Data Sharing for Advanced TV Advertising," Comcast Corp. Press Release, Business Wire Inc., 21 Dec. 2018. www.businesswire.com/news/home/20181221005530/en/Comcast-Collaborates-Industry-Partners-Blockgraph-Software-Jumpstart, accessed 15 Feb. 2019.

140. "Fujitsu Develops Blockchain-based Software for a Secure Data Exchange Network," Press Release, Fujitsu Ltd., 5 June 2017. www.fujitsu.com/global/about/resources/news/press-releases/2017/0605-01.html, accessed 6 Dec. 2017.

141. David Knight, interviewed by Mark van Rijmenam, 4 May 2017.

142. David Sønstebø, "IOTA Data Marketplace," *Iota Blog*, 28 Nov. 2017. blog.iota.org/iota-data-marketplace-cb6be463ac7f, accessed 11 Dec. 2017.

143. Zeljko Panian, "Some Practical Experiences in Data Governance," *World Academy of Science, Engineering, and Technology* 62 (2010): 939–946. citeseerx.ist.psu.edu/viewdoc/download?doi=10.1.1.190.6948&rep=rep1&type=pdf, accessed 24 Feb. 2021.

144. Vijay Khatri and Carol V. Brown, "Designing Data Governance": 148–152.

145. Ibrahim Alhassan, David Sammon, and Mary Daly, "Data Governance Activities: An Analysis of the Literature," *Journal of Decision Systems* 25, no. sup1 (2016): 64–75. www.tandfonline.com/doi/full/10.1080/1246012 5.2016.1187397, accessed 22 Feb. 2021.

146. Paul P. Tallon, "Corporate Governance of Big Data: Perspectives on Value, Risk, and Cost," *Computer* 46, no. 6 (2013): 32–38. IEEE, ieeexplore.ieee.org/document/6519236, accessed 22 Feb. 2021.

147. Kristin Wende, "A Model for Data Governance-Organizing Accountabilities for Data Quality Management," Conference Paper, 18th Australasian Conference on Information Systems (ACIS 2007), Toowoomba, Australia, 5–7 Dec. 2007. www.alexandria.unisg.ch/67284, accessed 6 Dec. 2016.

148. Anne Cleven and Felix Wortmann, "Uncovering Four Strategies to Approach Master Data Management."

149. Anne Cleven and Felix Wortmann, "Uncovering Four Strategies to Approach Master Data Management."

150. Jude Umeh, "Blockchain Double Bubble or Double Trouble?" *ITNOW* 58, no. 1 (March 2016): 58–61. academic.oup.com/itnow/article-abstract/58/1/58/2392029, accessed 24 Feb. 2021.

151. James Condos, William H. Sorrell, and Susan L. Donegan, "Blockchain Technology: Opportunities and Risks," Vermont State Legislature, 15 Jan. 2016. legislature.vermont.gov/assets/Legislative-Reports/blockchain-technology-report-final.pdf, accessed 6 Dec. 2017.

152. Kristin Wende, "A Model for Data Governance-Organizing Accountabilities."

153. Alex Hern, "Google's DeepMind Plans Bitcoin-Style Health Record Tracking for Hospitals," *The Guardian*, Guardian News & Media Ltd., 9 March 2017. www.theguardian.com/technology/2017/mar/09/google-deepmind-health-records-tracking-blockchain-nhs-hospitals, accessed 3 Dec. 2017.

154. Cade Metz, "Google DeepMind's Untrendy Play to Make the Blockchain Actually Useful," *WIRED*, Condé Nast, 11 March 2017. www.wired.com/2017/03/google-deepminds-untrendy-blockchain-play-make-actually-useful, accessed 6 Dec. 2017.

155. Craig Mundie, "Privacy Pragmatism: Focus on Data Use, Not Data Collection," *Foreign Affairs*, March–April 2014. www.foreignaffairs.com/articles/2014-02-12/privacy-pragmatism, accessed 3 Dec. 2017.

156. Alex Pentland, *Social Physics: How Good Ideas Spread—The Lessons from a New Science* (New York: Penguin Press, 2014).

157. George Slefo, "Comcast Says Marketers Can Make TV Ad Buys with Blockchain Tech," *AdAge*, Crain Communications, 20 June 2017. adage.com/article/digital/comcast-marketers-make-tv-ad-buys-blockchain-tech/309486, accessed 1 Dec. 2017.

158. Mike Gault, "Implementing Data Governance at Internet Scale," *Guardtime*, 28 Feb. 2014. guardtime.com/blog/implementing-data-governance-at-internet-scale, accessed 17 Oct. 2017; and Ahto Buldas, Andres Kroonmaa, and Risto Laanoja, "Keyless Signatures' Infrastructure: How to Build Global Distributed Hash-Trees," Build Global Distributed Hash-Trees," Lecture Notes, Nordic Conference on Secure IT Systems, Springer, Berlin, Heidelberg, 2013. doi.org/10.1007/978-3-642-41488-6_21, accessed 6 Dec. 2017.

159. Mike Gault, "Implementing Data Governance at Internet Scale."

160. Eric Piscini et al., "Blockchain & Cyber Security: Let's Discuss," *Performance Magazine* 24 (29 May 2017). Deloitte Ireland, www2.deloitte.com/content/dam/Deloitte/lu/Documents/financial-services/

performancemagazine/articles/lu-blockchain-and-cybersecurity-lets-discuss-092017.pdf, accessed 6 Dec. 2017.

161. Richard Kissel, ed., "Glossary of Key Information Security Terms," Internal Report 7298r2, National Institute of Standards and Technology Interagency, May 2013. nvlpubs.nist.gov/nistpubs/ir/2013/NIST. IR.7298r2.pdf, accessed 6 Dec. 2017.

162. Kelly McLaughlin, "Google and Facebook Fall for $100 Million Phishing Scam: Internet Giants Are Duped into Sending Cash to Lithuanian Conman," *Daily Mail*, Associated Newspapers Ltd., 28 April 2017. www.dailymail.co.uk/~/article-4455652/index.html, accessed 29 April 2017.

163. Omri Barzilay, "Three Ways Blockchain Is Revolutionizing Cybersecurity," *Forbes.com*, Forbes Media LLC, 21 Aug. 2017. www.forbes.com/sites/omribarzilay/2017/08/21/3-ways-blockchain-is-revolutionizing-cybersecurity, accessed 18 Oct. 2017.

164. "Publications: Technology, Peace, Conflict," Danube Tech GmbH, 2017. danubetech.com/download.html, accessed 6 Dec. 2017. See also Markus Sabadello, "A Universal Resolver for Self-Sovereign Identifiers," *DIF Blog*, Decentralized Identity Foundation, 1 Nov. 2017. medium.com/decentralized-identity/a-universal-resolver-for-self-sovereign-identifiers-48e6b4a5cc3c, accessed 1 Dec. 2017.

165. Jill Richmond, "Advancing Cybersecurity with Blockchain Technology," *Nasdaq.com*, Nasdaq Inc., 26 April 2017. www.nasdaq.com/article/advancing-cybersecurity-with-blockchain-technology-cm780007, accessed 1 Dec. 2017.

166. Omri Barzilay, "Three Ways Blockchain Is Revolutionizing Cybersecurity."

167. Richard Kissel, ed., "Glossary of Key Information Security Terms."

168. David Treat et al., "Blockchain Security Made Simple," Accenture, 2017. www.accenture.com/t20170215T065935Z__w__/us-en/_acnmedia/PDF-43/Accenture-Blockchain-POV.pdf, accessed 6 Dec. 2017.

169. David Treat et al., "Blockchain Security Made Simple."

170. Richard Kissel, ed., "Glossary of Key Information Security Terms."

171. Tim Berners-Lee, "Re-decentralizing the Web—Some Strategic Questions," Keynote Address, Free Video Download, The Internet Archive, 8 June 2016. archive.org/details/DWebSummit2016_Keynote_Tim_Berners_Lee, accessed 6 Dec. 2017.

172. Jonathan Taplin, *Move Fast and Break Things*; Jamie Doward and Alice Gibbs, "Did Cambridge Analytica Influence the Brexit Vote and the US

Election?" *The Guardian,* Guardian News & Media Ltd., 4 March 2017. www.theguardian.com/politics/2017/mar/04/nigel-oakes-cambridge-analytica-what-role-brexit-trump, accessed 4 Sept. 2017.

173. Zhangxi Lin, Andrew B. Whinston, and Shaokun Fan, "Harnessing Internet Finance with Innovative Cyber Credit Management," *Financial Innovation* 1, no. 5 (9 June 2015). doi.org/10.1186/s40854-015-0004-7, accessed 6 Dec. 2017.

174. Zennon Kapron, "Measuring Credit: How Baidu, Alibaba and Tencent May Succeed Where Facebook Failed," *Forbes.com,* Forbes Media LLC, 17 March 2017. www.forbes.com/sites/zennonkapron/2016/03/17/measuring-credit-how-baidu-alibaba-and-tencent-may-succeed-where-facebook-failed, accessed 4 Sept. 2017.

175. "Just Spend," *The Economist,* Economist Newspaper Ltd., 17 Nov. 2016. www.economist.com/news/finance-and-economics/21710292-chinas-consumer-credit-rating-culture-evolving-fastand-unconventionally-just, accessed 4 Sept. 2017.

176. Celia Hatton, "China 'Social Credit': Beijing Sets Up Huge System," *BBC News,* British Broadcasting Corp., 26 Oct. 2015. www.bbc.com/news/world-asia-china-34592186, accessed 4 Sept. 2017.

177. Celia Hatton, "China 'Social Credit': Beijing Sets Up Huge System."

178. Masha Borak, "China's Social Credit System: AI-driven Panopticon or Fragmented Foundation for a Sincerity Culture?" *TechNode,* TechNode Global, 23 Aug. 2017. technode.com/2017/08/23/chinas-social-credit-system-ai-driven-panopticon-or-fragmented-foundation-for-a-sincerity-culture, accessed 4 Sept. 2017.

179. Cheang Ming, "FICO with Chinese Characteristics: Nice Rewards, but Punishing Penalties," *CNBC.com,* NBCUniversal, 16 March 2017, updated 17 March 2017. www.cnbc.com/2017/03/16/china-social-credit-system-ant-financials-sesame-credit-and-others-give-scores-that-go-beyond-fico.html, accessed 4 Sept. 2017.

180. Cheang Ming, "FICO with Chinese Characteristics."

181. Cheang Ming, "FICO with Chinese Characteristics."

182. David Birch, interviewed by Mark van Rijmenam, 24 April 2017.

183. David Birch, interviewed by Mark van Rijmenam, 24 April 2017.

184. "Our Solution: Streamlining Digital Identity," Cambridge Blockchain, 2017. www.cambridge-blockchain.com/news/category/Press-Release, accessed 6 Dec. 2017.

185. Daniel Gasteiger, interviewed by Mark van Rijmenam, 24 April 2017.

186. Lee Rainie, "The State of Privacy in Post-Snowden America," Pew Research Center, Pew Charitable Trusts, 21 Sept. 2016. www.pewresearch.org/fact-tank/2016/09/21/the-state-of-privacy-in-america, accessed 19 Oct. 2017.

187. Natasha Singer, "Sharing Data, but Not Happily," *New York Times*, New York Times Co., 4 June 2015. www.nytimes.com/2015/06/05/technology/consumers-conflicted-over-data-mining-policies-report-finds.html; and Martha C. White, "Credit-Card Fine Print Is Too Smart for Most Americans," *Time*, TIME USA LLC, 8 Sept. 2016. time.com/money/4481284/credit-card-agreements-fine-print, both accessed 19 Oct. 2017.

188. Deborah Bothun, Matthew Lieberman, and Anand S. Rao, "Bot.Me: A Revolutionary Partnership: How AI Is Pushing Man and Machine Closer Together," Consumer Intelligence Series, *PwCArtificialIntelligence.com*, PricewaterhouseCoopers International, 2017. pwcartificialintelligence.com, accessed 24 Feb. 2021.

189. Deborah Bothun, Matthew Lieberman, and Anand S. Rao, "Bot.Me: A Revolutionary Partnership."

190. "What Consumers Really Think about AI," *Pega.com*, n.d. www1.pega.com/system/files/resources/2017-11/what-consumers-really-think-of-ai-infographic.pdf, accessed 8 Aug. 2018.

191. Louis Columbus, "10 Charts that Will Change Your Perspective on Artificial Intelligence's Growth," *Forbes.com*, Forbes Media LLC, 12 Jan. 2018. www.forbes.com/sites/louiscolumbus/2018/01/12/10-charts-that-will-change-your-perspective-on-artificial-intelligences-growth/#371a41124758, accessed 24 Aug. 2018.

192. "Outlook on Artificial Intelligence in the Enterprise," *NarrativeScience.com*, Feb. 2019. narrativescience.com/wp-content/uploads/2019/02/Research-Report_Outlook-on-AI-for-the-Enterprise.pdf, accessed 4 March 2019.

193. John Markoff, "Computer Wins on *Jeopardy!* Trivial, It's Not," *New York Times*, New York Times Co., 16 Feb. 2011. www.nytimes.com/2011/02/17/science/17jeopardy-watson.html, accessed 7 March 2019.

194. "Korean Air Is Using Watson to Search Vast Amounts of Data to Improve Operational Efficiency and On-Time Performance," IBM Corp., n.d. www.ibm.com/watson/stories/airlines-with-watson, accessed 28 Aug. 2018.

195. "Machine Learning on AWS," Amazon Web Services, Amazon Inc., n.d. aws.amazon.com/machine-learning, accessed 28 Aug. 2018.

196. Google to Acquire Nest," Announcement, Alphabet, 13 Jan. 2014. abc.xyz/investor/news/releases/2014/0113.html, accessed 28 Aug. 2018.

197. "Amazon.com to Acquire Kiva Systems Inc.," Announcement, Amazon Inc., 19 March 2012. SEC, www.sec.gov/Archives/edgar/data/1018724/000119312512122135/d318297dex991.htm, accessed 28 Aug. 2018.

198. "The World's Most Valuable Resource Is No Longer Oil, but Data," *The Economist*, Economist Newspaper Ltd., 6 May 2017. www.economist.com/leaders/2017/05/06/the-worlds-most-valuable-resource-is-no-longer-oil-but-data, accessed 5 Sept. 2018.

199. Sumeet Santani, "Why Data Is the New Oil," *Infospace*, Syracuse University iSchool, 26 Feb. 2018. ischool.syr.edu/infospace/2018/02/26/why-data-is-the-new-oil, accessed 9 Sept. 2018.

200. Dylan Curran, "Are You Ready? Here Is All the Data Facebook and Google Have on You," *The Guardian*, Guardian News & Media, 30 March 2018. www.theguardian.com/commentisfree/2018/mar/28/all-the-data-facebook-google-has-on-you-privacy, accessed 9 Sept. 2018.

201. Tom Simonite, "Some Start-ups Use Fake Data to Train AI," *WIRED*, Condé Nast, 25 April 2018. www.wired.com/story/some-startups-use-fake-data-to-train-ai, accessed 15 Sept. 2018.

202. Steven Russolillo, "Initial Coin Offerings Surge Past $4 Billion—and Regulators Are Worried," *Wall Street Journal*, Dow Jones & Co., 14 Dec. 2017. www.wsj.com/articles/initial-coin-offerings-surge-past-4-billionand-regulators-are-worried-1513235196, accessed 25 Sept. 2018.

203. Satoshi Nakamoto, "Bitcoin: A Peer-to-Peer Electronic Cash System," White Paper, *Bitcoin.org*, 1 Nov. 2008. www.bitcoin.org/bitcoin.pdf, accessed 20 Sept. 2018.

204. Maria Korolov, "AI's Biggest Risk Factor: Data Gone Wrong," *CIO.com*, IDG Communications, 13 Feb. 2018. www.cio.com/article/3254693/artificial-intelligence/ais-biggest-risk-factor-data-gone-wrong.html, accessed 21 Sept. 2018.

205. Emel Aktas and Yuwei Meng, "An Exploration of Big Data Practices in Retail Sector," *Logistics* 1, no. 2 (12 Dec. 2017): 1–28. MDPI, www.mdpi.com/2305-6290/1/2/12, accessed 24 Sept. 2018.

206. Bob Tapscott, interviewed in person by Anjan Vinod, 14 May 2018.

207. Brigham Hyde, "Five Predictions for AI and Real-World Data in Oncology," *Forbes Technology Council*, Forbes Media LLC, 14 Aug. 2018.

www.forbes.com/sites/forbestechcouncil/2018/08/14/five-predictions-for-ai-and-real-world-data-in-oncology/#67a3d77441ec, accessed 2 Dec. 2018.

208. Bob Tapscott, interviewed in person by Anjan Vinod, 14 May 2018.

209. Bob Tapscott, interviewed in person by Anjan Vinod, 14 May 2018.

210. Besir Kurtulmus and Kenny Daniel, "Trustless Machine Learning Contracts; Evaluating and Exchanging Machine Learning Models on the Ethereum Blockchain," *Algorithmia*, Algorithmia Research, 26 Feb. 2018. algorithmia.com/research/ml-models-on-blockchain, accessed 15 Sept. 2018.

211. Wessel Reijers, Fiachra O'Brolcháin, and Paul Haynes, "Governance in Blockchain Technologies & Social Contract Theories," *Ledger Journal* 1 (2016): 134–151. www.ledgerjournal.org/ojs/index.php/ledger/article/download/62/51, accessed 24 Sept. 2018.

212. Henry Kim, interviewed via telephone by Anjan Vinod, 29 May 2018.

213. Ponemon Institute and McDermott Will & Emery, "The Race to GDPR: A Study of Companies in the United States and Europe," *International Association of Privacy Professionals*, April 2018. iapp.org/media/pdf/resource_center/Ponemon_race-to-gdpr.pdf, accessed 26 Sept. 2018.

214. Vitalik Buterin, "DAOs, DACs, DAs and More: An Incomplete Terminology Guide," *Ethereum Blog*, Ethereum, 6 May 2014. blog.ethereum.org/2014/05/06/daos-dacs-das-and-more-an-incomplete-terminology-guide, accessed 27 Sept. 2018.

215. Marc Peter Deisenroth and Jun Wei Ng, "Distributed Gaussian Processes," *Journal of Machine Learning Research*, Workshop and Conference Proceedings 37 (2015): 1–10. Proceedings of Machine Learning Research Press, proceedings.mlr.press/v37/deisenroth15.pdf, accessed 7 March 2019. Presented at the 32nd International Conference on Machine Learning in Lille, France, this paper builds on Gaussian processes (GP), which "allow for flexible modelling without specifying low-level assumptions in advance." GPs have helped to advance such areas as active learning, data visualization, geostatistics, optimization, robotics and reinforcement learning, and spatiotemporal modelling. Distributed Gaussian process models are "conceptually simple: they split the data set into small pieces, train GP experts jointly, and subsequently combine individual predictions to an overall computation."

216. George Polzer, interviewed online by Anjan Vinod, 3 Dec. 2018.

217. Toufi Saliba, interviewed via telephone by Anjan Vinod, 16 Nov. 2018.

218. Toufi Saliba, interviewed via telephone by Anjan Vinod, 16 Nov. 2018.

219. George Polzer, interviewed online by Anjan Vinod, 3 Dec. 2018.

220. Dominique Guinard and Vlad Trifa, *Building the Web of Things* (Shelter Island, NY: Manning, 2016).

221. Kevin Ashton, "That 'Internet of Things' Thing," *RFID Journal,* 22 June 2009. www.rfidjournal.com/articles/view?4986, accessed 21 Oct. 2017.

222. Dominique Guinard and Vlad Trifa, *Building the Web of Things.*

223. Ahmed Banafa, "Three Major Challenges Facing IoT," *IEEE IoT Newsletter,* 14 March 2017. iot.ieee.org/newsletter/march-2017/three-major-challenges-facing-iot, accessed 21 Oct. 2017.

224. This is where the new version of IP, IPv6 helps as its address space is far bigger than the number of things ever produced by mankind.

225. Paul Baran, "Introduction to Distributed Communications Networks," Part I, *On Distributed Communications*, Memorandum RM-3420-PR, US Air Force Project Rand, Rand Corporation, Aug. 1964. www.rand.org/pubs/research_memoranda/RM3420.html, accessed 3 March 2021.

226. Veena Pureswaran and Paul Brody, "Device Democracy Saving the Future of the Internet of Things," IBM Corp., July 2015. www-935.ibm.com/services/multimedia/GBE03620USEN.pdf; Ahmed Banafa, "Three Major Challenges Facing IoT," *IEEE IoT Newsletter,* 14 March 2017. iot.ieee.org/newsletter/march-2017/three-major-challenges-facing-iot; Konstantinos Christidis and Michael Devetsikiotis, "Blockchains and Smart Contracts for the Internet of Things," *IEEE Access* 4 (10 May 2016): 2292–2303. *IEEE* Xplore *Digital Library* (16042927), all accessed 21 Oct. 2017.

227. Dominique Guinard, "The Politics of the Internet of Things," *TechCrunch,* Verizon Media, 25 Feb. 2016. techcrunch.com/2016/02/25/the-politics-of-the-internet-of-things, accessed 21 Oct. 2017.

228. Dominique Guinard, Vlad Trifa, and Erik Wilde, "A Resource Oriented Architecture for the Web of Things," Swiss Federal Institute of Technology, Zurich, 2010. www.vs.inf.ethz.ch/publ/papers/dguinard-things-2010.pdf; Dominique Guinard and Vlad Trifa, "Towards the Web of Things: Web Mashups for Embedded Devices," Proceedings of the International World Wide Web Conference, Madrid, Spain, 20 April 2009. webofthings.org/wp-content/uploads/2009/03/guinard_physical_mashups_cameraready.pdf, all accessed 23 Oct. 2017.

229. "Web of Things Standards," *WebofThings.org,* n.d. webofthings.org/standards, accessed 21 Oct. 2017.

230. See IPFS.io/#why. Juan Benet, "IPFS, Content Addressed, Versioned, P2P File System," InterPlanetary File System, 2017. github.com/ipfs/papers/raw/master/ipfs-cap2pfs/ipfs-p2p-file-system.pdf, accessed 21 Oct. 2017.

231. Sean Gallagher, "IoT Garage Door Opener Maker Bricks Customer's Product after Bad Review," *Ars Technica*, Condé Nast, 4 April 2017. arstechnica.com/information-technology/2017/04/iot-garage-door-opener-maker-bricks-customers-product-after-bad-review, accessed 21 Oct. 2017.

232. James Halliwell, "How the Blockchain Will Change FMCG," *The Grocer*, 26 April 2017. www.thegrocer.co.uk/supply-chain/how-the-blockchain-will-change-fmcg/551923.article, accessed 21 Oct. 2017.

233. James Halliwell, "How the Blockchain Will Change FMCG."

234. "About Provenance," *Provenance.org*, Project Provenance Ltd., n.d. www.provenance.org/about, accessed 8 March 201.

235. Modum, n.d. modum.io; Information from European Union Institutions, Bodies, Offices, and Agencies, "Guidelines of 5 November 2013 on Good Distribution Practice of Medicinal Products for Human Use GDP 2013/C 343/01," *Official Journal of the European Union*, 5 Nov. 2013. eur-lex.europa.eu/LexUriServ/LexUriServ.do?uri=OJ:C:2013:343:0001:0014:EN:PDF, both accessed 21 Oct. 2017.

236. Alex Preston, "The Death of Privacy," *The Guardian*, Guardian News & Media, 3 Aug. 2014. www.theguardian.com/world/2014/aug/03/internet-death-privacy-google-facebook-alex-preston, accessed 21 Oct. 2017.

237. "Regulation (EU) 2016/679 of the European Parliament and of the Council of 27 April 2016 on the protection of natural persons with regard to the processing of personal data and on the free movement of such data, and repealing Directive 95/46/EC," *Official Journal of the European Union*, 27 April 2016. eur-lex.europa.eu/eli/reg/2016/679/oj, accessed 21 Oct. 2017.

238. Vitalik Buterin, "Privacy on the Blockchain," *Ethereum Blog*, Ethereum, 15 Jan. 2016. blog.ethereum.org/2016/01/15/privacy-on-the-blockchain; Guy Zyskind, Oz Nathan, and Alex "Sandy" Pentland, "Decentralizing Privacy: Using Blockchain to Protect Personal Data," SPW '15 Proceedings, 2015 IEEE Security and Privacy Workshops, Washington, DC, 21–22 May 2015. dl.acm.org/citation.cfm?id=2867781, both accessed 21 Oct. 2017.

239. Yves-Alexandre de Montjoye, Laura Radaelli, Vivek Kumar Singh, and Alex "Sandy" Pentland, "Unique in the Shopping Mall: On the Reidentifiability of Credit Card Metadata," *Science* 347, no. 6221 (30 Jan. 2015): 536–539.

240. "Twitter Usage Statistics," *Internet Live Stats*, Real Time Statistics Project, 9 March 2021. www.internetlivestats.com/twitter-statistics/#rate.

241. Dave Evans, "The Internet of Things," Cisco Systems Inc., April 2011. www.cisco.com/c/dam/en_us/about/ac79/docs/innov/IoT_IBSG_0411FINAL.pdf, accessed 24 Oct. 2017.

242. Team Register, "Nest Bricks Revolv Home Automation Hubs, Because Evolution," *The Register*, 5 April 2016. www.theregister.co.uk/2016/04/05/nest_bricks_revolv_home_automation_hubs; John Aldred, "Eye-Fi Unbrick Their X2 Cards to Give Us What We Should Have Had in the First Place," *DIY Photography*, 1 Sept. 2016. www.diyphotography.net/eye-fi-unbrick-x2-cards-give-us-first-place, accessed 24 Oct. 2017.

243. Jessica Rich, "What Happens When the Sun Sets on a Smart Product?" FTC.gov, Federal Trade Commission, 13 June 2016. www.ftc.gov/news-events/blogs/business-blog/2016/07/what-happens-when-sun-sets-smart-product, accessed 24 Oct. 2017.

244. Juan Benet, "IPFS, Content Addressed, Versioned, P2P File System," *IPFS*, 2017. github.com/ipfs/papers/raw/master/ipfs-cap2pfs/ipfs-p2p-file-system.pdf, accessed 21 Oct. 2017.

245. Cyberblock, "Top 9 Market Cap Blockchains Ranked in Order by Transaction Speed," *Steemit.com*, Steemit Inc., ~Feb. 2017. steemit.com/cryptocurrency/@cyberblock/top-9-market-cap-blockchains-ranked-in-order-by-transaction-speed-lets-see-where-steem-fits-in, accessed 24 Oct. 2017.

246. We used cryptofees.net when we wrote this chapter in Oct. 2017.

247. Dominik Schiener, "A Primer on IOTA," *IOTA Blog*, 21 May 2017. blog.iota.org/a-primer-on-iota-with-presentation-e0a6eb2cc621, accessed 24 Oct. 2017. Vitalik Buterin, "Privacy on the Blockchain," *Ethereum Blog*, Ethereum, 15 Jan. 2016. blog.ethereum.org/2016/01/15/privacy-on-the-blockchain, accessed 21 Oct. 2017.

248. "Ambrosus," White Paper, *Ambrosus.com*, 2017. ambrosus.com/assets/Ambrosus-White-Paper-V8-1.pdf, accessed 24 Oct. 2017.

249. Mark Russinovich, "Introducing the Confidential Consortium Framework," Video, *YouTube.com*, Microsoft Cloud Channel, 10 Aug. 2017. www.youtube.com/watch?v=8s6JMmGJ-dY&feature=youtu.be, accessed 24 Oct. 2017.

250. Dominik Schiener, "A Primer on IOTA"; and Serguei Popov, "The Tangle." *IOTA.org*, 3 April 2016. iota.org/IOTA_Whitepaper.pdf, accessed 24 Oct. 2017.

251. Refer to Serguei Popov, "The Tangle," See iota.org/IOTA_Whitepaper.pdf for a detailed description of the tangle.

252. Dominik Schiener, "A Primer on IOTA."

253. See Brooklyn Microgrid, www.brooklyn.energy.

254. Other examples are Filament and ElectricChain.

255. For example, see the ITU DLT focus group, www.itu.int/en/ITU-T/focusgroups/dlt/Pages/ToR.aspx, or the W3C Interledger initiative, interledger.org, both accessed 24 Oct. 2017.

256. Gavin Wood, "Polkadot: Vision for a Heterogeneous Multi-chain Framework," Draft 1, *Polkadot.network*, n.d. polkadot.network/PolkaDotPaper.pdf, accessed 24 Oct. 2017. "Hyperconnect the World," ICON Foundation, 2017. icon.foundation/en, accessed 14 Nov. 2017.

257. Karl O'Dwyer and David Malone, "Bitcoin Mining and Its Energy Footprint," Irish Signals and Systems Conference 2014 and 2014 China-Ireland International Conference on Information and Communications Technologies (ISSC 2014/CIICT 2014), 25th IET, 26 June 2013. IEEE Xplore Digital Library (14485315), ieeexplore.ieee.org/document/6912770, accessed 24 Oct. 2017.

258. "Bitcoin Energy Consumption Index," *Digiconomist*, as of 31 Oct. 2017. digiconomist.net/bitcoin-energy-consumption.

259. Dominik Schiener, "A Primer on IOTA."

260. Marco Iansiti and Karim R. Lakhani, "The Truth about Blockchain," *Harvard Business Review*, Harvard Business School Publishing Co., Jan.–Feb. 2017: 118–127. hbr.org/2017/01/the-truth-about-blockchain, accessed 24 Oct. 2017.

261. The Web Thing model is a generic model to represent the data of a thing in an IoT platform. It is an official, open, and used by a number of platforms such as the EVRYTHNG IoT platform. W3C Member Submission available here: www.w3.org/Submission/wot-model.

262. For instance, BigChainDB, see www.bigchaindb.com.

263. See www.hyperledger.org and www.corda.net.

264. Dominik Schiener, "A Primer on IOTA."

265. C. Dwight Klappich, Noha Tohamy, John Johnson, and Andrew Stevens, "Seven Things that Supply Chain Leaders Need to Know about

Blockchain," *Gartner.com*, Gartner Inc., 24 Feb. 2017. www.gartner.com/doc/3620517/seven-things-supply-chain-leaders, accessed 24 Oct. 2017.

266. Alan E. Pisarski, ed., "A Journey through American Transportation: 1776 – 2017," *DOT 50th Anniversary*, US Department of Transportation, 1 April 2017. www.transportation.gov/50/timeline, accessed 28 July 2019.

267. Cameron Eittreim, "Will Autonomous Cars Kill Car Culture as We Know It?" *Cameron Eittreim Blog*, Medium Corp., 10 July 2019. medium.com/@eittreimcameron/will-autonomous-cars-kill-car-culture-as-we-know-it-b119ab72b19a; M.R. O'Connor, "The Fight for the Right to Drive," *The New Yorker*, Condé Nast, 30 April 2019. www.newyorker.com/culture/annals-of-inquiry/the-fight-for-the-right-to-drive, both accessed 28 July 2019.

268. Gwyn Topham, "Pay-Per-Mile Road Tax Plan Wins £250,000 Wolfson Economics Prize," *The Guardian*, Guardian News & Media Ltd., 13 July 2017. www.theguardian.com/business/2017/jul/13/pay-per-mile-road-tax-plan-scoops-wolfson-economics-prize, accessed 4 June 2019.

269. Paul Buchanan, Kieran Arter, Lucy Dean et al., "Pricing for Prosperity," Wolfson Economics Prize and Policy Exchange, Volterra Partners LLP and Jacobs UK Ltd., June 2017. policyexchange.org.uk/wp-content/uploads/2017/07/Volterra-Jacobs-Pricing-for-Prosperity-Revised-Submission.pdf, accessed 28 July 2019.

270. Kirsten Korosec, "Waymo Launches Self-Driving Car Service Waymo One," TechCrunch, Verizon Media, last updated 8 Jan. 2019. techcrunch.com/2018/12/05/waymo-launches-self-driving-car-service-waymo-one, accessed 18 Oct. 2018.

271. Mark Phelan, "Detroit Leads, Tesla Lags in Trillion-Dollar Race or Robot-Car Business," *Detroit Free Press*, Gannett USA Today Network, 13 March 2019. www.freep.com/story/money/cars/mark-phelan/2019/03/13/waymo-ford-chrysler-apple-tesla-autonomous-car/3142974002, accessed 29 March 2019.

272. Andrew J. Hawkins, "Waymo's Autonomous Cars Have Driven 8 Million Miles on Public Roads," *The Verge*, Vox Media Inc., 20 July 2018. www.theverge.com/2018/7/20/17595968/waymo-self-driving-cars-8-million-miles-testing, accessed 28 July 2019.

273. David Morris, "Today's Cars Are Parked 95% of the Time," *Fortune.com*, Fortune Media IP Ltd., 13 March 2016. fortune.com/2016/03/13/cars-parked-95-percent-of-time, accessed 18 Oct. 2018.

274. Warwick Goodall et al., "The Rise of Mobility as a Service," *Deloitte Review*, no. 20 (Deloitte University Press, 2017): 112–129. www2.deloitte.

com/content/dam/Deloitte/nl/Documents/consumer-business/deloitte-nl-cb-ths-rise-of-mobility-as-a-service.pdf, accessed 18 Oct. 2018.

275. Chris Ballinger, interviewed via telephone by David Mirynech, 10 Dec. 2018.

276. Chris Ballinger, interviewed via telephone by David Mirynech, 10 Dec. 2018.

277. Warwick Goodall et al., "The Rise of Mobility as a Service."

278. Alan Ohnsman, "Honeymoon's Over? GM Cruise Said to Turn to Uber as Lyft Alliance Cools," *Forbes.com*, Forbes Media LLC, 18 Oct. 2017. www.forbes.com/sites/alanohnsman/2017/10/18/honeymoons-over-gm-cruise-said-to-turn-to-uber-as-lyft-alliance-cools/#540d18cb3b15, accessed 18 Oct. 2018.

279. Greg Bensinger and Chester Dawson, "Toyota Investing $500 Million in Uber in Driverless-Car Pact," *The Wall Street Journal*, Dow Jones & Co. Inc., last updated 27 Aug. 2018. www.wsj.com/articles/toyota-investing-500-million-in-uber-in-driverless-car-pact-1535393774, accessed 18 Oct. 2018.

280. Susan Crawford, "Autonomous Vehicles Might Drive Cities to Financial Ruin," *WIRED*, Condé Nast, 20 June 2018. www.wired.com/story/autonomous-vehicles-might-drive-cities-to-financial-ruin, accessed 18 Oct. 2018.

281. Susan Crawford, "Autonomous Vehicles Might Drive Cities to Financial Ruin."

282. Susan Crawford, "Autonomous Vehicles Might Drive Cities to Financial Ruin."

283. Andrew J. Hawkins, "Not All of Our Self-Driving Cars Will Be Electrically Powered—Here's Why," *The Verge*, Vox Media Inc., 17 Dec. 2017. www.theverge.com/2017/12/12/16748024/self-driving-electric-hybrid-ev-av-gm-ford, accessed 23 Oct. 2018.

284. Chris Ballinger, interviewed via telephone by David Mirynech, 10 Dec. 2018.

285. Satoshi Nakamoto, "Bitcoin: A Peer-to-Peer Electronic Cash System," *Bitcoin.org*, 1 Nov. 2008. bitcoin.org/bitcoin.pdf, accessed 23 Oct. 2017.

286. Stan Higgins, "Ethereum IoT Project Wins $100k in Dubai Blockchain Hackathon," *CoinDesk*, Digital Currency Group, 14 Feb. 2017. www.coindesk.com/ethereum-iot-project-wins-100k-dubai-blockchain-hackathon, accessed 25 Oct. 2018.

287. Oaken Innovations, "UAE GovHack: Tesla and Tollbooth on Blockchain," Video, *YouTube.com*, 7 Jan. 2017. 00:03:00. www.youtube. com/watch?v=lKJrTeNQGZE, accessed 16 June 2018.

288. Oaken Innovations, "UAE GovHack: Tesla and Tollbooth on Blockchain."

289. Randy Cole, interviewed via telephone by David Mirynech, 10 Aug. 2018.

290. Randy Cole, interviewed via telephone by David Mirynech, 10 Aug. 2018.

291. For a sample of Kapsch TrafficCom's patented tolling solutions, see "USPTO Patent: Full-Text and Image Database," United States Patent and Trademark Office, Department of Commerce, n.d. patft.uspto.gov/ netacgi, accessed 4 Aug. 2019.

292. Mark Roberti, "How Do RFID-Based Toll-Collection Systems Work?" Ask The Experts Forum, *RFID Journal*, Emerald Expositions LLC, 30 Sept. 2013. www.rfidjournal.com/blogs/experts/entry?10743, accessed 16 Aug. 2019.

293. Hillary Chabot, "Cyber Experts Warn of Driver Risk for E-ZPass Hack, Track," *Boston Herald*, MediaNews Group Inc., 18 Nov. 2018. www. bostonherald.com/2015/09/14/cyber-experts-warn-of-driver-risk-for-e-zpass-hack-track, accessed 16 Aug. 2019.

294. Randy Cole, interviewed via telephone by David Mirynech, 10 Aug. 2018.

295. Ashley Lannquist, "Introducing MOBI: The Mobility Open Blockchain Initiative," *Blockchain Pulse: IBM Blockchain Blog*, IBM Corp., 25 June 2018. www.ibm.com/blogs/blockchain/2018/06/introducing-mobi-the-mobility-open-blockchain-initiative, accessed 28 Oct. 2018.

296. Ashley Lannquist, "Introducing MOBI: The Mobility Open Blockchain Initiative."

297. Chris Ballinger, interviewed via telephone by David Mirynech, 10 Dec. 2018.

298. John Gerryts, interviewed via telephone by David Mirynech, 24 June 2018.

299. "Lemon Law Basics," Consumer Protection, *Findlaw.com*, Thomson Reuters Corp., n.d. consumer.findlaw.com/lemon-law/lemon-law-basics. html, accessed 16 Aug. 2019.

300. John Gerryts, interviewed via telephone by David Mirynech, 24 June 2018.

301. John Gerryts, interviewed via telephone by David Mirynech, 24 June 2018.

302. "CryptoKitties Craze Slows Down Transactions on Ethereum," *BBC News*, British Broadcasting Corp., 5 Dec. 2017. www.bbc.com/news/technology-42237162, accessed 6 Nov. 2018. See also Olga Kharif, "CryptoKitties Mania Overwhelms Ethereum Network's Processing," *Bloomberg Technology*, Bloomberg LP, 4 Dec. 2017. www.bloomberg.com/news/articles/2017-12-04/cryptokitties-quickly-becomes-most-widely-used-ethereum-app, accessed 16 Aug. 2019.

303. "CryptoKitties Craze Slows Down Transactions on Ethereum."

304. "CryptoKitties Craze Slows Down Transactions on Ethereum."

305. Mansoor Iqbal, "Uber Revenue and Usage Statistics (2019)," *Business of Apps*, Soko Media, 10 May 2019. www.businessofapps.com/data/uber-statistics, accessed 6 Nov. 2018.

306. Ayssa Hertig, "How Will Ethereum Scale?" *CoinDesk*, Digital Currency Group, n.d. www.coindesk.com/information/will-ethereum-scale, accessed 6 Nov. 2018.

307. Vaibhav Saini, "Difference between SideChains and State Channels," *Hacker Noon*, Artmap Inc., 23 June 2018. hackernoon.com/difference-between-sidechains-and-state-channels-2f5dfbd10707, accessed 6 Nov. 2018.

308. Vaibhav Saini, "Difference between SideChains and State Channels."

309. Uber, "How Surge Pricing Works," Uber Technologies Inc., n.d. www.uber.com/en-CA/drive/partner-app/how-surge-works, accessed 10 Nov. 2018.

310. "The Raiden Network," The Raiden Network, n.d. raiden.network, accessed 10 Nov. 2018; and Ray Fontaine, "Plasma: An Innovative Framework to Scale Ethereum," *CoinCentral*, Coincentral.com LLC, 7 July 2018. coincentral.com/plasma-an-innovative-framework-to-scale-ethereum, accessed 4 Nov. 2019.

311. "The Raiden Network," as of 10 Nov. 2018.

312. Brian Curran, "What Is Sharding? Guide to this Ethereum Scaling Concept Explained," *Blockonomi*, Kooc Media Ltd., 22 March 2019. blockonomi.com/sharding, accessed 2 April 2019.

313. Brian Curran, "What Is Sharding? Guide to this Ethereum Scaling Concept Explained."

314. Aion Community, n.d. aion.network/community, accessed 5 Nov. 2018. This is now the Open Application Network.

315. Sudhir Khatwani, "What Is Atomic Swap and Why It Matters? [Must Know]," *CoinSutra*, last updated 13 Oct. 2018. coinsutra.com/atomic-swap/, accessed 5 Nov. 2018.

316. "White Papers," Aion, n.d. aion.network/developers/#whitepapers; "Cosmos White Paper," *COSMOS Network*, Tendermint Inc., n.d. cosmos.network/resources/whitepaper; and "ICON Hyperconnect the World," White Paper version 1.2, *ICON*, ICON Foundation, last updated Jan. 2018. icon.foundation/resources/whitepaper/ICON_Whitepaper_EN.pdf, all accessed 7 Aug. 2019.

317. Polkadot, n.d. polkadot.network/, accessed 4 Aug. 2019.

318. John McCann and Mike Moore, "5G: Everything You Need to Know," *TechRadar*, Future US Inc., last updated 29 July 2019. www.techradar.com/news/what-is-5g-everything-you-need-to-know, accessed 16 Nov. 2018.

319. John McCann and Mike Moore, "5G: Everything You Need to Know."

320. Ray Sharma, Public Talk at UWO by David Mirynech, 24 Nov. 2018.

321. Bijan Khosravi, "Autonomous Cars Won't Work—Until We Have 5G," *Forbes.com*, Forbes Media LLC, 25 March 2018. www.forbes.com/sites/bijankhosravi/2018/03/25/autonomous-cars-wont-work-until-we-have-5g/#f60970e437e0, accessed 12 Nov. 2018.

322. Bijan Khosravi, "Autonomous Cars Won't Work—Until We Have 5G."

323. Jon Martindale, "What Is an ASIC Miner?" *Digital Trends*, Designtechnica Corp., 12 April 2018. www.digitaltrends.com/computing/what-is-an-asic-miner, accessed 12 Nov. 2018.

324. Bijan Khosravi, "Autonomous Cars Won't Work—Until We Have 5G."

325. Bijan Khosravi, "Autonomous Cars Won't Work—Until We Have 5G."

326. Bijan Khosravi, "Autonomous Cars Won't Work—Until We Have 5G."

327. Bijan Khosravi, "Autonomous Cars Won't Work—Until We Have 5G."

328. David Shephardson, "Trump Administration Looks to Speed 5G Networks, Ease Hurdles," *Reuters*, Thomson Reuters Corp., 28 Sept. 2018. www.reuters.com/article/us-usa-tech-5g/trump-administration-looks-to-speed-5g-networks-ease-hurdles-idUSKCN1M82UN, accessed 12 Nov. 2018.

329. David Shephardson, "Trump Administration Looks to Speed 5G Networks, Ease Hurdles."

330. Bijan Khosravi, "Autonomous Cars Won't Work—Until We Have 5G," p. 14.

331. Bijan Khosravi, "Autonomous Cars Won't Work—Until We Have 5G," p. 14.

332. Todd Spangler, "Facebook Under Fire: How Privacy Crisis Could Change Big Data Forever," *Variety*, Penske Business Media LLC, 2018. variety.com/2018/digital/features/facebook-privacy-crisis-big-data-mark-zuckerberg-1202741394, accessed 21 Nov. 2018.

333. Sam Frizell, "What Is Uber Really Doing with Your Data?" *Time*, TIME USA LLC, 19 Nov. 2014. time.com/3595025/uber-data, accessed 21 Nov. 2018.

334. Sam Frizell, "What Is Uber Really Doing with Your Data?"

335. Sam Frizell, "What Is Uber Really Doing with Your Data?"

336. "Privacy Policy," *EU GDPR.org*, Trunomi, n.d. eugdpr.org/privacy-policy, accessed 16 Nov. 2018.

337. Wade Rosado, "Data Detour: Analytics Will Move Transportation Forward," *WIRED*, Condé Nast, n.d. www.wired.com/insights/2014/07/data-detour-analytics-will-move-transportation-forward, accessed 16 Nov. 2018.

338. Wade Rosado, "Data Detour," p. 16.

339. Wade Rosado, "Data Detour," p. 16.

340. Gideon Greenspan, "The Blockchain Immutability Myth," *CoinDesk*, Digital Currency Group, 9 May 2017. www.coindesk.com/blockchain-immutability-myth, accessed 20 Nov. 2018.

341. "GDPR Right to Be Forgotten," Intersoft Consulting, n.d. gdpr-info.eu/issues/right-to-be-forgotten, accessed 20 Nov. 2018.

342. The European Parliament and the Council of the European Union, "General Data Protection Regulation," 2016. publications.europa.eu/en/publication-detail/-/publication/3e485e15-11bd-11e6-ba9a-01aa75ed71a1/language-en, accessed 4 Aug. 2019.

343. Nelson Petracek, "What Zero-Knowledge Proofs Will Do for Blockchain," *VentureBeat*, VentureBeat Inc., 16 Dec. 2017. venturebeat.com/2017/12/16/what-zero-knowledge-proofs-will-do-for-blockchain, accessed 22 Nov. 2018.

344. Nelson Petracek, "What Zero-Knowledge Proofs Will Do for Blockchain."

345. Joseph Lubin, interviewed via telephone by Don and Alex Tapscott, 30 July 2015.

346. Don Tapscott and Alex Tapscott, *Blockchain Revolution* (New York: Penguin Portfolio, 2018): Ch. 1.

347. Jon Russel, "Former Mozilla CEO Raises $35M in Under 30 Seconds for His Browser Start-up Brave," *TechCrunch*, Verizon Media, 1 June 2017. techcrunch.com/2017/06/01/brave-ico-35-million-30-seconds-brendan-eich, accessed 12 Dec. 2018.

348. Jon Russel, "Former Mozilla CEO Raises $35M."

349. "Facebook 57," *Fortune.com*, Fortune Media IP Ltd., last updated 16 May 2019. fortune.com/fortune500/facebook, accessed 12 Dec. 2018.

350. Don Tapscott and Alex Tapscott, *Blockchain Revolution*

351. "White Paper," DOVU, April 2018. dovu.io/resources.html, accessed 12 Dec. 2018.

352. Chris Ballinger, interviewed via telephone by David Mirynech, 10 Dec. 2018.

353. John Gerryts, interviewed via telephone by David Mirynech, 24 June 2018.

354. Michael K. Spencer, "Google's Chief Futurist Says Basic Income Will Spread Worldwide by the 2030s," *Hacker Noon*, Artmap Inc., 16 April 2018. hackernoon.com/googles-chief-futurists-says-basic-income-will-spread-worldwide-by-the-2030s-af5b9ef41aa, accessed 22 Nov. 2018.

355. Guest Writer, "The 5 Worst Examples of IoT Hacking and Vulnerabilities in Recorded History," *IoT for All*, 10 May 2017. www.iotforall.com/5-worst-iot-hacking-vulnerabilities, accessed 24 Nov. 2018.

356. Susan Carney, "Cybersecurity in Self-Driving Cars: U-M Releases Threat Identification Tool," MCity, The Regents of the University of Michigan, 4 Jan. 2018. mcity.umich.edu/cybersecurity-self-driving-cars-u-m-releases-threat-identification-tool, accessed 12 Dec. 2018.

357. Guest Writer, "The 5 Worst Examples of IoT Hacking."

358. Guest Writer, "The 5 Worst Examples of IoT Hacking."

359. Guest Writer, "The 5 Worst Examples of IoT Hacking."

360. Francis Dinha, "How to Secure the Internet of Things," *Forbes.com*, Forbes Media LLC, 13 April 2018. www.forbes.com/sites/forbestechcouncil/2018/04/13/how-to-secure-the-internet-of-things/#5a38fab91cbb, accessed 25 Nov. 2018.

361. Susan Carney, "Cybersecurity in Self-Driving Cars."

362. Susan Carney, "Cybersecurity in Self-Driving Cars."

363. Andre Weimerskirch and Derrick Dominic, "Assessing Risk: Identifying and Analyzing Cybersecurity Threats to Automated Vehicles," *MCity*, The Regents of the University of Michigan, 19 Dec. 2017. mcity.umich. edu/wp-content/uploads/2017/12/Mcity-white-paper_cybersecurity.pdf, accessed 12 Dec. 2018.

364. Francis Dinha, "How to Secure the Internet of Things."

365. Arnab Chattopadhyay, "IoT Security Using Blockchain," *Sogeti*, Capgemini, n.d. www.uk.sogeti.com/content-hub/blog/iot-security-using-blockchain, accessed 26 Nov. 2018.

366. Aran Davies, "How to Secure the Internet of Things with Blockchain," *DevTeam.Space*, 12 March 2018. www.devteam.space/blog/how-to-secure-the-internet-of-things-iot-with-blockchain, accessed 26 Nov. 2018.

367. Aran Davies, "How to Secure the Internet of Things with Blockchain."

368. Ameer Rosic, "5 High Profile Cryptocurrency Hacks," *Blockgeeks*, Blockgeeks Inc., 2017. blockgeeks.com/guides/cryptocurrency-hacks, accessed 26 Nov. 2018.

369. Ameer Rosic, "5 High Profile Cryptocurrency Hacks."

370. Ray Kurzweil, "The Law of Accelerating Returns," *KurzweilAI.net*, Kurzweil Technologies Co., 7 March 2001. www.kurzweilai.net/the-law-of-accelerating-returns, accessed 18 Dec. 2018.

371. Will Knight, "What Uber's Fatal Accident Could Mean for the Autonomous-Car Industry," *MIT Technology Review*, Massachusetts Institute of Technology, 19 March 2018. www.technologyreview. com/s/610574/what-ubers-fatal-accident-could-mean-for-the-autonomous-car-industry, accessed 8 Dec. 2018.

372. Will Knight, "What Uber's Fatal Accident Could Mean for the Autonomous-Car Industry."

373. Parker O'Very, "3 Ways Self-Driving Cars Will Affect the Insurance Industry," *VentureBeat*, VentureBeat Inc., 26 Jan. 2018. venturebeat. com/2018/01/26/3-ways-self-driving-cars-will-affect-the-insurance-industry, accessed 8 Dec. 2018.

374. Parker O'Very, "3 Ways Self-Driving Cars Will Affect the Insurance Industry."

375. Parker O'Very, "3 Ways Self-Driving Cars Will Affect the Insurance Industry."

376. Will Knight, "What Uber's Fatal Accident Could Mean for the Autonomous-Car Industry."

377. Will Knight, "What Uber's Fatal Accident Could Mean for the Autonomous-Car Industry."

378. Tom Stone, "Road Rules Platform for Safe Autonomous Vehicle Deployment Launched by Inrix," *Traffic Technology Today.com*, Mark Allen Group Ltd., 17 July 2018. www.traffictechnologytoday.com/news/autonomous-vehicles/road-rules-platform-for-safe-autonomous-vehicle-deployment-launched-by-inrix.html, accessed 18 Dec. 2018.

379. Tom Stone, "Road Rules Platform for Safe Autonomous Vehicle Deployment Launched by Inrix."

380. Tom Stone, "Road Rules Platform for Safe Autonomous Vehicle Deployment Launched by Inrix."

381. Tim Stickings, "World's First Flying Car that Can Turn into a Plane in Less than a Minute and Soar along at 100mph Is Going on Sale in the US Next Month," *Daily Mail*, dmg media, 26 Sept. 2018. www.dailymail.co.uk/sciencetech/article-6210205/Worlds-flying-cars-set-market-pre-sales-month.html, accessed 16 Jan. 2019.

382. Tim Stickings, "World's First Flying Car."

383. Glenn Chapman, "Buzz Grows on 'Flying Cars' Head of Major Tech Show," *Phys.org*, Science X Network, 4 Jan. 2019. phys.org/news/2019-01-cars-major-tech.html, accessed 5 Aug. 2019.

384. Glenn Chapman, "Buzz Grows on 'Flying Cars' Head of Major Tech Show."

385. Andrew J. Hawkins, "Uber's 'Flying Cars' Could Arrive in LA by 2020—and Here's What It'll Be Like to Ride One," *The Verge*, Vox Media, 8 Nov. 2017. www.theverge.com/2017/11/8/16613228/uber-flying-car-la-nasa-space-act, accessed 20 Jan. 2019.

386. Jeff Holden and Nikhil Goel, "Fast-Forwarding to a Future of On-Demand Urban Air Transportation," *Uber Elevate*, Uber, 27 Oct. 2016. www.uber.com/elevate.pdf, accessed 20 Jan. 2019.

387. Michael Ramsey and Kimberly Harris-Ferrante, "Maverick* Research: Flying Autonomous Vehicles—The Next Big Thing that Isn't," *Gartner.com*, Gartner Inc., 18 Sept. 2017. www.gartner.com/doc/3802871/maverick-research-flying-autonomous-vehicles, accessed 24 Jan. 2019.

388. Jeff Holden and Nikhil Goel, "Fast-Forwarding to a Future of On-Demand Urban Air Transportation."

389. Jeff Holden and Nikhil Goel, "Fast-Forwarding to a Future of On-Demand Urban Air Transportation."

390. Jeff Holden and Nikhil Goel, "Fast-Forwarding to a Future of On-Demand Urban Air Transportation."

391. Jeff Holden and Nikhil Goel, "Fast-Forwarding to a Future of On-Demand Urban Air Transportation."

392. "Bill Gates Quotes," *BrainyQuote*, BrainyQuote.com, n.d. www.brainyquote.com/quotes/bill_gates_404193, accessed 3 Feb. 2019.

393. Christoph Jentzsch, CEO, Slock.it, "Building a Decentralized Sharing Economy on Top of Ethereum," *YouTube.com*, Devcon3, 4 Nov. 2017. www.youtube.com/watch?v=iRtG_6pYqGE, accessed 22 Nov. 2017.

394. Harry Campbell, and Christian Perea, "What's the Real Commission that Uber Takes from Its Drivers?" *The Rideshare Guy*, 25 July 2016. therideshareguy.com/whats-the-real-commission-that-uber-takes-from-its-drivers-infographic, accessed 22 Nov. 2017.

395. Gregory Maxwell, "eBitcoin the Enabler: Truly Autonomous Software Agents Roaming the Net," *Bitcoin Forum post*, 6 Dec. 2011. bitcointalk.org/index.php?topic=53855.msg642768#msg642768, accessed 3 Oct. 2017.

396. Stephan Tual, interviewed by Alan Majer, 11 Sept. 2017.

397. Mike Hearn, "Mike Hearn: Autonomous Agents, Self-Driving Cars and Bitcoin," Video, *YouTube.com*, Turing Festival, 23 Aug. 2013, uploaded 26 March 2017. www.youtube.com/watch?v=MVyv4t0OKe4, accessed 22 Nov. 2017.

398. Vitalik Buterin, "Bootstrapping a Decentralized Autonomous Corporation: Part I," *Bitcoin Magazine*, 19 Sept. 2013. bitcoinmagazine.com/articles/bootstrapping-a-decentralized-autonomous-corporation-part-i-1379644274, accessed 22 Nov. 2017.

399. Vitalik Buterin, "Ethereum: The Ultimate Smart Contract and Autonomous Corporation Platform on the Blockchain," *Vitalik.ca*, 19 Dec. 2013. Wayback Machine, web.archive.org/web/20131219030753/http://vitalik.ca/ethereum.html, accessed 22 Nov. 2017. For further reading, see Wayback Machine, web.archive.org/web/20150627031414/http://vbuterin.com/ultimatescripting.htmlhttp://vitalik.ca/general/2017/09/14/prehistory.html.

400. Stephan Tual, interviewed by Alan Majer, 11 Sept. 2017.

401. Stephan Tual, interviewed by Alan Majer, 11 Sept. 2017.

402. Stephan Tual, interviewed by Alan Majer, 11 Sept. 2017.

403. Christoph Jentzsch, "The History of the DAO and Lessons Learned," *Slock.it Blog*, 24 Aug. 2016. blog.slock.it/the-history-of-the-dao-and-lessons-learned-d06740f8cfa5, accessed 22 Nov. 2017.

404. Christoph Jentzsch, "The History of the DAO and Lessons Learned."

405. Christoph Jentzsch, "The History of the DAO and Lessons Learned."

406. Christoph Jentzsch, "Decentralized Autonomous Organization to Automate Governance," *Slock.it*, Slock.it UG, n.d. download.slock.it/public/DAO/WhitePaper.pdf, accessed 22 Nov. 2017.

407. Stephan Tual, interviewed by Alan Majer, 11 Sept. 2017. While the DAO was an independent entity, it had eight named curators, among them Vitalik Buterin, Christian Reitweissner, and Vlad Zamfir.

408. Stephan Tual, communications with Alan Majer, 13 Oct. 2017.

409. Matthew Leising, "The Ether Thief," *Bloomberg Markets*, Bloomberg Finance LP, 13 June 2017. www.bloomberg.com/features/2017-the-ether-thief, accessed 11 Dec. 2017. 12 million ETH at a price of $1,862.70 would be worth ~$22.4 billion, as of 9 March 2021. coinmarketcap.com/currencies/ethereum.

410. Cade Metz, "The Biggest Crowdfunding Project Ever—The DAO—Is Kind of a Mess," *WIRED*, Condé Nast, 6 June 2016. www.wired.com/2016/06/biggest-crowdfunding-project-ever-dao-mess/, accessed 22 Nov. 2017.

411. Christoph Jentzsch, "The History of the DAO and Lessons Learned."

412. Cade Metz, "The Biggest Crowdfunding Project Ever—the DAO—Is Kind of a Mess."

413. Nathaniel Popper, "A Hacking of More than $50 Million Dashes Hopes in the World of Virtual Currency," *New York Times*, New York Times Co., 17 June 2016. www.nytimes.com/2016/06/18/business/dealbook/hacker-may-have-removed-more-than-50-million-from-experimental-cybercurrency-project.html, accessed 22 Nov. 2017.

414. For the full anatomy of the attack, see Matthew Leising, "The Ether Thief," *Bloomberg Markets*, Bloomberg Finance LP, 13 June 2017. www.bloomberg.com/features/2017-the-ether-thief, accessed 11 Dec. 2017.

415. BokkyPooBah, "Which Accounts Are Involved in Mounting the Recursive Call Vulnerability Attacks on the DAO?" *StackExchange*, 18 June 2016. Community updated 13 April 2017. ethereum.stackexchange.com/questions/6224/which-accounts-are-involved-in-mounting-the-recursive-call-vulnerability-attacks, accessed 22 Nov. 2017.

416. These Robin Hoods are not to be confused with users of the Robinhood investing app. robinhood.com/us/en/support/articles/our-story.

417. David Z. Morris, "The Bizarre Fallout of Ethereum's Epic Fail," *Fortune.com*, Fortune Media IP Ltd., 4 Sept. 2016. fortune.com/2016/09/04/ethereum-fall-out, accessed 22 Nov. 2017. However, the story doesn't end there. A group of miners did not accept the fork, splitting away from the main blockchain in an "alternate universe" where the attack did happen, in effect creating another digital currency, Ethereum Classic.

418. Debate in the aftermath continued. Even the SEC weighed in over a year later, in July 2017, concluding that DAO tokens were "securities" but that in this case it would not press any charges. See "SEC Issues Investigative Report Concluding DAO Tokens, a Digital Asset, Were Securities," Press Release 2017-131, *SEC.gov*, US Securities and Exchange Commission. www.sec.gov/news/press-release/2017-131.

419. Stephan Tual, interviewed by Alan Majer, 11 Sept. 2017.

420. Stephan Tual, interviewed by Alan Majer, 11 Sept. 2017.

421. "The Ethereum Computer," *Slock.it*, Slock.it UG, 2017. Wayback Machine, web.archive.org/web/20170429033912/https://slock.it/ethereum_computer.html, accessed 26 Feb. 2021.

422. Slock.it staff, communications with Alan Majer, Oct. 2017.

423. Share&Charge formally launched on 1 May 2017.

424. Stephan Tual, "Share&Charge Launches Its Mobile App, On-Boards over 1,000 Charging Stations on the Blockchain," *Slock.it Blog*, Slock.it UG, 1 May 2017. blog.slock.it/share-charge-launches-its-app-on-boards-over-1-000-charging-stations-on-the-blockchain-ba8275390309, accessed 22 Nov. 2017.

425. Stephan Tual, "Share&Charge Launches Its Mobile App, On-Boards over 1,000 Charging Stations on the Blockchain."

426. Stephan Tual, "Share&Charge Launches Its Mobile App, On-Boards over 1,000 Charging Stations on the Blockchain."

427. Simon Jentzsch, "Share&Charge Smart Contracts: The Technical Angle," *Slock.it Blog*, Slock.it UG, 30 April 2017. blog.slock.it/share-charge-smart-contracts-the-technical-angle-58b93ce80f15, accessed 9 March 2021.

428. Stephan Tual, "Share&Charge Launches Its Mobile App, On-Boards over 1,000 Charging Stations on the Blockchain."

429. Simon Jentzsch, "Share&Charge Smart Contracts: The Technical Angle."

430. Harry Campbell and Christian Perea, "What's the Real Commission that Uber Takes from Its Drivers?" David Z. Morris, "Uber's New Fare System Raises Its Cut while Angering Drivers," *Fortune.com*, Fortune Media IP Ltd., 20 May 2017. fortune.com/2017/05/20/uber-new-pricing-angry-drivers, accessed 22 Nov. 2017.

431. Vitalek Buterin, "The Not-so-Paranoid Case for Decentralization," *YouTube.com*, Meetup Presentation (London), 30 March 2015. www.youtube.com/watch?v=tjxkdniYtkc, accessed 25 Sept. 2017.

432. "This will take place within a 'permissionless' environment, encouraging network effects through a free and easy onboarding of manufacturers' smart objects onto the USN." See "The Ethereum Computer," *Slock.it*, Slock.it UG, 2017. Wayback Machine, web.archive.org/web/20170429033912/https://slock.it/ethereum_computer.html, accessed 26 Feb. 2021.

433. Christoph Jentzsch, CEO, Slock.it, "Building a Decentralized Sharing Economy on Top of Ethereum."

434. Global Solution Networks, "10 Types of Global Solution Networks," GSNnetworks, n.d. gsnetworks.org/ten-types-of-global-solution-network, accessed 22 Nov. 2017.

435. Christoph Jentzsch, "Blockchains Acquires Slock.it," *Slock.it Blog*, Slock.it UG, 3 June. 2019. blog.slock.it/blockchains-acquires-slock-it-4b3a0276893d, accessed 9 March 2021.

436. "Our Story: The Blockchains Vision," *Blockchains.com*, Blockchains LLC, n.d. www.blockchains.com/our-story, accessed 9 March 2021.

437. Stephan Tual, interviewed by Alan Majer, 11 Sept. 2017.

438. For example, see the latest Share&Charge charging pole events at etherscan.io/address/0xb642a68bD622D015809bb9755d07EA3006b85843, accessed 5 Oct. 2017.

439. Primavera De Filippi, "Ethereum: Freenet or Skynet?" Berkman Klein Center Luncheon Series, 15 April 2014. cyber.harvard.edu/events/luncheon/2014/04/difilippi, accessed 22 Nov. 2017.

440. Stephan Tual, "Share&Charge Launches Its Mobile App, On-Boards over 1,000 Charging Stations on the Blockchain."

441. Vitalek Buterin, "The Not-so-Paranoid Case for Decentralization."

442. Vitalek Buterin, "The Not-so-Paranoid Case for Decentralization."

443. Indeed, some have blamed the Solidity language itself for the difficulty in identifying anti-patterns like the ones that caused the attack on the DAO.

444. Stephan Tual, interviewed by Alan Majer, 15 Sept. 2017.

445. Stephan Tual, interviewed by Alan Majer, 15 Sept. 2017.

446. Don Tapscott and Alex Tapscott, *Blockchain Revolution* (New York: Penguin Random House LLC, 2016).

447. Jonathan Kats and Yehuda Lindell, *Introduction to Modern Cryptography* (Boca Raton, FL: CRC Press, 2015); and Ghassan O. Karame and Elli Androulaki, *Bitcoin and Blockchain Security* (Boston and London: Artech House, 2017).

448. In general, smart contracts are arbitrary complex programs that may rely on security of cryptographic protocols used outside of blockchains. The conditions that trigger payments then rely on the security of those protocols. For instance, users implement smart contracts for auctions that rely on bidders properly holding/executing certain bids/payments, perhaps using cryptographic keys that are completely external to the blockchain.

449. A universal quantum computer is a quantum computer that can be programmed or configured to implement reliably an arbitrary quantum algorithm or program. The known powerful quantum attacks on cryptography require such a fault-tolerant device capable of universal operations.

450. N-bit RSA numbers are semi-primes (the products of two large primes) having size used in RSA-based public key schemes. R.L. Rivest, A. Shamir, and L. Adleman, "A Method for Obtaining Digital Signatures and Public Key Cryptosystems," *Communications of the ACM* 21 (1978): 120–126; NIST, "Digital Signature Standard (DSS)," Federal Information Processing Standards, Gaithersburg, 2013.

451. "Quantum resistant" or "quantum safe" means designed to be safe against quantum attacks. This requires using cryptographic tools known or believed to be resilient to quantum attacks.

452. Michele Mosca, "Cybersecurity in an Era with Quantum Computers: Will We Be Ready?" *Cryptology ePrint Archive: Report 2015/1075*, Waterloo, ON, 2015. eprint.iacr.org/2015/1075.pdf, accessed 26 Feb. 2021.

453. Technically, by *impossible*, we mean computationally hard, i.e., the running time of any known classical algorithm for key recovery (breaking) is exponential in the length of the key.

454. The 10 minutes required on average for validation of a block applies to the current Bitcoin blockchain, where the agreement protocol is based on proof of work. There are other blockchain agreement protocols in which

the validation is done via other agreement schemes, and which may be significantly faster, at the (possible) cost of less understood security assumptions.

455. Companies can also deploy so-called *private* blockchains, i.e., blockchains that are visible only from the interior of the company, with no outside exposure whatsoever. However, their use is still debatable. In this chapter, we focus our attention only on *public* blockchains, i.e., blockchains visible in principle to everyone.

456. By *Internet of Things*, we mean sensors and other small devices that are connected to the Internet and collect and/or transmit data via the network.

457. Technically, by *infeasible*, we mean computationally hard, i.e., the running time of any known classical algorithm for key recovery (breaking) is exponential in the length of the key.

458. R.L. Rivest, A. Shamir, and L. Adleman, "A Method for Obtaining Digital Signatures and Public Key Cryptosystems."

459. Eric W. Weisstein, "Abelian Group," *MathWorld: A Wolfram Web Resource,* n.d. mathworld.wolfram.com/AbelianGroup.html, accessed 2 Nov. 2017.

460. Jonathan Kats and Yehuda Lindell, *Introduction to Modern Cryptography*.

461. Peter W. Shor, "Polynomial-Time Algorithms for Prime Factorization and Discrete Logarithms on a Quantum Computer," *SIAM Journal on Computing* (1997): 1484–1509.

462. User wallets do not reveal directly the public keys they contain, but only "addresses," which are obtained from the public key via a series of hash function applications. Therefore, the public key is not directly visible to the network, but only its hash, which is believed to be resistant against a quantum attack. The public key must be broadcasted only when the user wants to spend money from his or her wallet, so the network can verify that indeed the money belongs to the respective user. Only at this stage is the public key fully revealed and thus potentially open to attack from a quantum computer.

463. Matthew Amy, Olivia Di Matteo, Vlad Gheorghiu, Michele Mosca, Alex Parent, and John Schanck, "Estimating the Cost of Generic Quantum Preimage Attacks on SHA-2 and SHA-3," arXiv:1603.09383 [quant-ph], *Selected Areas of Cryptography*, 2016. arxiv.org/pdf/1603.09383.pdf.

464. A quadratic speedup is nonetheless remarkable. Imagine trying to find a particular book in a library of 1,000,000 books shelved randomly. Any human or conventional machine would need an order of 1,000,000-time

steps (i.e., the intervals between events such as the browsing of each book one by one). A quantum computer could perform the same search quadratically faster, in only 1,000-time steps. Lov Grover discovered this scheme in 1994, and so we know it as Grover's quantum search algorithm. See Lov K. Grover, "Quantum Mechanics Helps in Searching for a Needle in a Haystack," *Physical Review Letters* (1997): 325–328. journals.aps.org/prl/abstract/10.1103/PhysRevLett.79.325.

465. It is estimated that the total power consumption in the Bitcoin network might surpass that of a small country like Denmark by 2020. See Vice Motherboard, "Bitcoin Could Consume as Much Electricity as Denmark by 2020," 29 March 2016. motherboard.vice.com/en_us/article/aek3za/bitcoin-could-consume-as-much-electricity-as-denmark-by-2020.

466. Jing Chen and Silvio Micali, "Algorand," arXiv:1607.01341 [cs.CR], 2016. arxiv.org/pdf/1607.01341.pdf; Tendermint, tendermint.com; and Hyperledger, www.hyperledger.org.

467. Oded Regev, "On Lattices, Learning with Errors, Random Linear Codes, and Cryptography," Proceedings of the Thirty-seventh Annual ACM Symposium on Theory of Computing (New York: Association for Computing Machinery, 2005): 84–93; David Jao and Luca De Feo, "Towards Quantum-Resistant Cryptosystems from Supersingular Elliptic Curve Isogenies," Bo-Yin Yang, ed., *Post-Quantum Cryptography*, Lecture Notes in Computer Science (Berlin, Heidelberg: Springer, 2011): 19–34; and Tsutomu Matsumoto and Hideki Imai, "Public Quadratic Polynomial-Tuples for Efficient Signature-Verification and Message-Encryption," Barstow D. et al., eds., *Advances in Cryptology, EUROCRYPT 1988*, Lecture Notes in Computer Science (Berlin, Heidelberg: Springer, 1988): 419–453; and Robert J. McEliece, "A Public Key Cryptosystem Based on Algebraic Coding Theory," *DSN Progress Report* (La Cañada Flintridge: Jet Propulsion Laboratory, 1978): 114–116.

468. "Post-Quantum Crypto Standardization—Call for Proposals Announcement," National Institute of Standards and Technology, *NIST. gov*, 15 Dec. 2016. csrc.nist.gov/groups/ST/post-quantum-crypto/cfp-announce-dec2016.html.

469. Miguel Herrero-Collantes and Juan Carlos Garcia-Escartin, "Quantum Random Number Generators," *Reviews of Modern Physics* 89, no. 1 (American Physical Society, 2017): 015004.

470. A cryptographically secure pseudo-random number generator uses an initial seed to generate deterministically the list of pseudo-random numbers. If an adversary somehow has access to the seed, he or she can faithfully reproduce the whole list of numbers, hence compromising cryptographic security.

471. Charles H. Bennett and Gilles Brassard, "Public Key Distribution and Coin Tossing," *Proceedings of the IEEE International Conference on Computers, Systems and Signal Processing* (New York: IEEE Press, 1984): 175–179.

472. E.O. Kiktenko, N.O. Pozhar, M.N. Anufriev, A.S. Trushechkin, R.R. Yunusov, Y.V. Kurochkin, A.I. Lvovsky, and A.K. Fedorov, "Quantum-secured Blockchain," arXiv:1705.09258 [quant-ph], Moscow, Calgary, Orsay, 2017.

473. Anne Broadbent and Christian Schaffner, "Quantum Cryptography beyond Quantum Key Distribution," *Designs, Codes and Cryptography* 78, no. 1 (2016): 351–382.

474. Jonathan Jogenfors, "Quantum Bitcoin: An Anonymous and Distributed Currency Secured by the No-Cloning Theorem of Quantum Mechanics," arXiv:1604.01383 [quant-ph], Linköping, Sweden, 2016.

475. The number 4.2 multiplied by 10 to the power of 21 as a power of two is approximately equal to two to the power of 71.8. In cryptography, the number in the exponent of the number of steps an adversary needs to perform in order to attack the system is called the *security parameter*. In other words, we can say that as of Aug. 2017, the proof-of-work system of the Bitcoin network offers approximately 71.8 bits of security.

476. See "Total Hash Rate (TH/s)," *Blockchain.com*, Blockchain Luxembourg SA, as of 9 March 2021. www.blockchain.com/charts/hash-rate.

477. A *preimage* is the inverse image of a hash.

478. The overhead is polynomial in the logarithm of the number of logical qubits and logical gates used in the computation and highly depends on which quantum error correcting code is used. As of today, the most promising quantum error correcting code is called the *surface code,* and it is based on topological error correction. For a comprehensive introduction, see Austin G. Fowler et al., "Surface Codes: Towards Practical Large-Scale Quantum Computation," *Physical Review A*, vol. 86, no. 3 (2012): 032324.

479. Christof Zalka, "Grover's Quantum Searching Algorithm Is Optimal," *Physical Review A*, vol. 60, no. 4 (1999): 2746.

480. Dr. David Jao, professor, faculty of mathematics at the University of Waterloo, and member of the Centre for Applied Cryptographic Research at the University of Waterloo, 2017.

481. David Jao and Luca De Feo, "Towards Quantum-Resistant Cryptosystems from Supersingular Elliptic Curve Isogenies."

482. An *asymptote* is "a straight line that continually approaches a given curve but does not meet it at any finite distance." *Oxford Dictionaries*, Oxford University Press, 2017. en.oxforddictionaries.com/definition/us/ asymptote, accessed 16 Nov. 2017.

483. Leslie Lamport, "Constructing Digital Signatures from a One-Way Function," *Technical Report SRI-CSL-98*, SRI International Computer Science Laboratory, 1979.

484. Ralph C. Merkle, "A Digital Signature Based on a Conventional Encryption Function," C. Pomerance, ed., *Advances in Cryptology - CRYPTO '87*, Lecture Notes in Computer Science (Berlin, Heidelberg: Springer, 1987): 369–378; and C. Dods, N.P. Smart, and M. Stam, "Hash Based Digital Signature Schemes," *Proceedings of the 10th International Conference on Cryptography and Coding* (Berlin, Heidelberg: Springer-Verlag, 2005): 96–115.

485. Dr. David Jao, interviewed by Vlad Gheorghiu, 7 Sept. 2017.

486. Dr. Manfred Lochter, Bundesamt für Sicherheit in der Informationstechnik, interviewed by Vlad Gheorghiu, 16 Sept. 2017.

487. Public key collisions are a major security flaw. If wallet B, newly added to the blockchain, happens to have the same address as an existing wallet A (i.e., having a public/private key collision or having a different public key that by chance hashes to the same address as the address of A), then B will be able to spend all of A's currency (and vice versa). Those issues appear whenever the random number generators used to generate the key pairs are not cryptographically secure, are poorly implemented, or are used inadequately (e.g., by reusing seeds).

488. Dr. Ghassan Karame, interviewed by Vlad Gheorghiu, 27 Sept. 2017.

489. Dr. Nadia Diakun-Thibault, interviewed by Vlad Gheorghiu, 25 Sept. 2017.

490. Dr. David Jao, interviewed by Vlad Gheorghiu, 7 Sept. 2017.

491. Stateful means that the protocol or server depends on the previous state of the application or process to function properly. As their name implies, stateless signatures do not need a server to keep track of a current state.

492. Johannes Buchmann, Erik Dahmen, and Andreas Hulsing, "XMSS—A Practical Forward Secure Signature Scheme Based on Minimal Security Assumptions," Cryptology ePrint Archive (Nov. 2011): 484.

493. "Open Quantum Safe," 2017. openquantumsafe.org.

494. "Cryptocurrency Market Capitalizations," *CoinMarketCap.com*, 9 March 2021. coinmarketcap.com/charts, accessed 3 March 2021.

495. 1 March 2016 through 21 Feb. 2018, "Cryptocurrency ICO Stats 2018,"
      CoinSchedule.com, 21 Feb. 2018. www.coinschedule.com/stats.html,
      accessed 21 Feb. 2018.

496. Ashley Lannquist, "Blockchain in Enterprise: How Companies Are
      Using Blockchain Today," *Blockchain at Berkeley Blog*, A Medium Corp.,
      18 Jan. 2018. blockchainatberkeley.blog/a-snapshot-of-blockchain-in-
      enterprise-d140a511e5fd, accessed 19 Feb. 2018.

497. Satoshi Nakamoto, "Bitcoin P2P e-Cash Paper," The Cryptography
      Mailing List, The Mail Archive, 1 Nov. 2008. www.mail-archive.com/
      cryptography@metzdowd.com/msg09959.html, accessed 19 Feb. 2018.

498. Joi Ito, "The Fintech Bubble," *Joi Ito Blog*, Movable Type, 14 June 2016.
      joi.ito.com/weblog/2016/06/14/-the-fintech-bu.html, accessed 19 Feb.
      2018.

499. Oscar Williams-Grut, "Apple's iPhone: The Most Profitable Product in
      History," *The Independent*, Independent Digital News & Media,
      29 Jan. 2015. www.independent.co.uk/news/business/analysis-
      and-features/apples-iphone-the-most-profitable-product-in-
      history-10009741.html; Lex Friedman, "The App Store Turns Five: A
      Look Back and Forward," *Macworld*, IDG Communications Inc., 8 July
      2013. www.macworld.com/article/2043841/the-app-store-turns-five-a-
      look-back-and-forward.html, both accessed 19 Feb. 2018.

500. Marco Tabini, "App Store Surpasses 50 Billion Downloads," *Macworld*,
      IDG Communications Inc., 16 May 2013. www.macworld.com/
      article/2038882/app-store-surpasses-50-billion-downloads.html,
      accessed 19 Feb. 2018.

501. Matt Murphy and Steve Sloane, "The Rise of APIs," *TechCrunch*, Verizon
      Media, 21 May 2016. techcrunch.com/2016/05/21/the-rise-of-apis; Bala
      Iyer and Mohan Subramaniam, "The Strategic Value of APIs," *Harvard
      Business Review*, Harvard Business School Publishing Co., 7 Jan. 2015.
      hbr.org/2015/01/the-strategic-value-of-apis, both accessed 19 Feb. 2018.

502. WiMAX is technically referred to by the Institute of Electrical and
      Electronics Engineers (IEEE) as 802.16, and LTE was standardized
      through the 3rd Generation Partnership Project (3GPP). Matt Hamblen,
      "WiMax vs. Long Term Evolution: Let the Battle Begin," *Computerworld*,
      IDG Communications Inc., 14 May 2008. www.computerworld.com/
      article/2535716/mobile-wireless/wimax-vs--long-term-evolution--let-
      the-battle-begin.html, accessed 19 Feb. 2018.

503. Matt Hamblen, "WiMax vs. Long Term Evolution: Let the Battle
      Begin"; MarketResearch.com, "The Wireless Telecommunication
      Carriers Market Is Expected to Reach over $1 Trillion in 2020,"

News Release, *Cision PR Newswire*, PR Newswire Association LLC, 14 Sept. 2017. www.prnewswire.com/news-releases/the-wireless-telecommunication-carriers-market-is-expected-to-reach-over-1-trillion-in-2020-300519774.html, accessed 19 Feb. 2018.

504. Between the acquisition of Clearwire, the $5-billion network buildout plan, and debatably even the acquisition of Nextel and their 2.5 GHz licenses. Dan Meyer, "Worst of the Week: A Bold Look Back at the Sprint WiMAX Network," *RCR Wireless News*, 1 April 2016. www.rcrwireless.com/20160401/opinion/worst-week-bold-look-back-sprint-wimax-network-tag2, accessed 19 Feb. 2018.

505. Lou Frenzel, "What's the Difference between the OSI Seven-Layer Network Model and TCP/IP?" *Electronic Design*, Informa USA Inc., 2 Oct. 2013. www.electronicdesign.com/what-s-difference-between/what-s-difference-between-osi-seven-layer-network-model-and-tcpip, accessed 9 March 2021.

506. Joel Monegro, "The Blockchain Application Stack," *CoinDesk*, Digital Currency Group, 30 Nov. 2014. www.coindesk.com/blockchain-application-stack, accessed 19 Feb. 2018.

507. Joel Monegro, "The Blockchain Application Stack"; David Xiao, "The Four Layers of the Blockchain," *David Xiao Blog*, A Medium Corp., 21 June 2016. medium.com/@coriacetic/the-four-layers-of-the-blockchain-dc1376efa10f; Joichi Ito, "The Fintech Bubble"; Arun Devan, "The Blockchain Technology Stack," *Steemit*, Steemit Inc., Oct. 2017. steemit.com/blockchain/@acdevan/the-blockchain-technology-stack; Vitalik Buterin, "On Silos," *Ethereum Blog*, Ethereum, 31 Dec. 2014. blog.ethereum.org/2014/12/31/silos; and Deloitte, "Blockchain Technology Stack," Deloitte Touche Tohmatsu India LLP, 2017. www2.deloitte.com/content/dam/Deloitte/in/Documents/industries/in-convergence-blockchain-tech-stack-noexp.pdf, all accessed 19 Feb. 2018.

508. "Cryptocurrency Market Capitalizations," *CoinMarketCap.com*, as of 19 Feb. 2018. coinmarketcap.com.

509. "Percentage of Total Market Capitalization (Dominance)," CoinMarketCap Charts, as of 9 March 2021. coinmarketcap.com/charts.

510. Timothy B. Lee, "Bitcoin Has a Huge Scaling Problem—Lightning Could Be the Solution," *Ars Technica*, Condé Nast, 4 Feb. 2018. arstechnica.com/tech-policy/2018/02/bitcoins-lightning-network-a-deep-dive, accessed 19 Feb. 2018.

511. Will Warren and Amir Bandeali, "0x: An Open Protocol for Decentralized Exchange on the Ethereum Blockchain," White Paper, *0xProject.com*, 21 Feb. 2017. 0xproject.com/pdfs/0x_white_paper.pdf, accessed 19 Feb. 2018.

512. Ashley Lannquist, interviewed by Christian Keil, 7 Feb. 2018; edited by email, 14 Feb. 2018.

513. Sarah Baker Mills, "Blockchain Design Principles," *IBM Design Blog*, A Medium Corp., 21 March 2017. medium.com/design-ibm/blockchain-design-principles-599c5c067b6e, accessed 19 Feb. 2018.

514. Sarah Baker Mills, "Blockchain Design Principles."

515. Reuters, "This Nasdaq-Backed Blockchain Startup Just Signed a Big Deal to Improve Security," *Fortune.com*, Fortune Media IP Ltd., 30 March 2017. fortune.com/2017/03/30/chain-thales-security-pact; Duncan Riley, "Gem Deploys Thales e-Security Hardware Security Modules for More Secure Bitcoin Wallets," *SiliconANGLE*, SiliconANGLE Media Inc., updated 28 Jan. 2015. siliconangle.com/blog/2015/01/28/gem-deploys-thales-e-security-hardware-security-modules-for-more-secure-bitcoin-wallet, both accessed 26 Nov. 2017.

516. We've included overlay networks within a larger blockchain protocol layer because we expect some overlays (e.g., Lightning Network) to become more or less synonymous with the core protocols they extend.

517. Justine Moore and Olivia Moore, "A VC's Take on Evaluating Cryptocurrencies," *Hacker Noon*, Artmap Inc., 29 Jan. 2018, updated 31 Jan. 2018. hackernoon.com/a-framework-for-evaluating-cryptocurrencies-e1b504179848, accessed 19 Feb. 2018.

518. While IOTA doesn't technically use a blockchain, it is still well within the family of decentralized technologies and therefore the scope of this chapter. We can think of their innovation—the directed acyclic graph (DAG), which they call a "tangle"—as an alternative structure to the *consensus* layer. Neha Narula, "Cryptographic Vulnerabilities in IOTA," *Neha Narula Blog*, A Medium Corp., 7 Sept. 2017. medium.com/@neha/cryptographic-vulnerabilities-in-iota-9a6a9ddc4367, accessed 19 Feb. 2018.

519. Neha Narula, "Cryptographic Vulnerabilities in IOTA."

520. David Dinkins, "Satoshi's Best Kept Secret: Why Is There a 1MB Limit to Bitcoin Block Size," *Cointelegraph*, 19 Sept. 2017. cointelegraph.com/news/satoshis-best-kept-secret-why-is-there-a-1-mb-limit-to-bitcoin-block-size, accessed 19 Feb. 2018.

521. In Feb. 2021, the average block size was 1.3 MB. See "Average Block Size," *Blockchain.com*, Blockchain Luxembourg SA, 26 Feb. 2021. blockchain.info/charts/avg-block-size?timespan=all, accessed 26 Feb. 2021.

522. "Visa Fact Sheet," Visa Inc., July 2019. usa.visa.com/dam/VCOM/global/about-visa/documents/visa-fact-sheet-july-2019.pdf, accessed 26 Feb. 2021.

523. "Block Size Limit Controversy," *Bitcoin Wiki*, 15 Dec. 2017. en.bitcoin.it/wiki/Block_size_limit_controversy, accessed 19 Feb. 2018.

524. Grace Caffyn, "What Is the Bitcoin Block Size Debate and Why Does It Matter?" *CoinDesk*, Digital Currency Group, 21 Aug. 2015, updated 25 Aug. 2015. www.coindesk.com/what-is-the-bitcoin-block-size-debate-and-why-does-it-matter, accessed 19 Feb. 2018.

525. Daniel Morgan, "The Great Bitcoin Scaling Debate—A Timeline," *Hacker Noon*, Artmap Inc., 3 Dec. 2017. hackernoon.com/the-great-bitcoin-scaling-debate-a-timeline-6108081dbada, accessed 19 Feb. 2018.

526. Grace Caffyn, "What Is the Bitcoin Block Size Debate and Why Does It Matter?"

527. Nathaniel Popper, "A Hacking of More than $50 Million Dashes Hopes in the World of Virtual Currency," *New York Times*, New York Times Co., 17 June 2016. www.nytimes.com/2016/06/18/business/dealbook/hacker-may-have-removed-more-than-50-million-from-experimental-cybercurrency-project.html, accessed 22 Nov. 2017.

528. Don Tapscott and Alex Tapscott, "Realizing the Potential of Blockchain: A Multistakeholder Approach to the Stewardship of Blockchain and Cryptocurrencies," White Paper, *WEForum.org*, World Economic Forum, June 2017, p. 16. www3.weforum.org/docs/WEF_Realizing_Potential_Blockchain.pdf, accessed 19 Feb. 2018.

529. Vitalik Buterin, Fred Ehrsam, and Chris Dixon, "a16z Podcast: Ethereum, App Coins, and Beyond," Podcast, *Blockchain & Cryptocurrencies*, Andreessen Horowitz, SoundCloud audio, 29:06, 28 Aug. 2016. a16z.com/2016/08/28/ethereum, accessed 19 Feb. 2018.

530. Vitalik Buterin, "A Proof of Stake Design Philosophy," *Vitalik Buterin Blog*, A Medium Corp., 30 Dec. 2016. medium.com/@VitalikButerin/a-proof-of-stake-design-philosophy-506585978d51, accessed 19 Feb. 2018.

531. "Bitcoin Energy Consumption Index" and "Comparing Bitcoin's Energy Consumption to Other Payment Systems," *Digiconomist*, as of 21 Feb. 2018. digiconomist.net/bitcoin-energy-consumption, accessed 21 Feb. 2018.

532. "Bitcoin Energy Consumption Index" and "Comparing Bitcoin's Energy Consumption to Other Payment Systems."

533. It's also particularly problematic for those who believe that governments are itching for excuses to outlaw cryptocurrencies. We think that most governments are still adopting a "wait and see" approach, as explained by Lawrence Orsini in "Distributed Power: How Blockchain Will Transform Global Energy Markets," foreword by Don Tapscott,

Blockchain Research Institute, 11 Oct. 2018. But it's not implausible to think governments may adopt a standard for blockchain like a carbon credit that drastically eats into blockchain mining margins.

534. CryptoMines, "Important Information from Today's Ethereum Dev Call and What It Means for Miners," *Reddit.com*, Reddit Inc., Aug. 2017. www.reddit.com/r/EtherMining/comments/6t56a0/important information from todays ethereum dev, accessed 19 Feb. 2018.

535. Toshendra Kumar Sharma, "Reasons behind Delay in Crucial Ethereum Update," *Blockchain-Council.org*, Blockchain Council, 6 Jan. 2018. www. blockchain-council.org/blockchain/reasons-behind-delay-in-crucial-ethereum-update, accessed 19 Feb. 2018.

536. Fabian Vogelsteller and Vitalik Buterin, "EIP-20: ERC-20 Token Standard," Ethereum Improvement Proposals, no. 20, Nov. 2015. eips. ethereum.org/EIPS/eip-20, accessed 25 Feb. 2021.

537. "Ethereum Tokens Market Capitalization," *Ethereum.io*, as of 9 March 2021. etherscan.io/tokens.

538. Alex van de Sande, "Let's Talk about the Coin Standard," *Reddit.com*, Reddit Inc., 2016. www.reddit.com/r/ethereum/comments/3n8fkn/ lets talk about the coin standard/?sort=new, accessed 19 Feb. 2018.

539. Hudson Jameson, "All Core Devs: Meeting 16," Recorded Meeting Agenda, *GitHub.com*, GitHub Inc., 19 May 2017. github.com/ethereum/ pm/blob/master/All%20Core%20Devs%20Meetings/Meeting%2016.md; Hudson Jameson, "ERC-20 Token Standard #610," Online Conversation, *GitHub.com*, GitHub Inc., 11 Sept. 2017. github.com/ethereum/EIPs/ pull/610, both accessed 19 Feb. 2018.

540. Hudson Jameson, "All Core Devs: Meeting 16."

541. "Ethereum Improvement Proposals" and "Ethereum Request for Comment," *Ethereum.org*, Ethereum Foundation, n.d. eips.ethereum.org/ all and eips.ethereum.org/erc, accessed 9 March 2021.

542. "Bitcoin Scaling Agreement at Consensus 2017," *Digital Currency Group Blog*, A Medium Corp., 23 May 2017. medium.com/@DCGco/bitcoin-scaling-agreement-at-consensus-2017-133521fe9a77, accessed 19 Feb. 2018.

543. Carl Shapiro and Hal R. Varian, "The Art of War," ManEc 387, Economics of Strategy, Marriott School, Brigham Young University, n.d. marriottschool.net/emp/Bryce/manec387/handouts/art of war.pdf, accessed 8 Feb. 2018.

544. Terry Gray, "Why Not ATM?" June 1999, revised Nov. 2000. staff. washington.edu/gray/papers/whynotatm.html; Tony Li and Carlos Ribeiro, "Why Did Asynchronous Transfer Mode (ATM) Lose to IP?" *Quora.com*, Quora Inc., 22 March 2014, modified 28 May 2014. www. quora.com/Why-did-Asynchronous-Transfer-Mode-ATM-lose-to-IP, accessed 19 Feb. 2018.

545. Erik Fair, "Asynchronous Transfer Mode Is Bad for Computer Networks," *Clock.org*, International Organization of Internet Clock Watchers, 29 Dec. 1997. www.clock.org/~fair/opinion/atm-is-bad.html, accessed 19 Feb. 2018.

546. Brian Behlendorf, interviewed via telephone by Don Tapscott and Kirsten Sandberg, 2 May 2017; quoted in Don Tapscott and Alex Tapscott, "Realizing the Potential of Blockchain: A Multistakeholder Approach to the Stewardship of Blockchain and Cryptocurrencies."

INDEX

0x, protocol exchanging ERC–20, 217
2WAY.IO, start-up, 64
4G (fourth generation wireless), 213
5G networks
  autonomous vehicles, and, 132,
  148–150, 161, 164
  incorporation of blockchain, into, 149
"51 percent attack" hack, 89, 156

A

access gates, Internet, 10–11
ACORNS (autonomous communication
  over redundant nodes), 139
AI (artificial intelligence)
  autonomous agents, and, 89–90
  blockchain, centralized,
    advantages with, 78–86
  blockchain, challenges and, 92–94
  blockchain, decentralized potential,
    86–92, 95
  blockchain democratization, and,
    82–85
  blockchain governance, and, 85–86
  blockchain immutability, and, 79–82
  DAO, and, 90–92
  data sets, 76–78, 85
  decentralized (DAI), type of, 86–92
  definition of, 74–75
  distributed economic entities, 91
  enterprise application growth, 74–75,
    95
  machine learning (ML) class, of, 74
  scaling problems, of, 92–93, 95
  see also DAI
  smart contract, 85–86
  symbolic class, of, 74
  training data, 75–76
  trivergence with IoT and blockchain,
  around data, 130
AION (Open Application Network), 147
AKASHA, blockchain-based social
  network, 34
algorithmic primitives, building blocks,
  blockchain, 192
Alibaba Alipay, 60–62
Alisie, Mihai, 34

Amazon, 15, 17, 19, 24, 75, 76, 82, 105,
  243
Ambrosus project, 117
Andreessen, Marc, 4, 210
Ant Financial, 60–62
API (application programming interface)
  digital signatures, common, 206
  economic gains, and, 213
  evolution of, APIs, 217
  external transaction interface, 174
  IoT platform exposure, 126
  local platforms, 127
  Mongero blockchain stack layer, 215
  open access, and, 8
  token interoperability, and, 227
  USN (Universal Sharing Network)
    comparison, 176
Apple Corporation
  App Store, launch, 212
  autonomous vehicles, 134
  deal with Amazon, 17
  iOS platform, 213
  oT space, 108
  iPhone, 212, 213
app-tokens, 20
Arduino board, 100
ARPANET (Advanced Research Projects
  Agency Network), 3
ASIC (application specific integrated
  circuits), 148
Association for Computing Machinery,
  89
asymmetric type, quantum computer, 198
ATM (asynchronous transfer mode), 230,
  231
autonomous agents
  AI representatives, as, 89–90
  DAI (decentralized artificial
    intelligence), and, 86–88
  DAO (Decentralized Autonomous
    Organization), creation as, 90–92
  decentralized architecture, open
    governance, and, 95
  distributed economic entities, 91
  latency issues on blockchain, start of
    process, 94
autonomous communication over
  redundant nodes (ACORNS), 139

296